Countryside Recreation, Access and Land Use Planning

OTHER TITLES FROM E & FN SPON

Amenity Landscape Management: A resources handbook
R. Cobham

Countryside Conservation
Second edition
B. Green

Countryside Management
P. Bromley

Countryside Recreation: a handbook for managers
P. Bromley

Ecology and Management of Coppice Woodlands
G. P. Buckley

The Ecology of Urban Habitats
O. L. Gilbert

Environmental Planning for Site Development
A. R. Beer

Fungal Diseases of Amenity Turf Grasses
Third edition
J. Drew Smith, N. Jackson and A. R. Woolhouse

The Golf Course: Planning, design, construction and management
F. W. Hawtree

Grounds Maintenance: A contractor's guide to competitive tendering
P. Sayers

Leisure and Recreation Management
Second edition
G. Torkildsen

Managing Sport and Leisure Facilities: A guide to competitive tendering
P. Sayers

Recreational Land Management
Second edition
W. Seabrooke and C. W. N. Miles

Spon's Grounds Maintenance Contract Handbook
R. M. Chadwick

Tree Form, Size and Colour: A guide to selection, planning and design
B. Gruffydd

For more information on these and other titles please contact:
The Promotion Department, E & FN Spon, 2–6 Boundary Row, London SE1 8HN. Telephone 071–865 0066.

Countryside Recreation, Access and Land Use Planning

Nigel Curry

Faculty of Environment and Leisure,
Cheltenham & Gloucester College of Higher Education, UK

E & FN SPON
An Imprint of Chapman & Hall

London · Glasgow · Weinheim · New York · Tokyo · Melbourne · Madras

**Published by E & FN Spon, an imprint of
Chapman & Hall, 2–6 Boundary Row, London SE1 8HN, UK**

Chapman & Hall, 2–6 Boundary Row, London SE1 8HN, UK

Blackie Academic & Professional, Wester Cleddens Road, Bishopbriggs, Glasgow G64 2NZ, UK

Chapman & Hall GmbH, Pappelallee 3, 69469 Weinheim, Germany

Chapman & Hall Inc., One Penn Plaza, 41st Floor, New York, NY10119, USA

Chapman & Hall Japan, Thomson Publishing Japan, Hirakawacho Nemoto Building, 6F, 1–7–11 Hirakawa-cho, Chiyoda-ku, Tokyo 102, Japan

Chapman & Hall Australia, Thomas Nelson Australia, 102 Dodds Street, South Melbourne, Victoria 3205, Australia

Chapman & Hall India, R. Seshadri, 32 Second Main Road, CIT East, Madras 600 035, India

First edition 1994

© 1994 Nigel Curry

Typeset in 10/12 Palatino by Florencetype Ltd, Kewstoke, Avon
Printed in Great Britain by TJ Press Ltd, Padstow, Cornwall

ISBN 0 419 15550 3

A catalogue record for this book is available from the British Library

Library of Congress Catalog Number: 93–74902

♾ Printed on permanent acid-free text paper, manufactured in accordance with the proposed ANSI/NISO Z39.48-1992 and ANSI/NISO Z39.48-1984

To the memory of Emma,
for her courage and love of nature

Contents

Preface

THE STRUCTURE OF THE BOOK

The purpose of this book is to evaluate contemporary countryside recreation and access policies and plans in England and Wales in the context of their historical antecedents. In doing this, the book develops five main propositions:

1. that the fragmented nature of the organizational structure for countryside recreation has inhibited the development and implementation of comprehensive policies and plans;
2. that the provision of countryside recreation and access facilities and opportunities has exhibited a confusion between the responsibilities and functions of the public sector and those of the market place and has been piecemeal and unco-ordinated as a result;
3. that policies and plans have not paid full regard to the social composition of recreation participation and have not fully taken into account people's preferences for recreation and access in the countryside;
4. that policy has generally been preoccupied with fears of a recreation explosion and the rights of the landowner, rather than the development of recreation opportunities, and has been unduly restrictive as a result;
5. that policies for recreation and access have had an unduly low priority in pressures for change in the countryside, particularly in relation to those in the conservation interest.

Chapter 1 examines these propositions in their historical context. Much of the deeper history of recreation and access is a story of the expression of people's preferences, often different among different social groups, and a failure of public policy to respond to them fully, commonly because of landowning interests in Parliament. Historically, many policies for countryside recreation and access were promulgated despite, rather than because of, public demands for provision.

Post-war affluence and increasing car ownership ensured a growth in countryside recreation and access participation among the middle classes. But this popularity would, it was presumed by policy-makers, lead to a recreation explosion that would despoil the very countryside that people had come to see. The articulation of this fear, dominant from the mid-1960s, was to ensure, right up to the present day, that both national recreation policies and the plans of local authorities would be overwhelmingly concerned with controlling the access 'problem' and not helping people to enjoy the countryside more fully. This fear of the recreation explosion, together with the protective interests of a land-owning Parliament, ensured that recreation and access had a residual priority in public policy.

Chapter 2 addresses the five propositions in the context of policies in the 1970s and 1980s. The 1949 National Parks and Access to the Countryside Act had made some provision for recreation and access in national parks just at a time when recreation was becoming more popular in the wider countryside. In addressing the problems of the 1920s and 1930s it had failed to anticipate the demands of the 1950s and 1960s. The Countryside Act of 1968, too, was aimed at solving the problems of the past and the slender recreation and access provisions contained within it were found to be too narrowly focused and insufficiently flexible for a modern era. As a result, innovations in countryside management ensued, almost entirely outside of a statutory framework, and what development for recreation did take place was done through the planning rather than the countryside Acts.

The 1970s also saw a burgeoning of agencies and ministries with part responsibilities for countryside recreation and access, leading to confusion, ineffectiveness and a further suppression of a recreation priority in public policy, as the first proposition of the book suggests. Some faltering steps in social provision were aired, but these were soon taken over by the fashion of the market place. Conservation remained centre stage in the countryside arena, and policies for recreation and access, particularly in land-use planning, remained restrictive.

Chapter 3 examines the second proposition of the book in more detail, in its contemporary context, by summarizing current recreation and access provision in the countryside. This is a story of the failure of government to come to grips with public access over private property rights, instead providing a few managed facilities to 'siphon off' the urban masses from the wider countryside which, as evidence suggests, is not really what people want. The confusion over whether countryside recreation really is a responsibility of the public sector has led to piecemeal provision by public, private and voluntary organizations, each often emulating the other.

Chapters 4 and 5, in addressing the third proposition of the book more closely, examine the nature of participation, preferences and social class. Despite an understanding of the nature of participation, through a number of surveys from the mid-1970s, there is still conflicting evidence about its exact extent and structure. Notwithstanding these limitations of data, countryside recreation participation appears to be clearly skewed towards the more affluent. Further there is evidence to suggest that this dominance of middle-class interests is largely as a result of preferences and not material deprivation. Because of this, social policies for countryside recreation, based on philanthropic good intent, always run the risk of actually being socially regressive if they are not taken up by the people for whom they are intended. The failure of policy here lies in not distinguishing preferences and constraints, and indeed, the supply-based nature of recreation and access policies may render them largely impotent in addressing the social structure of participation.

Chapters 6 and 7 address the fourth proposition of the book in evaluating the nature of land-use planning for rural leisure. A tradition of restrictive control-based policies is demonstrated in examining government advice for land-use planning, policies in structure plans and policies of the more recent informal countryside strategies. Earlier plans are restrictive chiefly because of the presumption of an inexorable participation growth – a presumption not borne out by fact. Later plans, in beginning to acknowledge that the recreation explosion might have never actually happened, have instead used the ethos of 'environmentalism' in the 1990 White Paper, 'This Common Inheritance' (Department of the Environment, 1990b), to ensure that recreation opportunities in their plans are not fully exploited.

In examining the fifth proposition of the book, Chapter 8 reviews contemporary policies for recreation relative to conservation at the national level, in local authorities and in management plans. It demonstrates that they reinforce the priorities established in the 1949 National Parks and Access to the Countryside Act, reaffirmed in the 1968 Countryside Act. Recreation still holds a residual priority to conservation, despite the fact that it is the resource sectors, particularly agriculture and forestry, that are the obvious culprits in the deterioration of the countryside, and not recreation. The chapter examines evidence of the damage that recreation causes to the countryside and finds the case against recreation largely unproven. This severely undermines the restrictive nature of land-use plans, irrespective of their inspirations based initially upon fears of a recreation 'explosion' and later on notions of 'environmentalism'.

The final chapter of the book examines contemporary national policies for countryside recreation and access in respect of the five propositions explored within it, and makes recommendations for the reformulation of these policies to the turn of the century.

PROMOTIONAL POLICIES BASED ON PUBLIC PREFERENCES

A principal proposition in this book suggests that public policy for countryside recreation and access has failed to take into account adequately the notion of public preferences. Further, concern about excessive use of the countryside for recreation purposes and the damage that this might cause has led, in the main, to policies based on control rather than opportunity. But is the notion of public preference nevertheless a defensible basis upon which to build countryside recreation policies of a less restrictive nature?

In a democratic system, the responsibility for public policy development is vested in the Parliamentary process rather than simply based on notions of public preference. This is important in the pursuit of the public good for essential commodities such as housing, food, health and employment where efficiency in their provision and equity in their distribution are clear national priorities.

But countryside recreation is not an essential commodity of this nature nor is it concerned primarily with law and order or defence. Many people have little interest at all in countryside recreation, even though others might suggest that it can 'do everyone good'. As one council officer involved in the West Pennine Moors Plan consultation remarked, people are not only ratepayers, they are also voters, and there are few votes in leisure (Centre for Leisure Research, 1986). It might therefore legitimately be considered that countryside recreation and access are areas of second-order importance in national policy terms, despite the fact that more narrowly within countryside policies they may be accorded an unduly low priority. As a policy area of second-order importance, it may be legitimate for public preferences to have a role in shaping policy.

Further, countryside recreation is a policy area that straddles both the market place (the success of which is based on responding to public preferences) and non-market sectors and it is therefore important at least to take public preferences into account in combination with broader public policy objectives.

Most persuasively, perhaps, accounting for public preferences in public policy for countryside recreation is important because if they are ignored, social policies are likely to be regressive, and land-use policies will develop restrictive provision that does not maximize human satisfactions. Ultimately, however, despite the need to take public preferences into account in the formulation of countryside recreation and access policies, they may still be of lesser importance to the public at large, than policies designed to procure better housing and living standards, better job opportunities and a safer environment for the nation as a whole. As Roberts (1979, p. 64) states:

Social class differences in the use of the countryside will narrow if and when social class differences themselves are tempered. As in education, attempts to equalize specifically recreational opportunities by tinkering with supply are unlikely to have their intended effects. Moreover, raising general standards of working class life will leave the individuals concerned free to make their own choices as to which of the deprivations currently endured they wish to alleviate.

DEFINING RURAL LEISURE

It is useful to define at the outset of this volume the areas of principal focus for the evaluation of public policies and plans, within the wider concerns of rural leisure. In broad terms, the notion of rural leisure encompasses a range of components that are distinctive although not exclusive. These components may be considered to fall into seven groups. The first is **countryside recreation**, which has been concerned with social-well being (and, earlier, public health) and with opportunities for the public enjoyment of the countryside. The second is **access**, which relates to the legal basis of rights over (usually private) land and exceptions. It may thus provide part of the means to achieving recreation objectives.

A third component of rural leisure is **sport**. Commonly this takes the form of more active and more capital-intensive countryside recreation but it is distinctive in terms of legislation, organizational structure and the demands that it places on the countryside. **Rural tourism** provides a fourth component which, critically, involves a stay away from home for one night or more (Clark, 1992). Rural tourism is not exclusively leisure-based, however, since business-related tourism also has a significant impact on rural economies. A fifth component relates to the **leisure activities and needs of the rural population itself**. Although not as widely researched, Glyptis (1992) has found these needs and activities to be discrete relative to the other four essentially migratory components.

The final two distinctive components of rural leisure relate to conservation. **Amenity conservation** is concerned with the aesthetic worth of the landscape and **nature conservation** with the scientific values of the countryside as an ecosystem. These are being consumed increasingly for recreation purposes as an end in themselves (McLaughlin and Singleton, 1979; Roorre, 1983). As Benson (1986) rightly claims, both are concerned with the provision of landscapes and ecosystems that make up the supply side of the rural leisure equation, with the other five components representing the demand for it.

As is apparent from this preface, this volume is principally concerned to evaluate policies and plans associated with the first two of these components of rural leisure – recreation and access. Even these two components have had distinctive pressures for change and legislative provision associated with them, a point that is reinforced throughout this volume. To the extent that none of these components of rural leisure is mutually exclusive, however, some consideration is given to sport and tourism, particularly in relation to participation and administrative structures considered in Chapter 2. The relationship between recreation, access, amenity and scientific conservation is considered explicitly in Chapter 8.

It should be noted, too, that this book is principally concerned with an evaluation of strategic policies and plans for recreation and access, rather than the detail of management and implementation, which has been considered more fully in other volumes (for example, Bromley, 1990). Thus, for example, while policies in structure plans and country-side strategies are fully assessed, the nature of proposals in local plans, national park plans and management plans are given more cursory attention.

Acknowledgements

This book derives from a series of research projects, the first of which was undertaken in 1982 when Gloucestershire County Council and the National Trust commissioned a survey of Crickley Hill country park as a means of reviewing the management plan for the site. A number of projects for the Countryside Commission followed, beginning with a period of secondment to the Recreation and Access Branch during 1984 and 1985, to assist in the analysis of the 1984 National Survey of Countryside Recreation. This was followed by a series of short projects that essentially provided inputs into the Commission's national recreation policy review, 'Recreation 2000', which became more widely known as 'Enjoying the Countryside'. These included a national recreation footpaths survey (1985), an analysis of recreation and access policies in county structure plans (1986) and a critique of recreation and access legislation (1986).

An additional 'academic perspectives on countryside recreation policy issues' contract was undertaken in 1986, with contributions from Dai Edwards, now of the Royal Agricultural College, Chris Gratton, now of the University of Tilburg, Niel Ravenscroft of Reading University, Ken Roberts of Liverpool University and Peter Taylor, now of the University of Sheffield. More recently, in 1991, an analysis was undertaken for the Commission, of the responses to their consultation paper 'Visitors to the Countryside' – part of the ongoing review of policies for 'Enjoying the Countryside' – which has again provided valuable information for this book.

In addition to these contracts, the Countryside Commission commissioned the editing of a book, 'A People's Charter?' (Blunden and Curry, 1990), undertaken with John Blunden of the Open University, with contributions from Theo Burrell, formerly national park officer for the Peak National Park, Gerald Smart, formerly chief county planning officer for Hampshire and professor of town and country planning at

University College, London, Roger Smith, a freelance journalist and member of the Ramblers' Association and Richard Steele, formerly director of the (then) Nature Conservancy Council, to evaluate the impacts of the 1949 National Parks and Access to the Countryside Act 40 years after its Royal Assent. This provided an opportunity to explore some of the historical antecedents of recreation and access policies that are further developed in the first two chapters of this volume. I would like to express my gratitude to the Countryside Commission for the opportunity to undertake all of these projects, and to those who contributed to their successful execution.

Various research staff have also made a valuable contribution both to these contracts and to the substance of the book. Alison Kohla, now with Dartmoor National Park, assisted in the evaluation of structure plan policies, and Mary Mitchell and Les Maas, both still at the Cheltenham and Gloucester College of Higher Education, with the evaluation of responses to the 'Visitors to the Countryside' consultation exercise. In particular I would like to thank Caroline Pack, now at the University of Warwick, for invaluable assistance in the updating of the structure plan and countryside recreation strategy evaluations contained in Chapters 6 and 7, and in the assessment of the environmental impact of recreation discussed in Chapter 8. Needless to say, all of the errors and omissions contained in this volume, that derive from all of their efforts, remain my own.

I would also like to thank the Department of Architecture and Planning, and particularly John Greer at the Queen's University of Belfast. They afforded me the hospitality of a room and nine weeks' space during the spring and autumn of 1992 while on an Allied Irish Banks Visiting Professorship in the Department, to break the back of a manuscript that was even then over two years overdue. In this respect, thanks are due to the publishers for their patience, and to my own institution, the Faculty of Environment and Leisure at the Cheltenham and Gloucester College of Higher Education, for allowing me the time to go to Belfast.

In addition, a number of people have provided comments on earlier drafts of the manuscript. Jeremy Worth, of the Countryside Commission, was most helpful in his comments on Chapter 4 and Roy Hickey and Paul Johnson, both also of the Commission, provided constructive criticism on Chapters 3 and 9. Caroline Mills and Stephen Owen, of the Cheltenham and Gloucester College of Higher Education made useful contributions to drafts of Chapters 1, 6, and 7. Again, despite all of this sound advice, the shortcomings of these chapters remain mine alone.

At a personal level, the hospitality of the family Kolbé during the summers of 1991 and 1992, at 'Les Bocages' in the Loire Valley, provided further invaluable opportunities for developing the manuscript without the normal distractions of family holidays. Most of all, fondest appreciation goes to my family, Tina, Jessica Rose, Stefan and Edward, who have had considerable problems in 'securing their rights of access' to me for a considerable period during the preparation of this book. I intend that they will be more successful in the future!

1

The historical context of countryside recreation and access

As Green (1985) has noted, the enjoyment of the countryside has never been universal. At different times in history, the countryside has been celebrated, revered and even feared. There was a crude kind of balance between recreation demand and supply prior to the enclosures of the eighteenth and nineteenth centuries. Common people had been able to roam over common land 'wastes' and the landowning classes had used their land extensively for country sports.

The enclosure movement served both to increase preferences for the enjoyment of the countryside and reduce its availability (Thomas, 1983). The chequerboard countryside was more attractive to people, but at the same time enclosed fields reduced the supply of accessible land, particularly of downland, woodland, marshland and heath. At the same time further lands were enclosed specifically for hunting purposes. People's places of recreation (and indeed sometimes sources of food) were further denied them by an increasingly restrictive and penal sequence of Game Laws up to the 1870s. Two sets of public policy in the eighteenth and nineteenth centuries – Enclosure Laws and Game Laws – thus served directly to restrict countryside recreation opportunities for the public (Table 1.1).

The Industrial Revolution of the nineteenth century further increased the demand or public preference for countryside recreation and threw its relationship with supply further out of balance. For the newly migrated urban population, the countryside provided both a vehicle to satiate its longing for a rural heritage and the fresh air to contrast its poor working conditions. The introduction of wakes weeks, during which factories closed, and bank holidays in 1871, allowed at least some leisure time for this indulgence.

It was around this time that people within the public sphere of influence began to formalize action to protect the supply of countryside recreation facilities and resources. The Commons and Open Spaces Preservation Society (later to include 'Footpaths' in its title and now the Open Spaces Society) was formed (Table 1.2) by Members of Parliament, barristers, philosophers, economists and social reformers to preserve the commons of Victorian England for public enjoyment. Even at this time, outdoor recreation was seen as an activity that was an important balancing element in people's lives – a social commodity or public good – and therefore its provision should fall into the public domain.

The Romantic and other artistic movements of the nineteenth and early twentieth centuries provide a third cause of an increase in public preference for the countryside. As all forms of creative endeavour became less tied to the services of the Church and the Crown, rural imagery became a popular preoccupation. In the early nineteenth century, Wordsworth and Byron extolled the virtues of the English countryside in verse and prose. Wordsworth even wrote a guide to his beloved Lake District, published in 1810, where he laid down the notion of a national park.

Later prose, including the Victorian novel, used rural imagery to create its power – the Brontës writing of Yorkshire and Hardy of Dorset, for example. Such imagery was reinforced in visual art with the nineteenth century providing a landmark in English landscape painting, for example through the work of Turner and Constable. And many popular musical composers – Elgar, Delius, Holst and later Vaughan Williams – had a common musical inspiration in pastoral England. Not surprisingly all of these developments and the fashionable nature of the arts themselves in Victorian England made the countryside a popular place to spend leisure time.

Table 1.1 Nineteenth century: changes in the supply and demand of countryside recreation

Increasing demands for countryside recreation	*Reducing supply of countryside recreation*
The Enclosures	The Enclosures
The Industrial Revolution	The Game Laws
The Romantic Movement	

Again, formal manifestation was given from this caucus to the importance of protecting the supply of the recreation resource. The National Trust was formed in 1895 as a derivative of the Commons and Open Spaces Society with artists and designers such as Ruskin, Hunt and Morris, as well as social reformers, among its early members.

1.2 WORDSWORTH AND OLMSTEAD: SHOULD THE COUNTRYSIDE BE FOR ALL?

Wordsworth was thus an early champion in promoting recreation in the English countryside. Indeed he saw countryside recreation as one of the principal purposes of an English national park. But he had very particular views about what kinds of participation patterns, in terms of numbers of people and their social class, he would like to see making use of the countryside in this way. As MacEwen and MacEwen (1982) note, in his *Guide to the Lakes* he saw the enjoyment of the Lake District to be 'for persons of pure taste' and definitely not for 'artisans, labourers and the humbler class of shopkeepers'. These would ruin the landscape by virtue of their numbers, a fact that concerned him particularly after the train came to Windermere (Donelly, 1986).

Thus, Wordsworth introduced both the notions of exclusion and social class into the activity of countryside recreation. Such recreation in his view should definitely not be for all. This notion was to be challenged later in the nineteenth century by a large number of ramblers' clubs, many of which had strong working-class origins, keen to seek access to the moorland and open country of northern England. But it was also challenged in the United States in the development of their national park movement. Yellowstone Park had been designated by Abraham Lincoln in 1872 and the General Grant National Park by 1901. These were to be 'inalienable for all time', and 'for enjoyment so as to leave them unimpaired for the enjoyment of future generations' (MacEwen and MacEwen, 1982). There was no hint of either exclusion or class segregation in this ethos.

Frederick Law Olmstead, considered to be the founding father of the American parks, was critical of the views of Wordsworth and people like him because of their condescending middle-class attitudes towards the exposure of the masses to landscape beauty. He felt that countryside recreation should be a non-exclusive classless opportunity. This ideal was to be compromised in England and Wales, but particularly in America, where the need for transport to reach and enjoy most 'unspoilt' countryside entailed a cost that ensured that most of such enjoyment would remain the preserve of the relatively better-off.

1.3 PRESSURE GROUPS, PARLIAMENTARY CONFLICT AND SOCIAL CLASS

Even during the nineteenth century, then, views were being expressed by influential people about who they would like to see in the countryside. Not surprisingly these views had their critics, many of whom were to form organized pressure groups to champion their desire for increased access in a climate of increasing recreation demand and reducing available supply. To balance these, other groups were formed essentially to represent the landowning interests associated with access, as Table 1.2 indicates.

Table 1.2 The formation of organized recreation and access groups

Pressure groups for increased recreation and access	
The Commons and Open Spaces Preservation Society	1865
The Highfield and Kinder Scout Ancient Footpaths Association	1876
The Cyclists' Touring Club	1878
The National Trust	1895
The Camping and Caravan Club	1901
The Caravan Club	1907
The Youth Hostels' Association	1930
The Ramblers' Federation	1930
The Ramblers' Association	1935
The Standing Committee on National Parks	1936
Pressure groups representing the landowning interest	
The British Association for Shooting and Conservation	1908
The British Field Sports Society	1930

1.3.1 Recreation and access in Parliament

The more radical of these access groups, essentially the more working-class rambling societies, formed an informal alliance with the more conservative and indeed more middle-class national parks movement that had been spawned by Wordsworth, to bring formal pressure on government to pass legislation for greater access to upland and mountainous areas. This pressure had its first significant impact in 1884 when James Bryce introduced the first Access to Mountains (Scotland) Bill into Parliament. This was to be the first coherent set of government policies towards public access in the countryside, calling as it did for free access to mountain and moorland without hindrance. This Bill suffered the same fate as 12 others that Bryce witnessed during his 27 years in a Parliament dominated by landowning interests – it was withdrawn through lack of support.

The first access Bill to reach a second reading in Parliament came in 1908. This was Charles Trevellyan's Access to Mountains Bill, which failed in Committee. He tried further unsuccessful Bills in 1926, 1927 and 1928 as did Ellen Wilkinson in 1930 and 1931 and Geoffrey Mander in 1937 and 1938. An Access to Mountains Act did reach the Statute in 1939 via a Private Member's Bill introduced by Arthur Creech Jones, but the policies that it contained simply strengthened the resolve of the access movement for further legislation.

This 1939 Act sought, as a Bill, to give access to uncultivated land, but during its passage, the landowning fraternity in Parliament with advice and guidance from Lawrence Chubb, the then Secretary of the Commons Open Spaces Preservation Society, managed to insert a 'trespass clause' which would have made it a criminal offence for the first time simply to be on open moorland that was classed as private land. After some negotiation this clause was removed from the Act, but in its place was inserted a wide range of offences that carried hefty fines. On balance, the Act provided policies that were even more restrictive for the rambler than if the Act had not been passed at all. The onset of war ensured
that it was never implemented, however, and it was repealed anyway in the passing of the National Parks and Access to the Countryside Act in 1949.

1.3.2 The middle classes and recreation

This long period of Parliamentary frustration where the development of recreation policies was continually thwarted was going on at a time when participation was becoming increasingly popular. And with this popularity, the formation of recreation groups burgeoned. Organizations such as the Cyclists' Touring Club, the Camping and Caravan Club and the Youth Hostel's Association (Table 1.2), together with the more established Commons and Open Spaces Preservation Society and National Trust were representative of those groups that had a strong middle-class caucus. They were by-and-large conservative organizations that exercised somewhat covert pressure for access reform. Although by no means exclusively so, they were often more at home pressing for change in the south of England and the home counties than the wilder northern parts of England and Wales.

Many urban commons and places of public recreation, particularly in London, were assuming greater importance for recreation at the same time as they were increasingly threatened by enclosure for building development and more intensive forms of farming. The Commons and Open Spaces Preservation Society played a particularly important role in protecting these areas. Although it lacked the resources itself to save commons from further enclosure, a founder and its chairman, Lord Eversley, was successful in persuading the Corporation of London to bring a suit challenging the legality of enclosures made in and around Epping Forest. The resultant success of this challenge allowed the Corporation, in 1882, to buy out the lords of the manor and manage the forest in perpetuity for public recreation and enjoyment.

Such an enclosure plan also had been proposed for Wimbledon Common (Lowe, Clark and Cox, 1991) which had met with objections from the local population. The metropolitan board of works proposed a similar solution to the Epping Forest case by buying up the rights of the manor, selling some of the land to cover its costs and preserving the rest as public open space. But there was some opposition even within the Commons, Open Spaces and Footpaths Preservation Society to Lord Eversley's views about such purchases providing a long-term solution to public access. It was argued that if the Epping Forest principle was applied all over London it would either incur massive public expenditure or a loss of public open space, neither of which was considered particularly acceptable. The only long-term solution (and here there was some alignment with the more working-class pressure groups of the north), would be to strengthen common rights in law in a manner which would guarantee both the public interest and public access.

1.3.3 The working class and access

Central to bringing forward such explicit organized pressure for legal reform, was a caucus of organizations, such as the Ramblers' Federation and its successor the Ramblers' Association. These groups had identifiable working-class origins and their main support came from the industrial centres of northern England (Centre for Leisure Research, 1986). Their preoccupation, therefore, was with access to the wilder open parts of upland Britain – the countryside on their doorstep – rather than lowland middle England.

This was at a time when over half the towns of England and Wales of over 50 000 population were situated on or near coalfields and the need for rural refreshment was central to the newly urbanized way of life. As J. B. Priestley (quoted in Blunden and Curry, 1985, p. 73) was to recall:

> however small and dark your warehouse or office was, somewhere inside your head the high moors were glowing, the curlews were crying, and there blew a wind that was as salty as if it came from the middle of the Atlantic. That is why we did not care very much if our city had no charm, for it was simply a place to go and work in until it was time to set off for Wharfdale or Wensleydale again.

This more radical and vociferous movement than that from the south can be traced back to the formation of the Hayfield and Kinder Scout Ancient Footpaths Association founded in 1876 (Hill, 1980), but it gained its real momentum after the First World War when war veterans were keen to exert their right to walk freely in their own land. The Manchester and Staffordshire Ramblers' Federations, for example, circulated candidates in the 1922 general election asking if they would support access legislation (Baker, 1924). As paid holidays and mass transport grew by the 1930s, there could be more than 10 000 people on the Derbyshire Peak on a summer weekend. Access had become a mass sport. Of itself, this led to the articulation of concerns about recreation overrunning the countryside, passionately expressed, for example, in William Ellis's (1928) *England and the Octopus*.

But of more enduring consequence was the fact that increasing participation led to the formation of innumerable local rambling clubs often under the aegis of left-wing political groups such as the Co-operative, Trades Union, Clarion and Labour movements. The formation of the Holiday Fellowship and the Co-operative Holidays Association also gave working people the opportunity to spend short periods in countryside areas. By the mid 1930s, as the Centre for Leisure Research (1986) notes, the central issue here concerned access to the countryside over private property rights. It cites Lowerson (1980, p. 9) describing rambling during this period as:

> A mass working class activity which resulted in a series of open clashes between the defenders of traditional rights of property on the one hand, and the assertive proponents of a different tradition on the other.

To counterbalance these two sets of middle-class and working-class organizations, the 'defenders of traditional rights of property', the landowners, also set up their own recreation societies such as the British Association for Shooting and Conservation and the British Field Sports Society. These were to be at loggerheads particularly with the more radical 'free access' groups in a tradition that has lasted into the 1990s.

1.3.4 Pressures for reform

Not surprisingly, perhaps, it was the northern working-class groups that escalated the pressure for access reform. With mass unemployment in the 1920s and 1930s, enforced leisure time placed an even greater demands on the countryside for recreational use. Much of this focused on the Peak District where, in the early 1930s, there was public access to less than 1% of open moorland. It was estimated at the time that over half of the population of England lived within 50 miles of the area (Hill, 1980).

It was in the Peak District that the idea of direct action was conceived. The Lancashire District of the British Workers' Sports Federation proposed a 'mass trespass' of Kinder Scout on the Duke of Devonshire's land on 24 April 1932. The idea behind this was one of a peaceful trespass of sufficient size that it could not be turned back by game-keepers. In the event, only six arrests were made for unlawful assembly and breach of the peace, five of whom were members of the Young Communist League. They were tried and found guilty by a jury of 11 landowners! Although a success in the ramblers' terms, it was widely felt in the press at the time that this trespass simply served to cause the abandonment of yet another access Bill proposed for that year. A lively account of the trespass is reported in Rothman (1982). To emphasize that these issues still have not been resolved today, the Ramblers' Association organized another mass trespass in the Derbyshire Peak, as well as in other counties as part of 'Forbidden Britain' day in September 1991.

After the Kinder trespass, the approach of the more conservative middle-class access groups on the one hand and the more militant working-class ones on the other became more distinct. The former tended to disassociate themselves from direct action and tried to negotiate with landowners and government directly. This was at a time, during the inter-war years, when the extension of rural bus services, and the increasing availability of the motor-cycle and motor car were opening up new horizons for the day-tripper and holiday-maker alike. No longer was the tripper to the Lincolnshire coast confined to Skegness, Mablethorpe or Cleethorpes. The full length of the sandhills was opened up, demonstrated by the appearance of car-parks and weekend and holiday homes (Blunden and Curry, 1985).

In fact, the conciliatory approach of the more conservative middle-class groups met with some success as it did much to convince the landowning community that some form of statutory access reform was required. In government too, the now Commons, Footpaths and Open Spaces Preservation Society was effective at emphasizing to the Ministry of Health the need to encourage the development of open-air recreation for health reasons (Curry, 1986a).

The more militant groups on the other hand began to develop a clearer public profile. During the 1930s they managed to place the access issue higher on the political agenda, particularly within the Labour Party (Stephenson, 1989), where many of those who were to hold ministerial posts in the post-war Labour Government were actively involved in the access movement (MacEwen and MacEwen, 1987). Their efforts were consolidated when many individual rambling clubs federated into the Ramblers' Association in 1936.

1.4 THE ACCESS ISSUE IN GOVERNMENT: A DISTINCTION BETWEEN RECREATION AND ACCESS POLICIES

Chiefly as a result of conservation lobbying rather than specifically that of the recreation groups, Ramsay McDonald's second Labour Government of 1929 set up a committee to explore the possibility of introducing national parks in Britain. This Addison Committee as it was called saw a clear conflict between conserving the countryside and allowing access, and representations to it made this notion more entrenched. The National Trust, for example, wanted to see parks closed to the public for the purposes of amenity conservation, whereas ramblers' groups wanted to see national parks principally used for recreation.

The vast majority of the evidence heard and received by the Addison Committee in 1929 and 1930 was about recreation and access. Addison's solution to the tensions between recreation and conservation demands was to propose two types of park. 'National reserves' were to be for conservation and 'regional reserves' were to be areas of countryside conveniently situated near to towns, with the primary purpose of public access. Significantly, this policy contained an ethos of separating recreation from conservation in policy terms, a distinction that was to residualize recreation in public policy. The recession in the economy during the 1930s ensured that the Addison proposals were never implemented.

Partly because of this, the Standing Committee on National Parks was formed in 1936, to sustain pressure on government for the introduction of national parks. This was a powerful organization made up of a wide range of both recreation and conservation pressure groups and did much to promote the national parks cause. Of particular impact was a pamphlet by John Dower entitled 'The Case for National Parks' which noted that it was in the most beautiful and rugged parts of our land, where the inherent desire for public enjoyment was greatest, that recreation was most restricted.

The Standing Committee was the first organization to introduce the notion of a National Parks Commission which they envisaged as having the function of producing maps of all footpaths and bridleways, and having the power to create new ones. Even at this stage, local authorities expressed opposition to the centralization of these powers. The persuasive nature of this campaign for national parks that embraced recreation as well as conservation objectives was again forestalled, this time by the Second World War.

The period of the war saw a plethora of government reports concerned with post-war reconstruction. Among these was the Scott Report on Land Utilisation in Rural Areas (Scott, 1942). This, although somewhat briefly, championed the cause of the recreationist in the countryside, not least because of pressure from the Ramblers' Association. In a memorandum to the Committee, the Association urged that there should be free access to all open land including coastal areas. The Scott Committee accepted that the countryside was the heritage of all and that therefore there should be the opportunity of access for all but it claimed that this should not interfere with the 'proper use of land in the national interest'. The Committee also recommended that local authorities should keep maps recording all public footpaths – a proposal that was to become one of the most important provisions of the 1949 National Parks and Access to the Countryside Act. The Committee's views on national parks too was that they should be principally for recreation.

Also, central to the development of government policies for countryside recreation and access were the reports of Dower (1945) and Hobhouse (1947a) into, respectively, the establishment and location of national parks. These parks were to have, according to Dower, 'ample provision for access and facilities for public open-air enjoyment'. He did not feel that two separate types of park for recreation and conservation were required as Addison had done, but rather that public enjoyment was the justification for wildlife and nature conservation. He had a good measure of government support in these views since by now many of the leading figures in the earlier working-class access movements of the 1930s were in positions of government power.

Lewis Silkin, Minister of Town and Country Planning, and Hugh Dalton, the Chancellor of the Exchequer, both had been actively involved in the Ramblers' Association. Indeed, by the time the 1949 National Parks and Access to the Countryside Act became law, Hugh Dalton was its president.

The Hobhouse Committee was set up to consider the implications arising out of Dower's proposals for national parks. He separated out a number of the issues associated with national parks and set up several sub-committees with more specific briefs. He himself chaired the committee that focused on Footpaths and Access to the Countryside. (Hobhouse, 1947b). In setting up this sub-committee, Hobhouse differentiated clearly, and formalized for the first time in government, the distinction between the principle of public enjoyment through recreation, which he was to amply consider in his main 'National Park Committee', and that of securing access over private land, and public rights of way. It was this differentiation that had been delimited earlier in the different objectives of the working-class 'access' pressure groups such as the Ramblers' Association and the more middle-class 'recreation' groups such as the Cyclists' Touring Club.

This double strand of recreation and access policies had also served to inhibit the formulation of legislation since it was difficult to determine the ministry within which the responsibilities for recreation and access should lie. Prior to the 1939 Access to Mountains Act, for example, no ministry was prepared to take on the recreation and access portfolios because of the succession of failed Acts during the 1920s and '30s. The 'footloose' nature of these responsibilities in government is considered further in Chapter 2, but from these origins of uncertain responsibility, jurisdiction over recreation and access has evolved very much in a fragmented and piecemeal way in government.

1.5 RECREATION AND ACCESS PRIORITIES IN PUBLIC POLICY

Although these wartime and post-war reports gave due regard to the development of countryside recreation and access policies, there was no hiding the fact that issues of countryside conservation held centre stage, at least in terms of political priorities, in all of the deliberations leading up to the 1949 National Parks and Access to the Countryside Act. This relative priority has been an important influence on the status of recreation policies since that time, an issue that is considered further in Chapter 8.

Despite this, Parliamentary concern for recreation and access did exist. Dower (1978, p. 3), for example, cites the principal purpose of the Trevelyan and Bryce Bills as being:

> that no person should be excluded or molested by the owner or occupier while walking or being . . . for the purposes of recreation or scientific or artistic study . . . on uncultivated mountains or moorland.

Although these Bills were unsuccessful, the government still put recreation into the terms of reference of the Addison Committee that would lead to the 'improvement of recreation facilities for all of the people'. This was echoed by the Scott Report which claimed that national parks should be 'for the enjoyment of the whole nation', a sentiment that found its way into the 1944 White Paper, *The Control of Land Use* (HMSO, 1944), where the assurance to the people of the enjoyment of the sea and the countryside in times of leisure was seen as being an important aspect of post-war reconstruction.

Dower's 1945 report embellished these notions to embrace a social dimension. Access to the countryside:

> should be for all people, and especially the young of every class and kind, from every part of the country and for the public at large and not just some privileged section of the community (Dower, 1978, pp. 4–5).

Dower felt that the public should have the right to wander at will subject to a minimum of regulations to prevent abuse and pertaining to a minimum of 'excepted areas'. These would not include grouse moors over which there had been such bitter controversy in the inter-war years.

Hobhouse too maintained that access to national parks should be 'for the whole nation'. Freedom to wander at will over mountain, moor rough grazing and uncultivated land would be very important. Landowners would actually have to apply for exemptions from a 'free access' provision only if they could show good cause. This was a turnaround indeed from the sentiments expressed in Parliament during the passage of the 1939 Access to Mountains Act. Such positive recreation policy proposals reached a high point in 1947 when the Footpaths and Access Special Committee, also chaired by Hobhouse, followed the same line as his main Committee, and in response, the Chancellor of the Exchequer, Hugh Dalton, stated that he was prepared to make available the then considerable sum of £50 million, 'to finance some of the operations necessary to give the public permanent access in national parks'.

Despite all of these positive policy intentions, there was a distinct air of the selectivity and exclusion in the sentiments of these reports that had been expressed by Wordsworth more than a hundred years before. Dower, in his report, had indeed suggested that some people would be better off pursuing their interests in an urban setting. Hobhouse too, wanted to exclude from all national parks those looking for all forms of mass entertainment. Neither Dower nor Hobhouse was expecting countryside recreation to be to the taste of all.

At the margin, it appears that both of these reports would favour conservation over recreation objectives if a choice had to be made between the two. Hobhouse, for example, cited in Dower (1978, p. 8), proposed that a progressive policy of national park management would be required to:

> ensure the peace and beauty of the countryside and the rightful interests of the resident population are not menaced by an excessive concentration of visitors, or disturbed by incongruous pursuits.

These measures of ambivalence towards countryside recreation were at variance with views from within the Scott Committee, however. One of its members, Professor Dennison, wrote a notorious minority report disagreeing with many of Scott's main conclusions. In response to a cautious approach to the development of rural access, he was clear about its paramount priority:

> In particular it is important not to attempt to preserve amenities which can only be preserved so long as full access to them is denied to those whose heritage they are (Scott, 1942, p. 115).

But it was the sentiments of Dower and Hobhouse that were to find their way into the 1949 legislation. Access to the countryside was to be for 'rural refreshment' and 'countryside contentment' rather than in the pursuit of activities that owed little to the natural environment. As the National Parks and Access to the Countryside Bill was given its second reading in the House of Commons, its principal architect Lewis Silkin, the Minister of Town and Country Planning, was to term it:

> A people's charter for the open air, for hikers and the ramblers, for everyone who loves to get out into the open air and enjoy the countryside. Without it they are fettered, deprived of their powers of access and facilities needed to make holidays enjoyable. With it the countryside is theirs to cherish, to enjoy and to make their own (Blunden and Curry, 1990, pp. 63–4).

But before it reached Royal Assent he had been persuaded to a degree by his more cautious Parliamentary colleagues. He ultimately concluded in relation to access in the Bill:

> A person's land is his land and I think that it is wrong to give the public an automatic right to go over all private land of a certain character (Blunden and Curry, 1990, p. 129).

This public policy for countryside recreation, emerging as it did through an alliance of powerful conservation groups and Parliamentary land-owners is well summed up by Dower (1978, p. 9):

> The countryside is for all, but only if they use it in a way which suits our perceptions of the countryside in its beauty and its quietude.

1.6 THE 1949 NATIONAL PARKS AND ACCESS TO THE COUNTRYSIDE ACT

When the 1949 Bill received Royal Assent, it contained provisions relating to the two broad aspects of countryside recreation and access that

Hobhouse had recognized – the opportunity for public enjoyment on the one hand, and the legal mechanisms by which public access over private land might be secured on the other. The first of these two aspects was reflected in the establishment of the national parks, and in the general spirit of the Act, to allow the urban population fuller enjoyment of the countryside. Such controversy as there was about these aspects of the Act centred on the organizational structure of the administration of the parks, rather than their inherent objectives (Cherry, 1975), and the costs of new recreation provision within them. The Treasury, for example, blocked the Ministry of Town and Country Planning's expenditure plans for hostel provision in the parks (Cherry, 1985).

As might be expected, it was the elements of the Act that concerned the legal procurement of the rights of access that were the most contentious. It was for these provisions that public pressure, at least from the more militant access organizations, had been the most vociferous. In the initial drafting of the Bill, nearly all of Hobhouse's recommendations from his Special Committee on Footpaths and Access were adopted. A national survey of existing footpaths and bridleways was to be undertaken, if possible every four years, by local authorities. The recording of rights of way on a 'definitive map' was to be completed and reviewed every five years but this was to prove an unrealistic target since its execution was to be dependent in many authority areas upon the voluntary effort of parish councils. Uneven spread and many geographical inaccuracies resulted.

Local authorities could also declare a public right of access to specific areas of 'open country', held to include mountain, moor, heath, down, cliff and foreshore. The designation of special Long Distance Footpaths was to be the responsibility not of local authorities, but of a National Parks Commission because they were to traverse many local authority boundaries. But these were to be given low-priority funding by the Treasury, and the first, the Pennine Way, was not opened until 16 years after the Act. They still represent less than 1% of public paths.

In general, the access provisions of the Bill were given cross-party support by the House of Commons at their Second Reading. H. D. Hughes, Labour Member for Wolverhampton West, summed up the feeling of the House by terming them 'a very important step in the long struggle for the common people to establish their right to freedom in their own land'. The only new clauses inserted in the Bill at this Second Reading related to the local authority provision of accommodation, meals and refreshments on Long Distance Routes (this was amended in the Lords so that it could take place only where no private alternative was available), and to the imposition of financial penalties to be imposed on those who displayed notices deterring the public from using public footpaths.

Again, predictably, the Clauses of the Act relating to access to private land met with less universal enthusiasm in the House of Lords. The hesitations of the landowning classes were well represented. Lord Cranworth, for example, envisaged an 'orgy of destruction' from any legislation that encouraged visitors to the countryside. The Earl of Radnor and the Duke of Rutland both felt that such encouragement of visitors would only increase conflicts with agriculture, and Lord Winster was concerned about areas of the countryside already damaged by visitor pressure (Blunden and Curry, 1990). More positively, Lord Carrington amended the Bill successfully so that local authorities could offer water recreation, but only where no-one else was prepared to, and a caucus of peers, including Viscount Maugham, Lord Hawke, Lord Merthyr and the Archbishop of York, managed to secure statutory provision for a 'country code' by which ramblers might respect the countryside (Table 1.3).

But despite all of these provisions concerning access over private land, it appeared that the passing of the Act had brought little fundamental change since the restrictive clauses of the 1939 Act. It had upheld the principle of the 1939 Act, that all access onto private land must be negotiated individually with the landowner. Whereas in the 1939 Act there had been negotiation between the rambler and landowner on pain of fine by the rambler for trespasses that had never previously been chargeable offences, the 1949 Act shifted the negotiating responsibilities with the landowner onto the local authority. In introducing provisions for Access Agreement and Access Orders, it had provided a mechanism by which landowners could be fully compensated in financial terms for relinquishing their rights of privacy. As a result, the Act eschewed the concept of a legal right of public access to open land, whether in a national park or not.

Table 1.3 The principal recreation and access provisions of the 1949 National Parks and Access to the Countryside Act

- The National Parks Commission was to encourage the provision of facilities for public enjoyment in national parks
- Access agreements and access orders could be made for 'open country'
- Any land could be compulsorily purchased for recreation and access
- Counties should survey and produce definitive maps of public rights of way and open country
- Long Distance Routes could be established
- The Country Code was introduced

The passing of the 1949 National Parks and Access to the Countryside Act thus set the tone for the five propositions of this book. Undoubtedly there was uncertainty, even in the preparation of the Act, as to which particular government ministry should have responsibility for the recreation and access portfolio. Certainly the policies contained in the Act were restrictive, since although specific provision for recreation and access was made, the Act, and indeed all Acts since, failed to achieve free access to open country, deferring instead, outside of the rights of way network and to an extent certain enlightened landowners such as the National Trust, to the notion of negotiating access with individual landowners. As a result, less than 2% of open country has access secured to it by these means (Curry, 1992b). Also, the Act was to reflect the views of Dower, Hobhouse and Scott in giving a clear priority to conservation over recreation.

The provisions of the Act were very much a compromise in terms of people's preferences, particularly for access to open land. Indeed, the history of the access movement to this time was one of attrition between an articulated and organized demand for recreation and access and the public policy response. The antecedents of the Act also had a class-based component with organized pressure for change having distinct working-class and middle-class origins. On the policy side, from Wordsworth to Hobhouse, there was a stated view that the countryside was perhaps not for the enjoyment of all, but rather for those who had the tastes and inclinations for quiet, even genteel enjoyment. Recreation and access were to be condoned only if they were to be peaceful and didn't disturb anyone.

1.7 RECONSTRUCTION, DESIGNATION AND AFFLUENCE: A FOURTH WAVE

By the early 1950s the period of post-war reconstruction was gaining momentum. The 'Macmillan era' gave new hopes of increasing material affluence, incomes and leisure time. These, and particularly the development of mass car ownership (which grew by over 9 million between 1950 and 1970), were to take over as the prevailing influences on countryside recreation participation. Affluence as a determinant of participation was also to shift the class structure of recreationists in the 1950s and 1960s. The strong working-class caucus that brought pressures to bear on government for the introduction of the 1949 Act had a less significant impact on the growth of recreation during this period. The social structure of recreation participation in the late twentieth century is explored more fully in Chapter 4.

Part of this diminution in the importance of active working-class pressure groups may have been due to the euphoria in the wake of the passing of the 1949 Act. It was also due in part to the concern of certain groups about the growth of leisure in the countryside. The Ramblers' Association, for example, was aware of signs of significant increases in leisure activity in the countryside during the Macmillan era, and deliberately chose to disassociate itself from the mass access movement (Blunden and Curry, 1990). It became more preoccupied with the implementation of the 1949 Act particularly in terms of charting the definitive map. The Association considered the car-based walker not to be a serious contender for membership, something that was to stem its growth considerably.

Thus, as soon as the 1949 Act received Royal Assent the issues relating to countryside, and access that it had attempted to address, altered. The mass recreationist as motorist was now concerned with opportunities adjacent to cities, in lowland rural England, and on the coast, rather than particularly in national parks. The unprotected countryside was now at risk, and many areas of local scenic interest, particularly associated with stretches of water, were becoming widely used and even congested. And there was no national policy to cope with these developments, save the country code!

As a result of this shift in orientation of both destinations and the social structure of participation, an awareness of the increasing pressures on the countryside that recreation and access could bring began to be voiced. Even in national parks as early as 1952, the third report of the National Parks Commission was expressing concern about increasing car ownership and leisure time (Cherry, 1975, p. 12):

> we are living in an age of transition when, for the first time a preponderantly urban population, largely unfamiliar with rural life, has acquired a considerable amount of leisure with the opportunity of using that leisure to satisfy the instinctive and wholesome desire to leave the city for the country.

The accent of public policy was beginning clearly to focus on recreation and access problems, rather than the satiation of public enjoyment.

Despite this early apprehension, the 1958 Royal Commission on Common Land recommended further developments in opportunities for public enjoyment. Among other proposals, it suggested extending a number of access provisions under the 1949 Act to common land and that local authorities should undertake positive management measures for common land to extend to public access. Such proposals, however, were never brought to Parliament.

By the mid-1960s the growth in rural leisure had reached a greater level of official concern. In 1963, a Ministry of Housing and Local Government memorandum expressed apprehension at the rapidly growing urban population with more money and more leisure time, and that future legislation should embrace the wider countryside and not just national parks as a result. This thinking was further influenced by two independent reports, one by Michael Dower, the son of the author of the Dower Report (1942), entitled 'A Fourth Wave, the Challenge of Leisure' (Dower, 1965). He predicted that industrialization, railway construction and the sprawl of car-based suburbs would be followed by a wave of 'gambolling humanity' brought to rural environments by motor-car. The prognosis was startling – a 19 million growth in the population by the year 2000 and a 26 million growth in cars on the road by 1980.

The second report came from the Countryside in 1970 Conference (Council for Nature, 1966). This too made stark predictions of recreation growth but, like Dower's, these were based on speculation and presumption because, as is noted in Chapter 4, this was at a time before any comprehensive surveys into the extent of countryside recreation had been undertaken. These presumptions were based much more on the American experience, where the Outdoor Recreation Resources Review Commission (1962) had shown a significant growth in recreation activities in the late 1950s. The Council for Nature (1965, p. 24) had warned of this growth in recreation as a threat to conservation:

> almost complete destruction of vegetation is taking place where the public congregate at weekends in large numbers . . . some control is necessary unless the places that they wish to visit are destroyed.

It was in this vein that Sir Keith Joseph, the then minister for Town and Country Planning, addressed the 1964 National Park authorities conference and suggested widening the powers of the National Parks Commission to the whole of the countryside. The new 'Countryside' Commission would become more professional (most of the work of the National Parks Commission was carried out by Commissioners themselves) and more specialist officer staff would be employed.

By the early 1970s, the Department of the Environment (1972) itself was echoing this concern about widespread recreation growth:

> We believe that the greatest impact (of countryside recreation) has yet to be seen: on the countryside and its rural, often vulnerable, landscape. We consider (in this report) what has to be done to cope with this problem (p. 56).

This was despite a full confession of the absence of data in support of this proposition:

A great deal of statistical data will be necessary and trends, potential and seasonal fluctuations must be established. Only in this way can the consequences of the escalation of recreational demands in rural areas be predicted and met and the attractive features which the visitor wishes to enjoy be protected (p. 58).

The House of Lords (1973) Select Committee on Sport and Leisure was to consider recreation just as much a threat to agriculture:

there will be certain parts of the country within less than a generation where one will have to accept that it is no longer possible to farm at all because of the pressure to come and look (p. 167).

This is ironic in the 1990s where the 1986 Agriculture Act now promotes countryside recreation as a significant means of farm diversification.

1.8 THE WHITE PAPER 'LEISURE IN THE COUNTRYSIDE': COUNTRYSIDE RECREATION SHOULD BE FOR ALL

Two conflicting notions thus characterized the development of recreation and access policies during the 1950s and 1960s. First, there was a political will to make up for some of the failings of the 1949 Act in relation to recreation opportunities. Labour and Conservative parties alike provided for new legislation in their 1964 manifestos (Curry, 1986a) which would place emphasis on promoting outdoor recreation. Second, there was the emerging fear of a recreation explosion. The short-lived Ministry of Land and Natural Resources introduced by the Labour Government in 1964 was undoubtedly under both of these influences in introducing in 1966 a White Paper entitled 'Leisure in the Countryside'.

Despite the caution expressed about the possibility of a recreation explosion this Labour Government White Paper was unashamedly dedicated to the development of further access for all. It was to champion the social worth of recreation and overcome the legalistic land-use problems that the 1949 Act had failed, in the main, to resolve, with the introduction of specific recreation sites. It proposed the development of country parks, picnic sites and transit camping sites in countryside areas less remote than national parks.

But the progress of the 1968 Countryside Act, which was to arise out of this Paper, reinstated a strong preservationist element into recreation policy. Even at the introduction of the 1967 Countryside Bill into Parliament, it contained only recreation and access functions for the soon-to-be formed Countryside Commission (Curry, 1986a). By the time it received Royal Assent, as is considered further in Chapter 8, its conservation clauses rivalled in importance those for recreation and access. The conservationists and landowners still held sway in Parliament.

At this time too, the distinction between recreation and access was reinforced. In the early 1960s Sir Keith Joseph had floated a 'private' idea for 'recreational areas' at the 1963 'Countryside in the 1970s' conference, mirrored in 1965 by a note from the Ministry of Land and Natural Resources to other departments, proposing 'countryside recreation sites'. These were to be the forerunners of country parks in the 1966 White Paper.

The year after the publication of 'Leisure in the Countryside', however, the Gosling Committee (1967) was to report on rights of way separately. The Committee was charged with a comprehensive examination of the 'present system of footpaths, bridleways and other rights of way'. This reflected the distinction established by Hobhouse 20 years earlier and was also to have an impact on the 1968 Countryside Act. The Act considered recreation (Clauses 1–10) and access (Clauses 15–21 and 27–31) separately. The almost universal separation of responsibility for these two components of rural leisure in the shire counties, with recreation functions invariably being carried out by planning or countryside departments and access by highways, has served to sustain this distinction since 1968.

1.9 THE 1968 COUNTRYSIDE ACT

As a result of the two conflicting notions behind the 'Leisure in the Countryside' White Paper, the resulting 1968 Countryside Act considered recreation as both an opportunity and a potential land-use problem. Niall McDermott, in moving the second reading of the Bill in 1967, described it as a:

> comprehensive Bill designed to tackle the problems of the country-
> side – problems which are increasing at an increasing pace (Curry,
> 1986a, p. 13).

Much of the tempering of positive powers for recreation and access came in the Committee stage of the Bill. It was at this stage that one of the Countryside Commission's new functions, to advise on the **problems** associated with recreation development, was inserted. Here too, although the Commission was empowered to encourage the provision of facilities, they were to be only for those **resorting** to the countryside and not for an, as yet, non-participant public. The Commission's functions, it was also stressed, were not meant to imply a duty on the part of the Commission to **promote** projects.

In addition, it was stressed at the Committee stage, the Commission's responsibility for the provision of facilities for enjoyment **of** the countryside certainly did not have to be **in** the countryside. And in the context specifically of experimental schemes for public enjoyment, the

Commission was to **facilitate** rather than **promote** them. Thus, when country parks, picnic sites and transit camping sites were introduced they had an air of 'provision with containment' about them. They were to serve the increasing needs of the urban population and therefore be close to urban centres. There was no need for them to be particularly beautiful but they should have both refreshments and shelter.

It was stressed too in the notes on Clauses to the Bill, that local authorities should distinguish them from urban and suburban parks in respect of serving a migratory rather than just a resident population since they were to cater for recreational overspill from one area to another. Indeed transit camping sites and picnic sites were to cater specifically for the 'motorist and others using the road' – the recreationist in transit. The 1937 Physical Recreation and Training Act had already made provision for camping sites for the benefit of residents of an area. Despite the fact that all three types of facility were of equal status (in grant-aid and compulsory purchase terms), subsequent policy has developed the provision of transit camping sites little.

Of other facilities for public enjoyment, the Act gave specific consideration to water recreation. It included the definition of water in 'open country' because, as the notes on Clauses maintained, 'water is becoming much more of a recreation focal point'. The British Waterways Board canal system was omitted from this definition since it had been covered by a 1967 White Paper, 'British Waterways: Recreation and Amenity'. The 1968 Act empowered statutory water undertakers to develop recreation facilities, and also considered the role of lakes in national parks. At the Committee stage of the Bill, a new clause was inserted, making provision for water-based recreation associated with country parks. As Chapter 7 indicates, water-based recreation has become a particularly important aspect of provision for local authorities in their structure plans.

Issues of access and public rights of way concerned with legal definitions and exceptions, as events leading up to the Act had foreshadowed, were kept quite separate from the somewhat constrained opportunities for enjoyment. Access clauses, for example, were concerned with extending the definition of 'open country' from the 1949 Act to include woodlands, rivers and canals and with extending financial assistance for Access Agreements and Orders outside of the boundaries of national parks and Areas of Outstanding Natural Beauty. Issues of rights of way related, on the other hand, to the erection and maintenance of signposts by highways authorities, the maintenance of stiles and gates, and time limitations of the restoration of footpaths.

In terms of the Countryside Commission's powers, too, it was to be able to **provide** and **improve** facilities for the enjoyment of the countryside but more forcefully was to **secure** public access for recreation.

Table 1.4 The principal recreation and access provisions of the 1968 Countryside Act

---

- Countryside Commission formed to have recreation and access duties over the whole of the countryside
- Country parks, picnic sites and transit camping sites to be introduced through grant aid, by public authorities and private individuals
- Finance for access agreements and access orders extended beyond national parks and Areas of Outstanding Natural Beauty
- Definition of 'open country' extended to include woodland, rivers and canals
- Highway authorities to introduce comprehensive signposting of rights of way

---

In both respects, the Commission was empowered to purchase land (Table 1.4).

The notes on Clauses to the 1968 Act clearly saw the new Commission as a resource planning agency. In this respect, uncertainties about grant-aid provision by the National Parks Commission under the 1949 Act were clarified. Grants to persons other than public bodies were to be restricted to projects which would not otherwise be financially self-supporting. Local authority grants on the other hand were to offer initial pump-priming monies beyond which the local authority and the consumer might be expected to cope. They placed an emphasis on initial capital costs (for refreshment buildings, car parks and so on) rather than running costs, for which 75% grant aid was available. Although in the Act this grant aid was not restricted to country parks it has, since that time, accounted for the vast proportion of its use. The 1974 Local Government Act reduced this level to 50% for local authorities and removed the need for ministerial approval on grant allocations.

The relationship between grant-aid eligibility and the commercial viability of any project became linked in the 1968 Act through the extent to which public bodies and local authorities were empowered to make charges for recreation facilities. The 1968 Act suggests that changes could be made by local authorities and other statutory undertakers for activities **within** country parks and associated parking. This has led to a prevailing view among local authorities and within the Countryside Commission that access **into** country parks and other recreation sites within public control should be free.

This free access criterion has been couched in terms of a social policy, despite the fact that such policies were not seen as being part of the Commission's jurisdiction under the 1968 Act. This, and other social policies for countryside recreation, however, have been shown to be less than successful during the 1970s and 1980s for reasons which are considered more fully in Chapter 5.

Thus, between 1950 and 1970, the propositions of this book can again be seen to be upheld. The 1968 Act introduced further changes to the organizational structure of countryside recreation, and the 'fear of the recreation explosion' was central to the tempering of the recreation and access provisions of the Act as it proceeded through Parliament. The provision of specific recreation facilities such as country parks turned out to be largely not what people wanted (Chapter 3) and, despite a broad measure of all party support, the resultant implementation of these recreation and access parts of the 1968 Act, chiefly through county councils and the structure plan and national park planning processes, was almost universally restrictive.

In short, the Act was concerned to redress the perceived problems of the 1950s and 1960s and not to anticipate those of the 1970s and 1980s. Even as the Act was passed, new issues were beginning to feature on the recreation and access planning agenda.

2

The 1970s and 1980s: tinkering with recreation and access supply

2.1 RECREATION MANAGEMENT AND INTERPRETATION

In tandem with the passing of the 1968 Act came the recognition that many issues of a smaller scale relating to countryside recreation were not amenable to being solved by the more formal planning mechanisms being proposed by the Act. As in 1949, the provisions of the 1968 Act were responding more to historical pressures than current issues, and to an extent in this respect, both Acts were out of date as soon as they had been passed.

2.1.1 Countryside management

In response to this 'smaller scale', and drawing from a number of planning studies on informal recreation, for example the Sherwood Forest Study (Countryside Commission, 1970), countryside management was conceived as a means by which liaison and goodwill could be created by local authorities entering into voluntary agreements with landowners. This would allow small-scale projects to be implemented not only with recreation, but conservation and multiple land-use objectives (Centre for Leisure Research, 1986).

This notion of countryside management was initiated even before the passing of the 1968 Act. In the Lake District and Snowdonia National Parks, Upland Management Experiments were introduced (Countryside Commission, 1976a, 1979b) and their success led to their extension to heritage coasts and the urban fringe into the 1970s. At the same time, planning policies for recreation control began to bite. As well as through the planning process, national policies for control were axiomatic:

Naturally such [recreation] uses must be carefully controlled if we are to successfully reconcile demands with the conflicting interests of farming, forestry, water supply and wildlife and avoid creating either a desert or a museum in the countryside (Department of the Environment, 1972, p. 57).

By the mid-1970s this 'containment' ethos led to a significant slowing down in new facility provision under the 1968 Act and to a large degree as a consequence of this, countryside management schemes became more widespread. For the urban fringe they had been formalized in 1972 with the introduction of the Urban Fringe Experiments in the Bollin Valley on the edge of Manchester (Countryside Commission, 1976b). These experiments extended the objectives of the upland management schemes beyond practical problem-solving to reconciling the interests of different user groups and were stimulated by a number of factors.

The first of these was that positive recreation management could solve a number of problems of the urban fringe simultaneously. Recreation developments were considered useful 'problem solvers' for areas of wasteland and farmland with an uncertain future. Further, the urban fringe was relatively under-exploited for recreation purposes. Second, recreation was considered a politically useful activity to stem further urban developments. Positive moves to enhance urban fringe environments could form a useful complement to containment policies. Third, those living in towns were increasingly keen to assist in practical tasks, either as voluntary wardens at sites or as conservation volunteers carrying out tasks such as fencing and the repairing of stiles and gates. Countryside management schemes were successful in stimulating the interest of the local community, but there was perhaps an element here of cost-effective management or even recreation management 'on the cheap'.

These factors were institutionalized into a notion of countryside management that was, strictly, outside the restrictive policies of the land-use planning system. Over 30 experiments on the urban fringe were eventually introduced by the 1980s. They covered the green belt areas of Greater Manchester, Tyneside, the West Midlands and London. Landscape renewal projects were introduced around the potteries and in South Staffordshire. In Hertfordshire five separate countryside management projects were introduced covering most of the green belt in the county (Countryside Commission, 1983). In a number of places, such experiments were particularly successful at considering recreation opportunities as part of a system that straddled local authority boundaries.

In some areas these experiments were formalized into management plans and even formed part of a framework for local subject plans as in the river valleys of the Tame, Mersey and Medlock, and the River Tees

Plan for Access and Recreation (Cleveland County Council, 1978). But they had shortcomings in a number of respects. First, they depended heavily on the competences and even charisma of an independent project officer who would be concerned with getting things done. These things were to embrace clearing and surfacing footpaths, renegotiating new footpath routes, developing small-scale tree planting, providing picnic sites in small woodland areas and so forth.

Second, as the Centre for Leisure Research (1986) notes, their success was based more on the common ground that could be established between certain agriculturalists and conservationists than with recreationalists seeking new forms of access. Third, many experiments were considered to be attempts to overcome poor levels of provision that were properly the responsibility of the local authority sector. Even where local authorities operated in partnership with some schemes, they often failed to execute their own undertakings, particularly in respect of landscaping. When dereliction was particularly severe, the effects of informal management mechanisms appeared to be little more than a cosmetic exercise.

Finally, the experimental nature of these projects ensured that they were short-term, and the adoption of countryside management services in areas where they were originally introduced has been dependent on the vagaries of the continued requirement of financial assistance through countryside grant allocations. This was thus a development in recreation provision based not so much on well-measured policies and plans but more on pragmatism and personality.

The fragility of this countryside management approach, being based as it was on voluntary agreements, was given a slightly stronger foundation in the early 1980s with the passing of the 1981 Wildlife and Countryside Act. Under this Act, local authorities could enter into a management agreement with a landowner who would then voluntarily refrain from certain agreed forms of land development. Thus they could be used, for example, for the maintenance or improvement of *de facto* permissive rights of way, but in truth they were less positive than the Access Agreement provisions of the 1949 Act that allowed for an increase in recreation opportunities rather than a reduction in their loss, but which had never been widely exploited.

By 1990, the Rights of Way Act offered little new for countryside management either, simply modifying the law on the ploughing and planting of footpaths and making the disturbance of rights of way, without lawful cause and offence. All in all, then, countryside management has been interpreted as failing to address the more fundamental problems of access. As Harrison (1991, p. 5) maintains:

The approach can be interpreted as a technocratic approach to the resolution of environmental problems that operates outside of the planning system. It did not seek to question why the conflicts had arisen in the first place. In practice, too, the approach based on partnership with local authorities and the voluntary sector provided a pragmatic solution to the (Countryside) Commission's own deteriorating resources.

2.1.1 Countryside interpretation

Running parallel with experiments in countryside management came, in the early 1970s, an increasing interest in the role of countryside interpretation. This growth in interpretation was strongly influenced by techniques pioneered in the USA which included self-guided trails, listening posts, fixed message repeaters, displays and even the practical undertaking of conservation tasks. In truth, however, these were developed as much for the imparting of the conservation message – developing an understanding of the processes occurring in the natural environment – as for public enjoyment *per se*. They would supplement 'control' mechanisms being developed in countryside management strategies, to reduce visitor impact.

The Countryside Commission's (1974a) advisory notes on country park plans had placed a strong emphasis on the role of interpretation at countryside recreation sites and more generally a number of studies had been commissioned during the 1970s to develop the interpretation base of particular sites (see, for example, Aldridge, 1975, and Stephens, 1978). In terms of capturing the public interest – at least the interest of the public who were enjoying the countryside through self-discovery rather than guided discovery, and regular users of the countryside – the success of the interpretation ethos was mixed. As the Centre for Leisure Research (1986) notes, most visitors, in fact, pay little attention to interpretation at individual sites. At Lochore Meadows Country Park (Countryside Commission for Scotland, 1982) for example, although 60% of visitors recalled leaflets being at the park, fewer than 30% read them and hardly anyone could remember anything about them one week later.

At Crickley Hill Country Park in Gloucestershire (Curry, 1983), in a survey relating to interpretation, around 80% of visitors made no use of the visitor centre, leaflet information and wardening services. This was due in part at least to the fact that many users used the park daily to walk the dog. A study by the Dartington Amenity Research Trust (1978) also concluded that interpretation may have no long-term effect on the visitor but also concluded that those who were most receptive to such facilities were those who were already most familiar with the ways of the countryside. They were also from the upper managerial occupations, a point that is considered further in Chapter 5.

Prince (1980), too, found that in the North Yorkshire Moors National Park interpretation facilities appealed only to a very narrow, more affluent and educated sector of the population (mirroring, he noted, the class of interpretation providers), and, as a result, questioned the use of interpretation even for conservation purposes. In examining features such as nature trails, visitor centres and landscape education boards, he found an over-emphasis on presentation to the detriment of communication and in terms of visitor appeal, many facilities were found to be educationally redundant. Prince concluded that a concentration of interpretation facilities in the countryside, as opposed to the town, for which provision had been made in the 1968 Act, has contributed to an alienation of the working class.

Thus, countryside management and interpretation represent somewhat *ad hoc* procedures. Countryside management is based on a mixture of personality, cash, goodwill, voluntary effort and grant aid. Interpretation is a borrowed idea that has contained a strong element of 'what people ought to have' rather than necessarily what they want. Fitton (1979) does suggest that interpretation has the potential to reduce conflicts in the countryside but suggests that this might more appropriately take place in the town rather than the countryside. But importantly, both management and interpretation have developed as informal mechanisms to fill a gap in recreation provision brought about by the lack of any clear statutory powers to regulate land use for recreation purposes under the 1968 Act.

2.2 RECREATION IN THE URBAN FRINGE

The failure of the 1949 Act effectively to consider recreation provision in areas anywhere but national parks gave the town and country planning system an opportunity to fill the breach. Patrick Abbercrombie, a co-founder of the (then) Council for the Preservation of Rural England, in his Greater London Plan advocated a system of outdoor recreation that included green wedges and green belts for public enjoyment as well as the containment of urban sprawl. It was thus the planning system rather than countryside legislation *per se*, that was beginning to address the recreational aspirations of the more middle-class southern pressure groups that had had a significant role prior to the 1949 Act.

These green belts and green wedges were introduced under the 1947 Town and Country Planning Act with similar dual functions to national parks – conservation (or more commonly because of their location, containment) and the development of recreation opportunities. Although they were to become reasonably successful at containing settlements, these areas were particularly threatened by townspeople seeking recreation simply by their popularity and proximity. This led to a degree of retrenchment on the part of urban fringe landowners, with the result that in many areas, recreation opportunities became more restrictive than had previously been the case. As Rubenstein and Speakman (1969, p. 10) note:

> Only about 5% of the Metropolitan Green Belt was available for recreation in 1960, nearly a third of it as golf courses having little general appeal (p. 10).

By the mid-1960s, though, the planning profession was responding to a degree to the problems of developing recreation in the green belt. In 1964, the Civic Trust prepared, for 18 constituent local authorities, a report on a Lea Valley Regional Park as an area of recreation, leisure, sport and entertainment for the people of north-east London. It was formally constituted under a Private Bill in 1969 – an 'Epping Forest' of the twentieth century. But the dominant response of the planning profession in these areas was to allow passive recreation only, on degraded or otherwise derelict land to avoid the use of working farm-land.

This notion of passive recreation only, in green belts as indeed in national parks, had come under fire from official sources in the 1960s, however. Dower (1978) notes the criticism of the Wolfenden Committee of the Central Council for Physical Recreation which reported in 1960 pressing for the development of more gregarious activities in the countryside. It concluded in connection with the desire for solitude, peace and quiet in the countryside that 'although the feeling is a natural one it is nevertheless selfish' (Central Council for Physical Recreation, 1960). The report, however, was based largely on the inherent virtues of more active pursuits than any comprehensive notion of what the public at large were likely to want to do. The dominance of passive countryside recreation was a strong characteristic of land-use policies in the 1970s and 1980s, a point that is considered more fully in Chapter 7.

By the 1970s, in many areas close to town where pressure for many different land uses were great, planning authorities began to move towards systems of land-use priority areas, to lessen conflicts. Some counties introduced agricultural priority areas where intensive activities such as country parks, golf courses and commercial sports activities were not to be allowed. Shoard (1978) maintains that it was agricultural intensification that caused the principal loss of recreation opportunities in areas close to towns in the 1960s and 1970s.

Occasionally, however, 'recreation priority areas' were established, such as in Hertfordshire, where, although agriculture was to remain the dominant land-using activity, more intensive recreation areas were also to be acceptable. It was in such areas that countryside management initiatives, discussed above, flourished. But as Harrison (1991) and Elson (1986) both note, this recreation role around towns and cities was used to justify both the implementation of green-belt policy, and as an excuse for many areas not achieving urban space standards proposed by the National Playing Fields Association.

Recreation 'policies' also sprang up from less likely sources. The Minerals Act of 1951 introduced for the first time after-use requirements on mineral workings. Minerals companies were to restore minerals sites once they had been worked, in an appropriate alternative use. The most popular of these was to be recreation, particularly where areas of water were involved.

This was to take on particular significance in structure plans, where water areas were considered among the most appropriate for the development of recreation. The fact that these after-use requirements were not made retrospective on minerals planning applications made them ineffective, however. This was because most minerals workings worked out up to the middle of the 1980s had had permissions given to them prior to 1951 and so after-use requirements did not apply.

During the 1960s and 1970s the presence of 80% and then 100% derelict land grants in the north of England gave an impetus for environmental improvement, the most common after-use for which was countryside recreation. This has allowed recreation budgets to develop tree planting, way marking and other facilities at a later stage. The Rother Valley regional park on the edge of Sheffield is one example of this, reclaimed from colliery pit heaps, and Blaydon Burn on the edge of Newcastle-upon-Tyne is another. By the 1981 Town and Country Planning (Minerals) Act minerals after-use requirements had been extended to 'aftercare' which required not just the restoration of minerals sites, but also their on-going management for recreation uses. Again, however, such conditions were not made retrospective.

In the context of derelict land grants and minerals restoration obligations, environmental improvement in the river valleys around Greater Manchester was to enhance urban fringe recreation opportunities greatly during the 1970s and 1980s. This was achieved through county-district co-operation with the county providing much of the finance and the districts producing statutory local plans for each of the valleys, embracing access improvements and increased provision for informal countryside recreation. Joint management committees were to provide policy consistency across each of the valleys.

Notwithstanding these successes in and around Manchester, the particular problems of the countryside around towns met with no formal government response in the 1970s, despite lobbying from landowners and public authorities alike. Partly as a result of this, the Countryside Commission conceived of the idea of promoting experiments in environmental improvement, recreation provision and farmland provision in the style of the Manchester river valleys. This would include funding from the major agencies investing in the urban fringe countryside and carried out making use of countryside management techniques pioneered in Bollin Valley.

In 1980 Operation Groundwork was thus launched around St Helens in Greater Merseyside and by 1982 a regional programme – Groundwork Northwest – was underway. Groundwork projects aim to establish a partnership between a range of organizations in the public, private and voluntary sectors. They are to play an enabling and catalytic role in bringing resources together to concentrate on countering industrial dereliction by putting wasteland to good use and by integrating farming. As a result of this general environmental remit, only a limited number of improvements relate to the upgrading of recreational facilities, with the possible exception of Rossendale, which has established its own access forum.

By 1985 the Groundwork scheme had gone national with the establishment of the National Groundwork Foundation, and trusts were set up outside the Northwest. An example of such was the Colne Valley Regional Park Groundwork Trust set up for the Park in the north-west of London in 1987, in an attempt to assist with flagging local authority funds, by setting itself a target of raising commercial funds and stimulating voluntary effort. Today there are 23 Groundwork Trusts nationwide.

Historically the Trusts have had a privileged position financially, being able to secure funds from local authorities and the Department of the Environment centrally, principally through derelict land grants, and the commercial sector. But since the abolition of the metropolitan county councils in 1986, these funds have been severely curtailed, and there is an increasing danger that the precarious nature of funding will severely limit the work of the Trusts into the future, leading to a new form of dereliction (Harrison, 1991).

Like countryside management, the work of Operation Groundwork has not been without its critics. The Centre for Leisure Research (1986) perceives them as often acting as a buffer between the local authority and the public and in many cases raising false expectations since their intentions are based more on aspiration than statutory responsibility. In addition, some concern has been expressed about the quasi-public sector status of Groundwork Trusts, since they have been regarded as potentially divisive of the voluntary sector, because of their privileged position in relation to funding and to local authorities. There have been fears too that successful Trusts could reduce the funding available to truly voluntary grass roots organizations. Their accountability has also been brought into question by Harrison (1991, pp. 146–7):

> unless there is an obvious mechanism for incorporating the work of the Trusts into the planning process, the Trusts run the risk of compensating for the failure of the local authorities and other public agencies, from carrying out their responsibilities.

Away from Operation Groundwork by the mid-1980s, urban fringe areas, particularly in the home counties, had become increasingly characterized by recreation and other non-agricultural pursuits. As farmers began to seek diversification opportunities, sport and recreation – from horsey culture to war games and farm parks – offered clear commercial opportunities often without the need to make recourse to planning approvals, or even quasi-public management schemes.

2.3 ORGANIZATIONAL OVERLAP

2.3.1 Burgeoning resource agency responsibilities

Also in the wake of the 1968 Countryside Act, the implementation of recreation policies and plans was to become more complex with the profusion of agencies having responsibility for countryside recreation and access (Table 2.1). Even prior to the Act, an Advisory Sports Council (to become an executive body, the Sports Council, in 1972) had been established, that was to champion the cause of 'planning standards' for recreation provision, that was to do much to divert local authorities from the more important role of assessing demands, in the production of structure plans.

Close on the heels of the formation of the Countryside Commission (where the 1968 Act saw the Commission's role of co-ordinating other agencies in respect of countryside recreation as being important), was the foundation of the English Tourist Board under the 1969 Development of Tourism Act. This introduced a regional planning function for tourism, by designating regional tourist boards both to develop tourism in the regions and encourage individual projects. The British Tourist Authority was also to have responsibility for attracting visitors from abroad to the British Countryside.

In the water sector too, the British Waterways Board was formed under the 1968 Transport Act to develop inland waterways specifically for recreation and amenity purposes. It now owns, operates and maintains most man-made inland waterways in England and Wales and is empowered to designate certain rivers and canals as 'cruising waterways' for powered boats. It can also provide for other facilities, for example, angling.

The Board was to be joined in 1974 by the now defunct Water Space Amenity Commission which was to liaise with the water industry more generally over the recreation potential of water. The Commission was set up as a result of the empowering of the regional water authorities to develop facilities for recreational use under the 1973 Water Act. This was undertaken particularly for reservoirs and disused mineral workings, but it remained a residual function of the authorities and, as a result, provision has remained patchy.

Under the 1967 Forestry Act, the Forestry Commission was empowered to develop recreation facilities in its own forests and to encourage recreation in private forests. This disposition had a deeper history in that the initial growth in Forestry Commission recreation interest stemmed from the inter-war years, when it was promulgated as a 'good relations' exercise in the face of extensive public protest over large coniferous planting in the Lake District (Harrison, 1991). By 1972, however, the Commission was making its responsibilities towards country-side recreation more explicit. The Treasury's (1972) cost-benefit study into forestry outlined the economically marginal nature of timber production alone and suggested that expanding the recreation activities of forests would enhance arguments for timber expansion.

The resultant Forestry Policy White Paper (HMSO, 1972) detailed the intention to enhance recreation provision in forests, introduced a recreation and conservation branch into the Forestry Commission's headquarters structure, and gave its regional conservancies a remit to produce conservancy recreation plans. A vigorous programme of the designation of National Forest Parks (the first of which had been introduced in 1936) and drives ensued and some forests such as the New Forest and the Forest of Dean were to be given particular recreation priorities.

In tandem with this development in the forestry sector, the Nature Conservancy Council (now English Nature) – reconstituted under the 1972 Nature Conservancy Council Act – was developing much more explicitly, through its annual reports, policies for a recreation component in the designation of national, forest and local nature reserves. Good management was to be the key here to the maintenance of nature conservation value and the development of guided trails, open days and so on became of increasing importance. Despite these new powers being given to, or enhanced in, a number of resource planning agencies, during the 1970s the development of recreation planning was piecemeal, unlike the responsibilities for conservation which, under the 1968 Act, were to be held by all government ministers.

2.3.2 Regionalism

These expanded powers for recreation were consolidated in 1973 with the House of Lords Select Committee on Sport and Leisure. This Committee held the view that leisure should be elevated in policy terms to the level of other types of social provision such as education and housing. This Committee provided a principal impetus for the introduction of a White Paper on Sport and Recreation in 1975.

The White Paper was concerned to broaden the base of recreational and sports facilities and was keen not to separate out town and country too strongly. Park systems to cover both the town and the country were advocated and it was considered that both the planning and organization of these were best done on a regional scale. The natural home of the 'leisure park', as the Select Committee called it, would be the urban fringe, and the best way to plan for such development was to bring the Sports Council and the Countryside Commission closer together and have some forum-based structure for the exchange of ideas.

This 'regionalization' was implemented through two Department of the Environment Circulars. Circular 47/76 (Department of the Environment, 1976b) regionalized the Sports Council and introduced eight Regional Councils for Sport and Recreation. Their main function was to co-ordinate provision through the preparation of regional recreation strategies. The councils themselves were to be an amalgam of all bodies in the region with an interest in recreation and sport and were to be serviced by the Sports Council regional offices with assistance from the Countryside Commission.

These councils were to have an ineffectual role into the 1980s, considered further in Chapter 6, and as a result, a ministerial review of them was undertaken between 1983 and 1986. This changed their terms of reference and membership slightly, but no revision of the terms of Circular 47/76 was proposed. These organizations were further supplemented in 1988 by 'Countryside and Water Recreation Policy Groups' set up again by the Sports Council (1988), the impacts of which have yet to become apparent.

The Department of the Environment's (1977) Circular 73/77 further consolidated this regionalization with the introduction of guidelines for the production of regional recreation strategies. These strategies were to help improve the range of opportunities for participation in sport and recreation in the regions. As Ferguson (1979) notes, there was no indication of how this was to be done and indeed any consideration of specific recreation sites was discouraged. These regional strategies were to assist in the co-ordination of recreation policies in structure plans but the first of them was published in the late 1970s after over half of the first round of structure plans had already been produced.

This Circular, together with the regionalization of the English Tourist Board in 1969 and the Sports Council in 1976, as well as the institution of the Regional Councils for Sport and Recreation in the same year, led the Countryside Commission to open regional offices in 1978. By this time national policy had in turn created a fairly comprehensive regional framework for countryside recreation, but this was coincident with the production of some of the first non-national policies for recreation, contained in structure plans, at a county level.

2.3.3 The local authority sector

In addition to these responsibilities of the national and regional resource agencies, the development of a two-tier system of town and country planning, discussed in a number of government reports in the late 1960s (Redcliffe-Maudé, 1969), was made law in the 1971 Town and Country Planning Act. This gave local authorities a statutory remit to consider recreation and tourism in both structure and local plans. They were, however, constrained to develop plans within their counties and districts, which more often than not concerned activity generated by people who came from elsewhere. From this time too, districts were to take on the responsibility for tourist information centres.

In 1972 the Local Government Act too, enacted in 1974, in strengthening the powers of national park authorities, introduced provisions for national park plans which were to be concerned with recreation and conservation management. Despite guidance notes from the Countryside Commission (1974b) these were to be very diverse in nature, some resembling structure plans more than management plans. This was at least in part because, unlike structure plans at that time, they did not require the formal approval of the Secretary of State. This strengthening of the powers of national park authorities often fragmented recreation and access functions between the park and the county.

The 1972 Local Government Act also changed the boundaries of local authorities and in many instances led to a reorganization of their internal structure. During the 1970s there was a growth in the development of multi-purpose leisure services departments, particularly in county and metropolitan authorities which, in the case of the latter, were disbanded with their abolition in 1986. As a legacy in metropolitan areas, a number of advisory units, such as the Greater Manchester Countryside Unit, have remained to provide a recreation input into the unitary development planning process that now exists in these areas.

The multi-purpose leisure departments in the counties undertook a number of policy and provision functions for countryside recreation but it was still the town and country planning departments that had the statutory responsibility for planning for recreation, and the county highways authorities that had a legal obligation over rights of way, footpaths, bridleways and other forms of access. To these could be added the parks and recreation and arts, amenity and library departments of the district authorities, that provided a structure for countryside recreation provision in local authorities every bit as complicated as that emerging at a regional level.

This pattern of fragmented responsibility in local authorities was found by the Centre for Leisure Research (1986) to reflect and reinforce a low priority for recreation and access provision generally and a lack of funding, especially for the rights of way functions of highways departments, in particular. They call for the consolidation of recreation and access functions into one department to reduce this residualization against other competing responsibilities.

Not only were there many departments within local authorities but, in recognition of the regional scale of countryside recreation, the 1968 Act had made provision for the setting up of advisory boards comprising separate local authorities where recreation 'regions' crossed local-authority boundaries. These have been set up in areas such as the North Pennines and the Cotswold Water Park and for many Areas of Outstanding Natural Beauty but authorities are reluctant to give them a higher priority than any of their internal functions. They have been most successful where they have been given some form of independent delegated status such as in the Lea Valley Regional Park.

Added to this, a number of less formal regional planning forums have been initiated, particularly in the south-east, that have a policy input to recreation planning. The south-east's 'Countryside Forum', for example, has an advisory function to local authorities in the region and includes representation from the Sports Council, the Countryside Commission and English Nature. It stands independent of, and has a broader remit than, the South East Regional Council for Sport and Recreation. The London Planning Advisory Committee, too, offers advice on matters relating to recreation and sport, although its advice inevitably is concordant with that of the south-east regional recreation strategy. The distinctive roles of these organizations, covering the same geographical area, is not always clear.

By the late 1970s, then, there had been several initiatives concerned to develop government activity for countryside recreation. These developments unlike in agriculture and forestry policy, for example, were spread across a number of agencies, most of which operated at a regional level but whose co-ordination was weak. It is this multiplicity and duplication of roles that has served, in part, to dissipate the effectiveness of recreation policy developments, supporting the first proposition of this book (p. xi).

2.3.4 Changing structures into the 1980s and 1990s

The 1980s saw a period of some stability in agency structure for country-side recreation and access, but on the other hand, some were to modify their functions. The 1981 Wildlife and Countryside Act changed the status of the Countryside Commission from being part of the civil service to being a grant-in-aid body – part of the 'public' service. This was to give it more independence but also possibly less of an influence in ministerial circles. Perpetual calls from the Commission during the 1980s for a White Paper on the 'Rural Estate' fell on deaf ears at the Department of the Environment.

Its independence, too, brought with it a change in the composition of its commissioners away from local government and the professions towards a membership based much more on the farming community (Lowe and Goyder, 1983). This was perhaps to have an influence on the movement of countryside recreation provision towards the market place but it also happened in parallel with a change in policy orientation at the Commission.

In truth, up to the 1980s, as part of the civil service, the Commission did not have an independent national policy towards recreation and access. It was constrained to supplying advisory notes and guidance on the distribution of grant aid. What policy there was could be found in fragmented statements in annual reports. Grant-in-aid status allowed the development of national policies independent of central govern-ment. In this context, consultation began in the spring of 1985 over a national policy statement to become known as 'Policies for Enjoying the Countryside'. Here, the Commission was concerned to make public enjoyment a higher policy priority, to consider the potential for a new 'Countryside Recreation Area' designation to move away from the notion of individual sites, to reconsider policies for sites, 'open country' and public rights of way, and to assess the management and resources required for the implementation of such policies.

By the mid 1980s a government agency set up in the early 1970s, the Manpower Services Commission sponsored by the Department of Employment, was also having a significant impact on countryside rec-reation. The direct job creation programmes of the Commission through the Community Programme, because they were not to displace local job markets, were largely orientated towards environmental improvements in the countryside and the urban fringe. Such programmes gave a great boost to the working of many voluntary organizations.

Despite an increasing use of voluntary effort in countryside manage-ment schemes, it was considered to have two principal problems. First, because the voluntary sector was not subject to the same degree of legal obligation as, say, the local authority sector was, the standard of

Table 2.1 Agencies involved in the planning of countryside recreation

Agency	Date of formation	Role
Rural Development Commission	1909	Responsible for the development of Tourism Development Action Plans in Rural Development Areas
Forestry Commission	1919	Responsible for recreation in state and private forests
National Parks Commission	1949 (now disbanded)	Responsible for recreation in national parks
British Waterways Board	1968	Responsible for recreation and amenity use of British inland waterways
Countryside Commission	1968	Facilitate enjoyment of the countryside
English Tourist Board	1969	Encourage tourism and the provision of facilities
British Tourist Authority	1969	Encourage visitors from abroad
Agricultural Development Advisory Service	1971 (now disbanded)	Farm-based recreation as a part of farm diversification
Nature Conservancy Council	1972 (now disbanded)	Recreation in nature reserves if no conflict with conservation
Sports Council	1972	Sport in the countryside (including walking)
Regional Water Authorities	1973 (now disbanded)	Responsible for water recreation in their regions
Manpower Services Commission	1973 (now disbanded)	Employment creation in recreation management, many rural tourism initiatives

implementation was very variable. Second, passing responsibility to the voluntary sector wrested control from the local authorities in the implementation of recreation developmental work.

In the event, the Manpower Services Commission direct labour force did little to overcome these problems, since it was inhibited by the transitory nature of employment under such programmes. It was difficult to plan programmes over a long time horizon which did not engender in employees a commitment to their work. The Manpower Services

Table 2.1 *continued*

Agency	Date of formation	Role
District Councils	1974	Recreation for the local population and (1991) recreation provisions in district development plans
County Councils	1974	Recreation and access provision for the wider population, and recreation policies in structure plans and countryside strategies
National Park Authority	1974	Recreation and enjoyment in national parks
Parish Councils	1974	Often given responsibility for the preparation of the definitive map
Water Space Amenity Commission	1974 (now disbanded)	Develop the recreation potential of the water industry
Regional Councils for Sport and Recreation	1976	Co-ordinate agency policies for recreation at the regional level
National Rivers Authority	1990	Recreation on the national river system
English Nature	1991	Replaced the functions of Nature Conservancy Council
ADAS, Food, Farming, Land and Leisure	1992	Farm-based recreation
United Kingdom Sports Commission	1993 (proposed)	Excellence in sport
English Sports Council	1993 (proposed)	Mass participation in sport

Commission was disbanded in 1988 and along with it the Community Programme that had created so much, albeit transitory, countryside management work (Curry and Gaskell, 1989). And in the wake of its demise, as with the Groundwork Trusts, was left a voluntary sector more cynical of its role, having been displaced by masses of otherwise unemployed people, for a comparatively short period of time.

By the early 1990s, further organizational changes for countryside recreation came with the formation of English Nature in 1991. Its responsibilities for recreation were no different than those of the Nature Conservancy Council which it had replaced, but its geographical jurisdiction was restricted to England. The privatization of the water industry under the 1991 Water Act, too, largely removed responsibility for recreation on water authority lands from the public sector altogether.

By April 1993, as a result of the Atkins *Review of Sport and Active Recreation* (1991), the structure of the Sports Council was also proposed for change. The Sports Council was to be superseded by an English Sports Council (with similar bodies for Wales and Scotland), with a principal concern for 'foundation' and mass participation levels of sport. But the pursuit of excellence and international levels of performance was to become the concern of a United Kingdom Sports Commission (Sports Council, 1992). By September 1993, however, these changes had been put on hold.

2.3.5 Ministerial responsibilities

If the organizational structure of government agency responsibilities for countryside recreation and access is complex and cumbersome, it is further complicated by partial and uncoordinated ministerial responsibilities for rural leisure. Historically, it has always been difficult to decide which ministry should have responsibility for countryside recreation. Even with the passing of the 1949 Act, there were uncertainties about whether the responsibility for its implementation should rest with the Ministry of Town and Country Planning because of the national importance of national parks. In 1968, too, the White Paper 'Leisure in the Countryside' had been sponsored by the Ministry of Land and Natural Resources, formed in 1964 by the new Wilson government. By the time the Act reached Royal Assent, the Ministry had been abolished.

At the beginning of the 1980s, the countryside recreation portfolio rested uneasily in a number of ministries. Education had responsibility for adult education, environmental education and the youth service. The Department of the Environment sponsored many of the agencies with some responsibility for countryside recreation and access, including the local authorities, the Countryside Commission and the Sports Council. The Department of Trade and Industry was in charge of the tourism sector, while the Employment Department presided over hours of work and the length of holidays.

By 1984 ministerial responsibility for the tourism industry had changed from the Department of Trade and Industry to the Department of Employment, emphasizing the importance of the industry to employment generation. Moves to change the quango structure of the industry – the Industry Minister proposed a merging of the British Tourist Authority and the English Tourist Board in 1983 – never came to pass.

Two years later, the 1986 Agriculture Act gave the Ministry of Agriculture direct recreation responsibilities in relation to farm diversification, adding to the complexity of ministerial responsibilities for countryside recreation depicted in Table 2.2. By 1990 increasing concern about the importance of developing a 'sport culture' in schools as a means of sustaining participation later in life led to a shift of the Sports Council from Environment to Education.

By the new government of 1992, a new Heritage Ministry – the 'Ministry for Fun' – had been created. As well as having a concern for broadcasting and the arts, it became the sponsoring ministry of the English Tourist Board, the Sports Council, and eventually, perhaps the UK Sports Commission, bringing about a second ministerial move for each of these agencies in less than seven years.

This fragmentation of countryside recreation and access responsibilities in government has undoubtedly contributed to its politically residual nature. A number of organizations, for example the Central Council for Physical Recreation (1991), have called for changes to improve its co-ordination. Certainly, the realignment of government responsibilities for rural leisure would be beneficial. Some kind of 'marriage' between the Ministry of Agriculture and the Department of the Environment over countryside issues would seem particularly useful, but the introduction of the Labour Party's notion of a Ministry for Leisure in their 1987 election manifesto would allow a better co-ordination of all of the components of rural leisure.

Table 2.2 The functions of central government departments in relation to countryside recreation[a]

Department	Function
Education	Policy for adult education, physical education, environmental education and the youth service. Sponsoring Ministry for the Sports Council, 1990–1992
Environment	Sponsoring Ministry for the Sports Council (to 1990), the Countryside Commission, English Nature, the National Rivers Authority and local authorities
Employment	Responsible for the tourist industry from 1986. Sponsoring Ministry for the Tourist Boards from 1984 to 1992. Guidelines on hours of work and holidays
Agriculture	Recreation responsibilities in farm diversification. Forest recreation via the Forestry Commission
Heritage	Sponsoring Ministry for tourism (English Tourist Board) and sport (Sports Council/Commission) from 1992. Responsible for arts and heritage
Trade and Industry	Sponsoring Ministry for the tourism sector to 1986

[a] Historically, the functions of the Department of the Environment have been held by similar ministries with frequently changing names, such as the Ministry of Works and Planning, the Ministry of Town and Country Planning and the short-lived Ministry of Land and Natural Resources.

2.4 FROM UNEASY STEPS IN SOCIAL PROVISION TO THE MARKET PLACE

During the 1970s there were also uneasy steps in social provision for countryside recreation. The 1968 Countryside Act, in having its recreation provisions weakened in fear of recreation growth, gave powers to the Countryside Commission that were principally to facilitate rather than to promote countryside recreation and access. It was to cater only for 'those resorting to the countryside' (Dower, 1978). This made targeting recreation development at specific people and specific areas rather difficult, although in early guidance documents (Countryside Commission, 1974a) priority for grant aid for country parks, at least, was given to areas close to urban centres.

The Sports Council, although having a clear jurisdiction over the more active forms of countryside recreation – walking in the countryside was considered the most popular sport of all – was not fettered by the facilitation-only ethic of the Countryside Commission. It was able in 1972 to develop a positive and promotional role for access to sport for all people – 'sport for all' – which inevitably made incursions into the countryside. Recognizing this somewhat passive role for the Countryside Commission in respect of developing countryside recreation and access for disadvantaged groups, the House of Lords Select Committee in 1973 had considered that:

> society ought to regard sport and leisure not as a slightly eccentric form of indulgence, but one of the community's everyday needs (p. xxvi)

and had recommended a 'recreation for all' role for the Commission, which was to include 'Recreation Priority Areas' for the disadvantaged in inner cities. Concern for the rural environment, however, ensured that this was not enthusiastically endorsed by government for rural areas and the 'disadvantaged' were catered for by the Sports Council, whose remit was not restricted to the countryside, through grant-aid to 'areas of special need'. The inner-city disadvantaged were to be catered for 'in situ' (Dower, 1978).

By the mid-1970s a number of groups were beginning to call for social policies for countryside recreation. The Town and Country Planning Association launched a campaign for recreation among the car-less (Curry, 1985c) and the English Tourist Board and the Trades Union Congress (1976) jointly developed the notion of 'social tourism' for the physically and mentally handicapped, the low paid and the elderly. The government's independent 'think tank' on the countryside, the Countryside Review Committee (1977) also came down in favour of the development of countryside recreation facilities for the socially disadvantaged.

The Countryside Commission (1981) was also undertaking a series of rural transport experiments to encourage the car-less into the country-side, and by the beginning of the 1980s the Chairman's Policy Group (1983), an amalgam of many of the chairpeople of the agencies in Table 2.1, with a concern for countryside recreation, was stressing the import-ance of social policies. These proposals, and attempts at developing policies for social recreation more generally, were to meet with limited success, a point which is considered in more detail in Chapter 5.

Despite protestations from the Chairman's Policy Group, echoing the sentiments of the House of Lords Select Committee on Sport and Leisure and the White Paper on Sport and Recreation during the 1970s, by the start of the 1980s, the new Thatcher era had caused a shift in the preoccupation of recreation policies away from social provision and towards a greater interest in market worth. The development of coun-tryside recreation began to be driven more by market strategies and investigations into pricing policies, as the real value of money available for expenditure on recreation by local authorities declined.

But to create markets it is necessary to restrict access so that charges for 'entrants' to the facility effectively can be made. Ironically, public agencies that were set up to promote access were now beginning to restrict it, not only in ability to pay terms, but also through ring fencing. As is discussed further in Chapter 3, there is a danger that this principle might extend to access areas traditionally of customarily considered as a public right (Lowe, Clark and Cox, 1991).

At Rufford Country Park in Nottinghamshire, for example, in the late 1970s a cost analysis of alternative projects within the park was under-taken, including a craft centre and interpretation centre as part of a marketing exercise (Coopers Lybrand Associates, 1979). This led to the selection of a desired mix of attractions which were priced and marketed along private sector lines.

The obligation too for the Forestry Commission to sell off lands under the 1981 Forestry Act further 'privatized' public access. Although these sales have to date been limited it has been those smaller tracts of amenity woodland, with the highest recreation potential, that have proved most attractive to purchasers. This has been compounded by the 1990 Water Act, taking water authority lands into the private sector increasing the threat of restricted access and its 'commoditization' for sale (Redburn, 1985).

For the tourism industry, too, it was the worth of the industry to the producer and to the local economy, rather than the consumer, that became the emphasis. Tourism planning was driven by assessments of employment potential and export earnings. Any social advantages of holidays articulated in the English Tourist Board and Trades Union Congress (1976) report on social tourism were absent from the 1987 Conservative Party manifesto.

Tourism in the mid 1980s became the industry par excellence for creating jobs. This was because of the labour-intensive nature of the industry and its seasonal peaks, rather than because the industry had a good employment structure. This perceived potential for the industry allowed government cash to be put into tourism and job market research, tourism training and tourism promotion. And for rural areas specifically, the Rural Development Commission was assisting local authorities in the introduction of Tourism Development Action Programmes in Rural Development Areas. Much tourism job market research and training was done through the (then) Manpower Services Commission's Local Collaborative Projects Schemes which were designed to identify and implement training. The large number of these meant project duplication on a significant scale. One particular limitation of these schemes was their concern only to identify training needs for those people already employed, rather than those people who wished to pursue qualifications to enter the industry.

2.5 THE IMPORTANCE OF RECREATION, ACCESS AND TOURISM IN GOVERNMENT

The low prioritization of rural leisure in government in the 1980s was manifest in three main factors. First, apart from the Cabinet Office's (1985) 'Pleasure, Leisure and Jobs', there have been no parallels since 1980 of the White Papers, Circulars, Select Committee Reports and other government documents of the 1960s and 1970s. In contrast, policies and proposals have been promulgated by several interest groups, ranging from the Ramblers' Association to the Association of Metropolitan Authorities (1986). These, like the Chairman's Policy Group of 1983, were all championing the cause of the social provision of recreation opportunities.

The Countryside Commission also produced specific leisure proposals – despite the Government's rejection of their appeal for a White Paper on the 'Rural Estate'. The Commission's earlier 'Access Charter' was accepted by government but this must be considered relatively ineffectual and, of particular political interest, of no real resource consequence. Their 'Enjoying the Countryside' policy initiative has had some influence on local authorities, particularly in steering them away from control policies a little and towards policies of more positive management, particularly through the production of informal countryside recreation strategies, but it wasn't significant enough to generate national policy reformulation in government.

Second, there has been little recreation and access legislation of significance since 1980. The 1986 Agriculture Act has given government agencies and private individuals alike scope to consider recreation opportunities as a means of agricultural diversification in the face of food surpluses. Recreation potential here results not so much from the altruistic notions of public enjoyment as out of economic necessity. The Act was part of the general spirit of pushing recreation into the market place. It was also for recreation that the 1981 Countryside (Scotland) Act introduced the Regional Park designation.

There have been two pieces of legislation concerning access since 1980. The 1981 Wildlife and Countryside Act contained provisions in relation to management agreements, the changing status of the Countryside Commission and the completion of the Definitive Map. The failure to complete these maps under the 1949 and 1968 legislation led, in the 1981 Act, to the more realistic but less satisfactory notion of their 'completion wherever possible' and into the 1990s many areas still remain uncharted. Meanwhile, some footpaths and other rights of way have been lost, and few created – possibly because of the preoccupation with documenting existing ones (Curry, 1992b).

In 1990 a second statute, the Rights of Way Act, was introduced. The maintenance of footpaths had been a problem since 1949, with as many as half of the recorded rights of way in England and Wales being blocked at any one time. The 1990 Act offers some clarification on this issue, but little significant change in access opportunities.

Characteristic of the 1980s, though, many Private Members' Bills, particularly in relation to improved access over common land, were unsuccessful. The Access to Commons and Open Country Bill and the Walkers (Access to the Countryside) Bill, both of which would have given unrestricted access to commons and open country, were terminated in 1982. The Sports Fields and Recreational Facilities Bill of 1985 also failed to proceed to an Act.

Legislative provisions for recreation and access have been distinct. The principal statutes referred to throughout this book are summarized in Table 2.3.

A third factor serving to ensure the low prioritization of rural leisure in government policy is that conservation has remained a clear priority over recreation in both legislative terms and through the stated priorities of government agencies such as the Countryside Commission. The White Paper 'This Common Inheritance' (Department of the Environment, 1990b) has served to reinforce this priority for the 1990s.

The situation is compounded by the relative strength and organization of recreation pressure groups where conflicts of interest both within and between groups with a recreation interest have often served to weaken their cause (Centre for Leisure Research, 1986). The

Table 2.3 Principal legislation for countryside recreation and access[a]

Act	Date	Provisions
Recreation and tourism		
Physical Recreation and Training	1937	Provision for camping sites for residents
Holidays with pay	1938	One week's paid holiday for all workers
Town and Country Planning	1947	Introduced Green Belts and green wedges
National Parks and Access to the Country- side	1949	Facilities for the enjoyment of national parks, including land purchase powers
Minerals	1951	Established after-use requirements to disused mineral workings – the most popular after-use was recreation
Forestry	1967	Empowered the Forestry Commission to provide recreation facilities in state forests
Countryside	1968	Clauses 1–10: Countryside Commission to be responsible for recreation facilitation in the whole of the countryside. Country parks, picnic sites and transit camping sites introduced
Transport	1968	Formed the British Waterways Board
Lea Valley Regional Park	1969	Established an authority for the development of a regional park from the Thames to Ware in Hertfordshire
Development of Tourism	1969	Introduced English Tourist Board and British Tourist Authority
Town and Country Planning	1971	Structure and local plans to contain recreation policies
Nature Conservancy Council	1972	Nature Conservancy Council given recreation possibilities
Local Government	1972	Introduced national park officers and national park plans
Water	1973	Empowered regional water authorities to provide countryside recreation facilities
Employment and Training	1973	Set up Manpower Services Commission
Local Government (Finance)	1974	Reduced grant-aid availability to public authorities for country parks and picnic sites

Table 2.3 *continued*

Act	Date	Provisions
Town and Country (Minerals)	1981	Introduced after-care requirements for mineral workings
Wildlife and Country-side	1981	Change in status for the Countryside Commission
Countryside (Scotland)	1981	Introduced regional parks in Scotland
Forestry	1981	Selling off the Forestry Commission lands to the private sector
Agriculture	1986	Gave agriculture ministers responsibility for recreation in the context of farm diversification
Water	1990	Removed much of the responsibility for recreation on water authority lands into the private sector
Access		
Access to Mountains	1939	Limited access to open land
National Parks and Access to the Country-side	1949	Introduced definitive maps, access agreements, access orders and long-distance routes
Countryside	1968	Clauses 15–21: extend definition of 'open country', Clauses 27–31: highways authorities to introduce signposting
Wildlife and Country-side	1981	Update of definitive maps, management agreements usable for access purposes
Wildlife and Country-side (Amendment)	1985	National parks to produce access maps
Rights of Way	1990	Restrictions on ploughing and cropping rights of way and made obstruction a legal offence
Water	1990	Secured access for some parts of water company land, but allowed charging for some customary access.
Water Resources	1991	Prohibited absolute restrictions on access to water company land.

[a] Many Bills for access during 1900–40 failed; many Bills for access to common land during 1940–90 failed.

Ramblers' Association and the Open Spaces Society remain, with a longevity of experience particularly in respect of the legal basis of access, as minority radical groups to fight the rural recreation and access cause outside government (Curry, 1988).

Thus the history of recreation and access provision has been characterized by inadequate statutes and the increasing use of informal mechanisms to fill the statutory vacuum. There has been a confusion over agency roles and planning functions extending to ministerial level. And there is still uncertainty as to which parts of the provision of recreation and access fall to the market place, and which are considered as either a *de facto* or a *de jure* right falling into the public domain. All of this points to recreation and access being an issue of second-order importance in government as the quote from Roberts in the Preface suggests. Certainly, the low political status of leisure generally presents substantial obstacles to any increase in public expenditure in this area (Coalter, Long and Duffield, 1986). In general terms this history is well summed up by the Centre for Leisure Research (1986, p. 13):

> Changing demands and emerging conflicts have tended to outrun policy responses so that the mechanisms of countryside management have tended to be slow to adapt – and have tended to be reactive rather than proactive (p. 13).

3

The provision of countryside recreation and access

3.1 AN UNEASY CO-EXISTENCE OF PUBLIC, PRIVATE AND VOLUNTARY PROVISION

The nature of provision for countryside recreation and access is a curious one since it is based on both the provision of facilities and the exercising of rights and it falls to both the public and the private sectors. The reasons for this duality of provision are complex, but from the first two chapters, some public provision can be justified on at least four grounds.

The first of these is that there has always been some opportunity to have access to the countryside and the state must ensure that these customary opportunities are not eroded. The second is that access to the countryside has been a traditional right of the individual relating in many instances to ancient laws, often unwritten, and the state should safeguard these rights and laws. Both of these justifications relate to public access.

In relation to specific recreation facilities, two other reasons for state intervention are often articulated. These are that for many facilities, the public realistically cannot be excluded, for example to open access areas in national parks or to many country parks, and therefore the state should take the responsibility for provision, because the private sector realistically cannot. Finally, the provision of state facilities comes about for social reasons – because countryside recreation is a good thing to have in a number of different respects – reasons that might be somewhat dubious, a point considered further in Chapter 5.

But countryside recreation is also a market commodity in many instances. A large number of stately homes, attractive gardens and wildlife parks opened, particularly during the 1970s, and proved very popular with the population at large. But their purpose has chiefly been for commercial gain rather than any altruistic notion of the general benefits of public enjoyment. This is a trend that is on the increase, as was noted in Chapter 2.

Because countryside recreation has these unusual characteristics of both public and private provision, there has been a certain ambivalence about public provision, based partly on the strength of the landowning interest in government, but also because of a genuine uncertainty about which types of recreation, at the margin, should be provided by the state on the one hand and the market on the other. Instances have even occurred where public provision has proceeded along commercial lines, as the Rufford Country Park case cited in Chapter 2 indicates.

The issue is further complicated by provision from the voluntary sector, from organizations such as the National Trust and the country wildlife trusts, which adhere to some of the principles of both the public and private sectors, with some voluntary organizations acting as agents for the public (local-authority) sector. In some cases there is also joint provision between public and private sectors where, for example, refreshment facilities at local-authority country parks are franchised to private companies. Joint provision between the public and voluntary sectors also exists at Crickley Hill Country Park in Gloucestershire, which is jointly owned by the county council and the National Trust.

All of this has led to a lack of co-ordination in the supply of opportunities for public enjoyment, which forms the basis for the second proposition of this book and is well summed up by Shoard (1978, p. 95):

Since the early 1950s, nobody in the United Kingdom has even begun to work out how the countryside as a whole could best be used to serve all of the recreation needs of the community. So instead of finding a range of facilities to improve his enjoyment of the countryside, the average citizen is confronted by a hotch potch of facilities designed for purposes other than enhancing his enjoyment: to minimise the impact of people on the countryside (like country parks and picnic sites), to enlist support for farmers (like farm open days) or to make money (like safari and wildlife parks, stately homes and 'pick your own' fruit farms).

This chapter, in reviewing the nature of the rural leisure resource, explores the relationship between public, private and voluntary provision and examines aspects of provision that fall uneasily between the three sectors.

3.2 PUBLIC AND VOLUNTARY RECREATION FACILITIES

Public recreation facilities in the countryside have existed throughout the twentieth century on a piecemeal basis, with the possible exception of National Forest Parks, the first of which was designated in 1936. The 1949 Act did little to formalize this, since no provision for facilities, as opposed to access, was contained within it. Certainly the Act did introduce national parks and Areas of Outstanding Natural Beauty and these, together with heritage coasts introduced some 20 years later provide potentially significant recreation resources. The recreational roles of these three designations are considered fully in Glyptis (1991). But these designations *per se* are less important in terms of public policy than the development of recreational opportunities within them. Three issues are important in this respect – the provision of specific facilities, the negotiation of access, and public policies for the control of private recreation development – each of which is considered in this chapter.

In relation to facilities, then, into the 1950s and 1960s, where they were to be tolerated they were, according to Dower (1978) to be for cheap holiday accommodation and facilities for the motorist in moderation, all of which were to avoid excessive concentration of incongruous pursuits. These sentiments found their way into the provision statements of many public bodies such as the Forestry Commission and the (then) water authorities.

The formalization of the provision of public facilities for recreation came with powers to designate country parks, picnic areas and transit camping sites under the 1968 Act. But even after their introduction, there was still some caution about positively promoting them to all sectors of the community. A number of policy statements into the 1970s reflect this. A Ministry of Housing and Local Government Circular in 1970 (MHLG, 1970b, p.4), for example, maintained that it was:

> The policy of the Government . . . to provide greater opportunities for members of the community to enjoy recreation in the forms for which they are interested.

The House of Lords Select Committee on Sport and Leisure (House of Lords, 1973, p. xxv) also proposed:

> the maximum opportunity to take part in . . . leisure activities according to the personal choice of the individual.

Despite being in not quite such strong terms, these sentiments were reflected in the White Paper on Sport and Recreation in 1975 (Department of the Environment 1975a, p. 1), which emphasized the need to:

> provide opportunities for those who wish to take part in sport and informal outdoor recreation.

Although more covert than the exclusionary statements of Wordsworth, Dower and Hobhouse, who were keen to restrict access to the countryside by the whole population as was noted in Chapter 1, these quotes from government sources all have key qualifying elements in them. They maintain, in turn, that recreation provision should be undertaken according to the population's 'interest', 'choices' and 'wishes'. There was, even by the mid-1970s, no intention to make the provision of countryside recreation facilities a universal objective for the population.

Despite this, between 1970 and 1980 some 156 country parks and 188 picnic sites were opened under the 1968 Countryside Act, chiefly by local authorities, grant-aided and approved by the Countryside Commission. It must be said, though, that most of these were designated prior to 1974, when grant aid for their development was reduced from 75% to 50% under the 1974 Local Government (Finance) Act. Also, between 1968 and 1974, 60% of these designations were made from existing *de facto* recreation sites to take advantage of grant aid. Only two transit camping sites, near Stroud and Exeter, for which provision was also made under the 1968 Act, have ever been introduced (Slee, 1982a).

Initially, when some public policy interest was at last beginning to be expressed about social provision for recreation, country parks were seen as having to be accessible. The Countryside Commission (1972, p.1), in its policy notes on country parks and picnic sites, stated that they should be 'readily accessible for motor vehicles and pedestrians'.

Only two years later, however, it was considered in Scotland at least, that this was no longer necessary. The Countryside Commission for Scotland (1974) stated that the original notion that a country park would probably be best situated fairly close to the main cities and towns was no longer part of the accepted thinking on the subject. For Scotland, the integration of a more holistic system of parks, from urban to rural, became a clear priority, and the notion of any social provision being achieved through the principle of accessibility was dismissed.

But whatever the principal purpose of country parks was considered to be, their impact has been minimal. As the Centre for Leisure Research (1986) notes, they probably account for less than 10% of informal recreation use and still less for sport. The 1990 National Survey of Countryside Recreation (Countryside Commission, 1992a) indicates that country parks account for only 4% of all countryside recreation trip destinations. It is thus considered that they have not materially affected the majority of visitors, who seek access to the wider countryside rather than managed attractions within it. This has led Glyptis (1991) to consider them as opportunistic and Patmore (1983) to term them sporadic and haphazard. Thus, as Harrison (1991) argues, local-authority provision for countryside recreation has centred on providing specific recreation facilities, which is misdirected in terms of the interests of the public. There is here a substantial gap between what providers thought people would like and what they actually wanted.

Outside the local-authority sector, public provision by the resource agencies also grew during the 1970s. Until 1973 the water authorities had pursued exclusionary policies with regard to their water catchment and associated lands. Their broader remit from this time, under the 1973 Water Resources Act, and improved filtration methods, did increase public-access opportunities although, as is considered below, these have been threatened by water privatization in 1990.

In the Forestry Commission, too, following the 1972 White Paper on Forest Policy, the number of Forest Parks, car parks, picnic sites, forest walks and interpretation facilities grew. The Commission also adopted a more permissive attitude to free access on foot on a wide scale. But again this has been tempered into the 1980s by the obligation to sell Forestry Commission lands into the private sector under the 1981 Forestry Act.

3.2.1 The voluntary sector

Where the direct public provision of facilities has been somewhat ambivalent and marginal, the provision by the voluntary sector, and particularly the National Trust, has been slightly more progressive. It owns 224 000 hectares of land in England and Wales, 20% of which is common land, and 8 000 km of coastline – one-sixth of the total. As an organization it has always attempted to integrate more fully the objectives of agricultural production, conservation and recreation on its own lands. Its recreation and access objectives are tempered only by the provision that they must not destroy the very properties that the Trust has a duty to protect. Recreation objectives therefore must be:

compatible with the needs of agriculture, forestry and the preservation of the landscape including the plant and animal life that inhabits it (National Trust, 1965, p. 4).

Much National Trust recreation provision is undoubtedly concerned with income generation and to that extent it represents a recreation resource on the cusp of public and private provision. Indeed income generation is often one of the conditions of donations of property to the Trust, to allow their preservation over time. In addition to the opening of specific facilities, the Trust also has a progressive policy towards public access to its lands, beyond just statutory public rights of way, considered more fully below.

As a result, many permissive *de facto* access opportunities exist on Trust lands, including access to farmland and woodland. But the overriding ethos of this provision, consistent with the Trust's declared aims, is to favour quiet enjoyment and air and exercise which ensures that visitors cause the least disturbance to each other's pleasure (Centre for Leisure Research, 1986).

3.3 ACCESS AND PUBLIC RIGHTS OF WAY

While the provision of public recreation facilities has been faltering, securing access over private land by the public sector remains, as it has always been, controversial. Press cuttings from one provincial newspaper over a ten-month period in 1989/90, for example, showed the depth of feeling about access rights among all actors in the access process (Figure 3.1). Many polemics have been written about the historical struggle for access (e.g. Hill, 1980; Stephenson, 1989) and about the current state of policy (Shoard, 1987, Godwin, 1990), and it is therefore important that the nature of access is fully understood. As Shoard (1978, p. 116) states:

> Public rights of way across private land in the countryside are historic and jealously guarded rights – part of the social contract of the countryside. . . . it is doubly important that ordinary people should understand their function.

Despite this, an extensive survey of both recreationists and landowners in terms of their knowledge of rights and obligations in respect of public rights of way, commons and 'open country' showed that it was exceedingly poor (Centre for Leisure Research, 1986). Within the context of this position, then, what does access for recreation purposes comprise?

Central to the problem of understanding the nature of access rights is that access for the purpose of **recreation** (a general right to roam) as opposed to a general right of passage has become an appendage to a larger body of highways legislation. Recreational access is thus peripheral in both highways legislation and in its implementation through highways departments of county councils, rather than through planning departments which commonly have the general responsibility for countryside recreation. Although, of itself, highways legislation is comprehensive, the significance of recreational access within it is slight. Both legislators and highways authorities have focused on non-recreational issues of passage and have rarely become seriously concerned with issues such as access to open country. Such access falls reluctantly within the remit of highways authorities who have no strong tradition in the sphere of recreational rights of access.

3.3.1 Definitions

In general terms, access to the countryside may be 'in law' – *de jure*, or 'through custom', or *de facto*. *De jure* access can be negotiated or imposed in law (for example through an access agreement, access order or a management agreement) or may be attributed to a customary route that has been used without challenge and there is a presupposition that permission had been given for its use some time in the past. *De jure* access may also occur with the owner's express permission, creating a permissive path, or through a lease, licence or a day ticket.

De facto access can occur with the informal permission of the landowner, but it is more common that the owner's permission has not been granted at all. Strictly, therefore, this is trespass. *De facto* access frequently extends to common land and publicly owned land, unless some *de jure* arrangements have been negotiated. The legal details of such arrangements can be found in the Centre for Leisure Research's (1986) publication, in Riddell and Trevelyan (1992) and, specifically for common land, Clayden (1992), but much of the concern of this chapter relates to *de jure* access (or the lack of it) associated with public rights of way. The issue of negotiated agreements and common land are considered separately.

3.3.2 Definitive map

Public rights of way are defined on the definitive map (where these have been completed) which was introduced in the 1949 National Parks and Access to the Countryside Act. It was to be prepared by county councils, for the entire county at one time, invariably at the beginning through enlisting the support of parish councils. Counties could also delegate powers for definitive map completion to district councils but this has not been widely exploited (Scott Planning Services, 1991). The maps were to be prepared in three stages – draft, provisional and confirmed. Objections were to be made at the provisional stage and the maps were to be reviewed every five years. Essentially they were to document all customary *de facto* routes to place them on a statutory *de jure* footing.

Progress in producing these definitive maps was slow because they were a low priority for many authorities, they were difficult to complete in their entirety for the county, and parish effort was variable. So in 1968, the Countryside Act got rid of the provisional stage in their formulation and reduced the number of classifications of types of public rights of way by reclassifying 'roads used as public paths' as 'byways open to all traffic'. By 1981 the persistent lack of map completions led the government to set a more realistic challenge. The Wildlife and Countryside Act of that year spoke not of completions, but simply

'Tackle footpath problem now" say Ramblers

THE Ramblers Association this week hit out at Gloucestershire County Council for its lack of action over the state of the public paths network in the county.

The association wants all those who walk for pleasure in the countryside to press candidates, if they are successful in next month's elections, to get the council to tackle the footpath problem with more staff and resources.

The association claims that, nationally, only £12 million is spent and that money spent on public paths is very cost effective.

Said Mr Tony Drake, Gloucestershire Footpath secretary for the Ramblers' Association: "It is only crumbs from the table that we ask for.

"When I see that Cheltenham spends four times more on its parks and open spaces than Gloucestershire spends on its paths, I wonder if there is a need for a sense of proportion."

The Ramblers are concerned that difficult cases are fudged and put aside due to the time involved to process to conclusion. They feel an example should be made of a few persistent offenders.

Mr Drake said that the staff for keeping the definitive maps of right of way up to date were way behind.

The definitive maps were 36 years old but work on redrafting and incorporation of legal changes seemed to have ground to a halt and new changes proposed for addition or upgrading of paths were not being processed quickly due to shortage of staff in the county solicitor's department

Escalation

Mr Drake said that although Gloucestershire County Council had increased its path budget in recent years, the escalation of interest in country walking had caused an ever increasing rate of complaints from the public about obstructed or cropped over paths.

This, he says, has left the county's rights of way section grossly understaffed in every aspect.

The Ramblers Association is starting legal action against the county council for failing to act on reports it has made to the county surveyor of 200 sites where footbridges are missing.

Expenses

Although the county has paid the Ramblers' expenses it has, says the association, failed to process the reports and put the work in hand due to staff being preoccupied with individual path problems.

The association claims there are no permanent work teams to maintain and improve paths, following the ending of the Community Programme scheme, which carried out many improvements using unemployed labour.

The current Employment Training scheme, it says, is much smaller and has an uncertain future.

Enforcement action over obstructions has been stepped up in the last year but there have still been no prosecutions over the ploughing laws or for crop obstruction, says Mr Drake.

10 Gloucestershire Echo, Wednesday, May 31, 1989

Hopes over footpaths row

NATIONAL Trust chiefs in Gloucestershire hope to resolve the Cotswolds footpath row within the next month.

Members of the conservation group, the Open Spaces Society, say the trust is breaking the law by blocking rights of way through the picturesque gardens of Hidcote Manor in Chipping Campden.

After the Trust applied to Cotswold District Council to change the routes, the society wrote to Gloucestershire County Council urging it to take legal action.

Mr. Cecil Pearse, regional director of the Severn region of the National Trust said: "The footpaths through Hidcote Manor is a very confusing issue.

"There has been a proposal for the diversion of the footpaths since the early 1980s

"But three attempts to have a diversion order made have resulted in three technical errors, one as recently as April.

"But we hope to have the matter resolved by June to put in a very satisfactory route around the garden

Gloucestershire Echo, Tuesday

Farmer's wife blasts 'hasty' path clearers

A FARMER'S wife today accused council workers of being "too hasty" when they mowed a quarter mile long path across a field of barley.

Mrs. Janet Newman claims the men from Gloucestershire County Council ignored her request to wait until her husband arrived before they began clearing a right of way.

Figure 3.1 Access is synonymous with conflict: press cuttings from ten months of the *Gloucestershire Echo* show the county council prosecuting farmers and landowners over access, farmers warning the council, the council warning farmers, the Ramblers' Association warning the council and the Open Spaces Society warning the National Trust.

Banker fined for blocking footpath

by Simon Crane

MERCHANT banker Charles Hambro has been fined hundreds of pounds for ploughing up a Gloucestershire footpath.

He was fined £200 and ordered to pay £122 in costs by Tewkesbury Magistrates after a prosecution brought by Gloucestershire County Council.

Now highway chiefs have promised to keep up their "get tough" policy on landowners who plough up public rights of way.

Apologised

Mr. Alan Seyers, prosecuting, told magistrates a rights of way officer went to check a field owned by Mr. Hambro in Teddington after a complaint from the parish council.

He said: "He found a headland path down one side of the field had been ploughed out over a length of almost half a mile."

When the officer called at Mr. Hambro's home, Dixton Manor, Gotherington, he had apologised and said he had done his best to reinstate the path, Mr. Seyers told the court.

Mr. Hambro, who was not present in court, pleaded guilty by letter to an offence under the Highways Act.

The highway authority dedited to get tough and turn to the courts after the number of complaints about rights of way in the county rose from 20 a month in 1987 to 65 a month so far this year.

Recently the council took direct action by moving in with its own equipment and cutting down crops growing over paths on 35 farms in the county.

After the court case, Mr. John Sumner, footpaths officer, said: "This was our first prosecution since the sharp rise in the number of complaints we have received from the public.

Prosecuted

"The court took a pretty serious view of the offence and we hope more people will now observe the law and the number of complaints will fall."

Mr. Hambro is the first to be prosecuted by Gloucestershire County Council under the authority's get tough policy on rights of way.

They are hoping court action will help stop farmers planting crops on footpath routes throughout the county and cut the number of complaints.

Deadline on paths law for farmers

FARMERS and landowners have been given a six week deadline to get used to new laws protecting public rights of way.

Under new legislation which came into force last month, restrictions on the ploughing or disturbing of paths are now much more stringent.

But after consultations between the National Farmers' Union, Country Landowners' Association and Mr John Sumner, public rights of way manager at Gloucestershire County Council, they have been given a settling in period until November 1.

Mr Sumner said: "We have agreed a joint approach to introducing the new law in Gloucestershire.

"Advice and guidance notes are being sent out to all farmers by the Ministry of Agriculture, Fisheries and Food but any farmer or landowner who wants specific advice should contact the public rights of way unit at Gloucester."

He added that a large number of people already observed the law, which states that cross-field footpaths that can be avoided, field edge paths and any other rights of way should not be ploughed or disturbed.

Tony Drake

But if it cannot be avoided the surface must be passable within 14 days.

Ramblers Association spokesman for Gloucestershire, Mr Tony Drake, said: "The deadline is fine, as long as they council does enforce the law once it has passed.

"At the moment we are keeping our eyes peeled to make sure we know about infringements, and we've already come across several which we will be reporting."

Farmer is fined for obstructing public footpath

by Mark Thomas

A FARMER has been fined £220 and ordered to pay £350 costs for growing crops over a Gloucestershire footpath and a bridleway in the second case of its kind in the county.

Richard Beldam, of East Lodge Farm, Stanton, pleaded guilty to two charges of obstructing a public highway.

And ramblers today welcomed the prosecution — brought by Gloucestershire County Council after calls for a crackdown from walkers.

The farmer had grown crops on his land over a bridleway at Stanton and over a footpath at Dumbleton, Chipping Campden magistrates heard

Mr David Rees, prosecuting, said council officers had twice visited each spot and found crops growing.

Mr Alan Thomas, defending, said the farmer had cut paths through his crops after the officers called but they turned up again and widened them.

Beldam refused to comment after being fined £100 for one offence and £120 for the other.

Chairman of the Gloucestershire branch of the Ramblers Association, Mr Tony Drake, said after the hearing: "This is a victory for people who want to walk the footpaths."

And the council's assistant public rights of way officer Mr Gerry Stewart said: "It is our current theme to look after rights of way."

obliged highways authorities to keep these maps under 'constant review' and introduced modification orders to allow specific changes to individual maps. This meant that, although the rights of way on maps were definitive at any one point in time, the maps themselves no longer were, since the status of individual paths became subject to a case by case 'rolling review'.

Lack of resources and priority (Ramblers' Association, 1987) leave these maps uncompleted for many parts of the country. In a survey by the Countryside Commission (Scott Planning Services, 1991), 70% of county authorities aimed to have them completed by 1995 but 14 authorities suggested that it would take longer than this, the worst being Devon, Cornwall, Northumberland and Suffolk.

But it is also the objections to individual proposals on definitive maps that have created an impasse in many areas. The 1981 Act did allow the Secretary of State for the Environment to direct the completion or abandonment of map reviews and up to 1985 (Ramblers' Association, 1985) it had required completions in 15 county councils, which involved the resolution of 1675 outstanding objections. It requested the abandonment of reviews, however, in a further 26 counties because the 15 000 outstanding objections were simply considered too large in number, and too expensive, to resolve (Centre for Leisure Research, 1986). This meant that, although the definitive map reviews were not to be completed, *de jure* rights of way would still be resolved on a case by case basis in these counties.

Nearly £14 million was spent on public rights of way during the 1986/87 financial year, but only 17% of this was spent on legal activities to secure access. Around 70% was disposed to maintenance, chiefly by highways authorities. Even the government bemoaned this level of expenditure with the (then) Environment and Countryside Minister, David Trippier, suggested that financial priorities for public rights of way, compared with the £1 billion of public funds spent on the tourism, leisure and recreation sectors generally, were all wrong (*Enjoying the Countryside Newsletter*, 1990).

3.3.3 Public rights of way

The 1981 Wildlife and Countryside Act now defines three types of public rights of way that may appear on the definitive map. These are: 'footpaths' which allow a right of way on foot; 'bridleways' which extend to horses and bicycles as well as access on foot, and 'byeways open to all traffic' that allow for access on foot, horse, bicycle and by vehicular traffic. In addition to these three categories, a number of other 'routes used as public paths' (RUPPs), designated under the 1949 National Parks and Access to the Countryside Act, still remain in existence. Their definition under the 1949 Act, although clear in terms of the right to walk and use bicycles and horses, was ambiguous in relation to vehicular traffic. Because of this, the 1968 Countryside Act directed the reclassification of RUPPs into one of the other three categories of public rights of way but this was particularly controversial in respect of a reclassification as 'byeways' which potentially allowed vehicular access to RUPPs that had previously not customarily experienced such use. Despite a reaffirmation of this reclassification process in the 1981 Act, many RUPPs still remain on the definitive map.

Surprisingly, perhaps, all of this recording of public rights of way does not ensure their use for recreation purposes. Their legitimacy still hangs on the historical legacy simply for their use as 'rights of passage'. Thus, in making decisions about whether to designate, divert or even to close them on the definitive map, the 1980 Highways Act does not require their use for recreational purposes to be taken into account.

In terms of obligations for public rights of way, highways authorities are to signpost them under the 1968 Countryside Act. A test case in the North Yorkshire Moors National Park, however, has suggested that to be legal, this requires prior notification to the landowner (*Farming News*, 1990b). Under the 1981 Wildlife and Countryside Act, definitive maps are to record public rights of way, and highways authorities, not landowners, are to safeguard and maintain them. Management agreements under the 1981 Act can be used as part of this safeguarding process.

The 1990 Rights of Way Act, in clarifying earlier legislation as a consolidation Act, places obligations on the landowner not to obstruct them, for example by growing crops on them; not to cause a nuisance around them; and restricts the extent to which they can be ploughed. Under this Act, restoring paths and removing crops must be paid for by the landowner or occupier, whether carried out by him/her or not. Paths may be disturbed by ploughing during cultivation, but must be restored within 14 days. In the Centre for Leisure Research (1986) survey of farmers, only 24% of them claimed to have ploughed public rights of way and most had restored them fully within 28 days. This provision for ploughing is particularly important and provided the principal impetus for the Act, since a survey by the University of Reading (1985) showed it to be the most common obstruction to footpaths, and even after 1987, when the Countryside Commission introduced the Ploughing Code, the Code was broken by a majority of farmers.

Rights over inland water have a less well-established legal framework than those over land, but are based on rights of navigation. Again these are historical, with commercial rather than leisure origins. Like rights of way, some rights of navigation are well established, and others hotly disputed (Telling and Smith, 1985). Conflicts arise between rights of navigation (for example, by canoeists) and sporting rights (for example, by anglers), and where sporting rights have been purchased, the conflict essentially becomes one of public versus private rights.

Access to water areas (lakes and reservoirs) as opposed to linear routes (rivers and canals) is likely to be secured by similar means to areas of land – access agreements and orders. But here, the privatization of the water sector is likely to inhibit the agreements that will be made. Access to water is generally considered more fully in Glyptis (1991).

3.3.4 Monitoring

A lack of use of some public rights of way and problems with the completion of the definitive map have led to significant losses over time. Rubenstein and Speakman (1969) noted that by the late 1960s, 1500 paths were being closed or diverted every year, and that this was, strictly, not outside the law. It has been suggested that between 1949 and 1990, some 48 000 km of public rights of way may have been lost, but because of their lack of definition, this can be only speculation (Blunden and Curry, 1990). Various attempts have been made to place the protection of public rights of way on a clearer statutory footing, such as MP Andrew Bennett's 1982 Walkers (Access to the Countryside) Bill, but these have been largely unsuccessful. The Countryside Commission (1990a) estimated that the rights of way network declined by between 5 and 35 km in 1983 and 1984, but that it actually increased through improved definitive map definition and negotiations associated with it by between 5 and 28 km in 1985 and 1986. Indeed, an element of the reduction in public rights of way may simply be due to more accurate estimates of their length, rather than actual losses.

Today it is estimated, and it can only be an estimate, that there are about 225 000 km of public rights of way in England and Wales. Some 76% of these are footpaths, 20% bridleways and the remaining 4% byways open to all traffic and RUPPs. They are most dense in Yorkshire and Humberside, and least dense in the South and East. In terms of highways authority obligations under the 1968 Act, only a third of public rights of way are signposted where they leave the road and only about 80% of them are accurately represented on the Ordinance Survey map. The Countryside Commission (1990e) survey of walkers found 15% of paths to be unusable, the principal obstructions being crops, ploughing, fences, hedges and walls. More than half of them were inaccessible, however, without the ability to use a map and the confidence to insist on walkers' rights. The Centre for Leisure Research's (1986) survey of walkers confirms that their biggest problem is an inability, for a variety of reasons, to follow footpaths, but despite this, 71% of them claimed to have no significant access problems.

From the farmer and landowner perspective, the Centre for Leisure

Research's (1986) survey of farmers found that 81% of them considered that they had public rights of way over their land, 90% of whom claimed that they spent time and money fulfilling their obligations towards them. They generally felt that the fulfilment of highway authority obligations towards public rights of way was poor.

3.3.5 Controversy

Difficulties in both the mechanisms for recording and defining rights of way and the objections by landowners, access groups and particularly local residents lie at the centre of the controversy of public access over private land. At the national level, the reliability of the definitive map has been some cause for concern. In 1987, for example, the Ramblers' Association took the Secretary of State for the Environment to court about definitive map provisions in the 1981 Wildlife and Countryside Act. This particular case ruled that the definitive map of rights of way is conclusive evidence of a right of way, and a landowner cannot now produce evidence to claim that a path should not have been put on the map in the first place.

As a result of this court ruling, a Private Member's Bill, the 'Definitive Map Modification Bill' sponsored by Sir Geoffrey Johnson-Smith and backed by the National Farmers' Union and the Country Landowners' Association aimed to change these provisions to allow a landowner to produce evidence to show that if a path was not a path at the date when it was put on the map, it can be expunged. The Open Spaces Society (1988d), for one, was worried that this would provide a loophole for many landowners, unless the evidence required is absolutely watertight. In the event, the Bill never proceeded to an Act.

At the level of individual disputes, objections, closure and diversion proposals, the conflicts between the landowner, local residents and the rambler are quite common, although around 80% of all changes to the definitive map are unopposed. In one celebrated case in 1988, where the film producer David Puttnam, then President of the Council for the Protection of Rural England, diverted paths over his land, even the ramblers' groups were at loggerheads. Figure 3.2 illustrates well the vociferous views of the Open Spaces Society about this particular diversion, but Figure 3.3 provides an equally terse response from the Ramblers' Association.

3.3.6 New forms of public rights of way

In order to exploit the rights of way network more effectively, a number of policies have been introduced to 'package' and publicize them. The most enduring of these has been the Long Distance Route introduced in

Puttnam's Privacy

David Puttnam, producer of the film *Chariots of Fire* and president of the Council for the Protection of Rural England (CPRE), has not behaved as a conservation chief should.

In March there was a public inquiry into the diversion of paths over his land at Kingsmead Mill, near Malmesbury in Wiltshire. These were Little Somerford Footpath 11 and bridleway 12, and St Paul Malmesbury Without Footpath 75. The parish council, local people and the Open Spaces Society objected. Deplorably, the Ramblers' Association did not.

The path, which changed from footpath to bridleway where it crossed the parish boundary midway along the proposed diversion, was about a quarter of a mile long. It ran past the house and across the River Avon. The proposed diversion went behind the mill, hidden from it and the river with its attractive waterfalls, by a high wall built by Mr Puttnam. It was longer and far less attractive! – and it had already been made.

A walker unsure of his rights would be deflected, by a series of signs, onto the proposed diversion and over the twee 'Willow Bridge', erected in 1984 where the diversion crossed the river.

The definitive map route was not waymarked. We deplore this attempt, by a landowner who should know better, to pre-empt confirmation of the diversion. How could we judge the merits of the diversion, when most walkers, other than locals, would not realise that the definitive route existed?

The order was faulty. One of the paths was being extinguished, yet had been included in the diversion order. We argued that the other should be withdrawn and remade correctly, and that change should not be contemplated until Mr Puttman had removed all the misleading signs and waymarked the definitive route.

At the inquiry, at which unusually eleven objectors appeared, Mr Puttnam – represented by counsel – complained of problems with security: the Wiltshire Constabulary had said that the presence of the path made it impossible to protect the house by an external beam. (Mr Puttnam had bought the mill in 1982, the path in situ.)

In his decision letter, the inspector, Major-General F. Michael Sexton, ignored our submission that the order was faulty. We shall take this up with the Department of the Environment. He sympathised heavily with Mr Puttnam's alleged 'security' problems. He considered the diversion to be less beautiful but not to the extent of outweighing its 'many other advantages'. And he found no fault in the landowner's efforts to encourage walkers onto the diversion. This, he said, was done 'specifically to establish the practicability and popularity of the route'. We wonder.

As we told CPRE, remembering our 1985 AGM when our too pro-military president Lord Onslow was not re-elected, even the best organisations have presidents who cause them embarrassment.

Figure 3.2 Objections over footpaths diversion: the Open Spaces Society took strong exception to diversions made by film producer David Puttnam who was at the time President of the Council for the Protection of Rural England. (Source: *Open Space*, 1988a.)

Puttnam's Path Change

Under the Heading 'Puttnam's Privacy' in the last *Open Space*, the author deplores the fact that the local Ramblers Association did not object to the proposed footpath/bridleway diversion at Kingsmead Mill, Little Somerford, near Malmesbury. The British Horse Society and the Trail Riders' Fellowship did not object either, but they were not mentioned.

For our part, we deplore being 'condemned' in this way without the courtesy of any prior consultation as to the reasons for our action. The article also failed to mention that the definitive route, namely bridleway 12, connected with footpath 75 by means of a ford which, at the time it was examined by the local RA committee, was carrying four feet of water, and is completely impassable by walkers for much of the year. It also omitted to mention that footpath 11 from the north comes to an abrupt end at the river, whereas the proposed diversion enables a link to be made with footpath 11, and brings some order to what can only be described as a chaotic system of rights of way.

These two factors were of sufficient importance to convince the local RA committee that, on balance, the proposed diversion order should not be opposed. It was the same committee which first brought the matter to the attention of the district council and so into the public domain.

Figure 3.3 Access controversies within ramblers' pressure groups: the Open Spaces Society's position was strongly contested by the Ramblers' Association. (Source: *Open Space*, 1988b.)

the 1949 Act although, as was noted in Chapter 1, the first of these, the Pennine Way, was introduced only 16 years after the passing of the Act. Despite this, some 2500 km of Long Distance Routes were designated during the 1970s and 1980s. They remain the only element of this 'packaging' process that actually has created, to a limited extent, new rights of way where necessary, to allow continuity of access over long distances (Figure 3.4).

During the 1970s and 1980s other forms of 'packaging', such as recreational footpaths and cycle ways, were introduced in various Countryside Commission statements but it wasn't until the late 1980s, in the wake of a series of rights of way monitoring reports (University of Reading, 1985; Ramblers' Association, 1985; 1987), that they were systematically reappraised. In the development of the Commission's 'Policies for Enjoying the Countryside', a rights of way agenda for action was published (Countryside Commission, 1989d), proposing new responsibilities for highways authorities, farmers and landowners, user groups and the Commission itself. Many of these proposals, particularly in relation to ploughing and obstruction, found their way into the 1990 Rights of Way Act.

This came in parallel with proposals to manage rights of way by dividing them into four groups (Countryside Commission, 1989c). Priority for investment was to go into the first two categories of more localized paths.

Parish paths and community paths are to be signposted from the road and marked on Ordinance Survey maps. They are to be kept open and legally protected, but not promoted. They are for those who wish to find their own way through the countryside. They also constitute a reservoir on which to draw for future development and promotion of walking and riding routes. Local walks and rides are also to be signed and fully waymarked but these will be promoted and developed for popular local use from home or a holiday base.

Regional routes are to be longer named paths offering more than a

---

Recreation facilities

Created under the 1968 Countryside Act

    Country parks
    Picnic sites
    Transit camping sites

Statutory public rights of way

Defined under the 1949 National Parks and Access to the Countryside Act

    Routes used as public paths

Defined under the 1981 Wildlife and Countryside Act

    Footpaths
    Bridleways
    Byways open to all traffic

'Packaged' rights of way

Created under the 1949 National Parks and Access to the Countryside Act

    Long Distance Routes

Created through a 1989 Countryside Commission Policy Statement

    Parish Paths
    Local Walks and Rides
    Regional Routes
    National Trails (replacing Long Distance Routes)

Figure 3.4 Public recreation and access provision

day's travelling, perhaps following a theme feature and with tourism potential. National trails are paths that have the quality and character to be truly national, allowing an extensive journey on foot, horseback or bicycle and capable of attracting tourist use from home or abroad. They are to replace Long Distance Routes but new ones will not be designated as such under the 1949 legislation unless this proves necessary for securing access.

It remains to be seen whether these proposals will either encourage a greater use of the public rights of way network or do much to ameliorate the conflicts associated with provision outlined above.

3.4 ACCESS AGREEMENTS, ORDERS, COMPULSORY PURCHASE AND TAX

The 1949 National Parks and Access to the Countryside Act empowered local planning authorities to secure access to 'open country' – mountain, moor, heath, down, cliff and foreshore by any of three measures – by agreement, order and compulsory purchase. This 'open country' definition was extended to cover woodland, rivers and canals in the Countryside 1968 Act.

Essentially, agreements allow the local authority to negotiate *de jure* access rights over private or common land with the landowner in exchange for cash payments or managerial services, or both. Access orders allow compulsion to be imposed on what would otherwise be an agreement although they do require Secretary of State approval. A more permanent securing of access rights can be obtained by the outright purchase of land. Despite these provisions, local councils have been reluctant to use these powers, and central government agencies have not historically coerced them to any great extent.

By 1974 access had been secured under these Acts to only 32 000 hectares, of which around 80% was in the Peak District National Park. By 1989 this had extended to only 34 000 hectares, still 80% of which was in the Peak Park. It has been suggested (Centre for Leisure Research, 1986) that this concentration of use is not entirely surprising, since it was the access controversies in the Peak District that were central in bringing them to statute in the first place. Even here, however, a study by Gibbs and Whitby (1975) showed that fewer than half of them were used primarily to obtain or safeguard access, the remainder being used to obtain greater control over visitors, or for amenity purposes.

Very little use of agreements indeed has been made in lowland England, at least in part because there is a much smaller amount of open country in this part of the country. In surveying their open country in the 1950s, Bedfordshire, Buckinghamshire and Hertfordshire, for example, felt that no agreements were necessary and they hadn't reviewed their position in the light of the 1968 Act by the late 1970s (Shoard, 1978). Despite the extension of the definition of 'open country' in 1968, no access agreements over lakesides had been secured by 1975. Only two agreements had been made for rivers – in 1971 by the Yorkshire Dales National Park for less than 2 hectares around the Aysgarth Falls and in 1973 by Cheshire County Council for 2.5 hectares around the river Weaver.

There has been little success, too, in securing agreements over woodland because of arguments for exclusion on the grounds of game, particularly pheasant, shooting. These arguments remain unproven since, as Shoard (1978) states, the two uses are not particularly incompatible, and satisfactory management can resolve any conflicts, as successful agreements in the Peak District National Park have shown.

Even with this very low use of access agreements and orders, it would appear that landowners are not entirely opposed to their deployment. Both the National Farmers' Union and the Country Landowners' Association told the House of Lords (1973) Select Committee on Sport and Leisure that they were a 'valuable instrument' since they entitled landowners to compensation for damage caused by walkers, and wardens were often provided to enforce bylaws and prevent damage. The perspective of both the CLA and the NFU was also observed by the Centre for Leisure Research (1986) who found that access agreements were considered favourably by both organizations in an otherwise ambivalent set of attitudes towards access. They were viewed principally to have income and management potential.

The Centre for Leisure Research's survey of farmers, in contrast, indicated that individual farmers and landowners generally view agreements with a degree of hostility, principally because any mechanism for increasing access to their land was considered to be undesirable. Other evidence (Blunden and Curry, 1990) indicates that farmers consider agreements as being intrusive, and they are often resisted on those grounds. Despite this, some successful new agreements for access have been negotiated with farmers under the Countryside Stewardship Scheme.

Access pressure groups have also opposed the use of access agreements and orders, principally on the grounds that access should be a right and not paid for. But some of the reasons for the lack of their use rests with local authorities. Part of their reluctance to use them has arisen as a result of their complicated legal basis and there has undoubtedly been some resistance on the part of landowning councillors on local authority committees: an attitude that might change in the context of a depressed agriculture industry. In this respect, the Occupiers Liability Act of 1984 was introduced to allow landowners a right to exclude liability from injury in an attempt to increase landowners' willingness to grant access. Few have been made aware of its existence, however.

There has also been a nervousness in the use of agreements because of their cost. Many agreements in the Peak National Park, for example, are coming up for renegotiation in 1993 and difficulties in successfully achieving these are feared on the grounds of compensation costs. It is also possible, though, that planners have not been made sufficiently aware of the potency of such agreements and orders, and this is a promotional job for the many national agencies with jurisdiction over rural leisure, not least the Countryside Commission, who have undertaken similar promotional work for public rights of way (Countryside Commission, 1992b).

The opening up of areas for public access has therefore not been a success in the wake of the two statutes that provided for it. Indeed it has not even compensated for losses arising from development and agricultural intensification. Shoard (1978) calls for a further use of these powers for all definitions of 'open country', especially in lowland England where their use is least but the demands are greatest, and for the extension of the definition of 'open country' to cover parkland.

3.4.1 Compulsory purchase

An alternative approach to these negotiated or directed rights is the outright purchase of land, compulsorily where necessary, for recreation purposes. Local authorities may do this under the 1949 Act and the Countryside Commission under the 1968 Act, specifically for experimental purposes. These powers have been used even less frequently than those for access agreements and orders, because local authorities fear a loss of goodwill, and again they are difficult to draw up in legal terms.

They have been occasionally deployed by local authorities, however, and the Centre for Leisure Research (1986) cites the case of Tamesdown Metropolitan Borough Council, which purchased Hobson Moor Quarry in 1983 for climbing purposes. The Countryside Commission has never exercised these rights of land purchase, but sometimes private groups have purchased, leased or even licensed land for recreational use. Parish councils, too, have used trusts for the purchase of land for recreation purposes, such as for parts of Churchdown Hill in Gloucestershire by the parish council in 1989.

3.4.2 Inheritance tax

In addition to all of these measures, access can be negotiated and existing access can be improved on individual estates of particular scenic quality in exchange for certain exemptions from inheritance tax under the 1975 Finance Act (Countryside Commission, 1990d). This provision has been used quite widely and it is estimated that some 150 private estates covering 134 000 hectares have taken advantage of it at a cost to the taxpayer of £140 million.

This arrangement has two significant shortcomings for improving access, however. First, the requirement is only that access to the land is adequate. This may or may not imply an increase in access. In addition, estate owners are frequently keen to keep any increased access on a permissive basis, rather than agree a new statutory right of way.

Second, tax matters are confidential and, despite pressure from the Ramblers' Association and some concern from the Countryside Commission, the Treasury has resisted giving publicity to the estates for which exemptions have been made. Since 1991 the Commission has been notified of such exemptions but essentially it is difficult to find out where these new access arrangements are (*Daily Telegraph*, 1992).

3.5 COMMON LAND

Common land is possibly the most contested recreation resource, despite perhaps being the oldest. Commons are areas of privately owned land over which certain other people than the owner may have rights, in common with the owner, to do things such as graze stock, collect wood and cut turf. Interestingly, however, most of the commons that were registered up to 1970 were registered without any common rights over them at all. Commons, by virtue of their open and unenclosed nature, are frequently available, in a *de facto* sense, to the public for recreation purposes. This does not, however, imply any *de jure* common rights of passage for all people. The principal problem associated with commons, in the context of recreation and access, is that they are so diverse in nature, status and origins that there is currently no comprehensive law to give commons proper protection and management.

Historically, common rights probably predate landownership itself. In Neolithic times, for example, Dartmoor was grazed in common. Over the centuries, though, farmers and lords of the manor successively enclosed land into private ownership and those areas left for common use were diminished (Open Spaces Society, 1988c). The first attempt to stall this 'privatization' was a 1593 statute which recognized people's needs, within three miles of London, for common land for recreation. This, however, did little to arrest the loss of common land elsewhere in the country. It was only in the nineteenth century that a national system of controlling the enclosure of commons was introduced, when landowners had to apply to Parliament before enclosing.

Some attempts were made to ameliorate commoners' losses, when the enclosure of common land intensified during the Agricultural Revolution. At this time, the enclosure of large tracts of land was supposed to be accompanied by a compensatory piece of land being allotted (the allotment) to the commoner, for recreation and other purposes. Between 1845 and 1865, however, the 16 000 hectares of land that was enclosed was accompanied by only 2500 hectares of allotments.

After 1865 cheap corn from America reduced the pressures for more enclosures in the countryside, and attention turned to common lands in urban areas. The Commons and Open Spaces Preservation Society, from 1865, saved the loss of many commons in and around London as was noted in Chapter 1. It was instrumental in bringing the 1876 Metropolitan Commons Act to statute, which allowed many recreation commons to be regulated by boards of conservators, and it also had a role to play in the Commons Act of 1899 which allowed many local authorities to manage and regulate commons.

In the twentieth century, the 1925 Law of Property Act (Section 193) gave members of the public, for the first time, full statutory right of access for 'air and exercise', to all common land falling into urban districts or boroughs that was covered by the 1876, 1899 and 1925 Acts. Additional rights extended to commons purchased for public open-space purposes by local authorities or the National Trust. Section 194 of the Act also introduced controls over the fencing of common land for the purpose of preventing anything which impeded public access to the land. By 1938 the total extent of commons covered by these provisions extended to 75 000 hectares.

These legislative provisions represented some progress in the protection, particularly, of urban commons, but they did little to stem the losses of common land in general, because of the uncertain nature of its status. In an attempt to resolve these issues, the Government set up a Royal Commission on Common Land which sat from 1955 to 1958. This Commission made three principal recommendations. First, all commons should be recorded and registered, to solve the uncertainty of their identification. Second, they should be open to the public as a statutory right, and finally, they should be properly managed. Legislation was only ever introduced for the first of these, and that was some seven years after the recommendations, but in fact none of the three was ever successfully implemented.

In respect of the first, the 1965 Commons Registrations Act allowed only a three-year registration period, and as a result, many commons were not registered and were lost. Despite the recreation precedents of the 1593 Act, nothing was done about statutory access to commons, with the result that 80% of common land still has no statutory public access rights today. Opposition to such access rights related to their potentially damaging effects on agriculture and the environment. The intention was that these effects would be minimized by good management practices, but no provision was made for this either. There were by 1980, for example, 4000 hectares of common that had no registered owner. These were placed in the care of the local authority, but they were given no powers of management.

Into the 1980s, then, the 1958 Commission had failed to have any significant impact on resolving the common-land problem in relation to statutory access. There were still estimated to be some 550 000 hectares (Countryside Commission, 1989e) of common land in England and Wales (common land is not recognized as such in Scotland and Northern Ireland), but its future remained uncertain. This land was still vulnerable to development by uses not in the public interest but local authorities were reluctant to oppose such activities, because the law relating to jurisdiction over them had still not been fully resolved.

As a result of these uncertainties and outside pressure, the Countryside Commission established the Common Land Forum, which reported in 1986 (Countryside Commission, 1986). The Forum was to seek agreement between a wide range of commons owners, commoners interests and user amenity groups and its report essentially repeated, though fine-tuned, the recommendations of the 1958 Commission.

In terms of access and management, the Forum proposed a five-year period for the development of management plans for commons, before the statutory right of access was introduced. These plans were to be developed by management associations made up of landowners, commoners and local authorities, and were to have environmental enhancement and sympathetic husbandry at the core of their objectives. Access problems, such as misbehaviour and damage, were to be controlled through by-laws.

County councils were to be given the powers to approve management schemes, and any departure of such schemes from the broad principles laid down by the Forum would have to be approved by the Secretary of State for the Environment separately. Counties were also to have the power to prosecute individuals for developments on common land not in the public interest (for example fencing), and were to be empowered to manage the 4000 hectares of ownerless land.

The Forum also put forward proposals for similar types of land to commons – village greens. All local inhabitants were to have the right of recreation on greens and local councils were to have the power to manage them and enforce the control of developments on them.

Despite the proposals of the Common Land Forum, the absence of any comprehensive national legislation as championed by the 1958 Royal Commission has led key interests in major areas of common land increasingly to consider legislation through private Bills relating to specific individual areas of common land. Thus the 1985 Dartmoor

Commons Act has responded to the access and management proposals of the Royal Commission by allowing the public statutory right of access to all commons in the Dartmoor National Park. It has also set up a commoners' council to implement management measures. In the wake of this Act, similar legislation for the Malvern Hills, the Malvern Bill, came before Parliament in the summer of 1993 and a Bill for Bodmin Moor was at that time being drawn up.

3.6 COMMON LAND: A CASE STUDY IN ACCESS CONFLICT

The fate of the Common Land Forum's report highlights well the enduring conflict between those seeking to secure access rights over land and those seeking to defend property rights. It went to environment ministers with an early plea for legislation. Just as the Forum was finishing its work, however, the Moorland Association was formed. This was a body of about 120 owners of grouse moor, mostly in Yorkshire and Durham, who felt that the Country Landowners Association had not represented their interests well on the Common Land Forum. Many of the members had seats in the House of Lords. In tandem with this association, the landowners employees set up a parallel organization called the Moorland Gamekeepers Association.

The Moorland Association made it clear that it did not like the Forum's recommendations about the statutory right of access to all commons, and the way in which they should be managed. This was despite representation on the Forum from sporting interests by Lord Peel, who was chairman of the North of England Grouse Research Project, and who secured some flexibility in access rights, where they could be shown to damage the sporting interests of the common.

The Forum's recommendations were produced in the form of a Government consultative Green Paper at the beginning of 1987, and the Moorland Association produced a two-volume document opposing it. The Countryside Commission subsequently sought to resolve the differences between the Moorland Association and the Forum's recommendations. This was attempted through the setting up of a working party, chaired by the Countryside Commission and made up of representatives from the Moorland Association and the Moorland Gamekeepers' Association representing landowning interests, and the Ramblers' Association and the Open Spaces Society representing public-access interests.

According to the Open Spaces Society (1988a), after four meetings of this group the Commission produced some proposals that provided a basis for discussion as far as the Ramblers' groups were concerned, but were unacceptable to the landowners' groups. The Commission then produced a new set of proposals that were much more along the lines of the Moorland Association's objections to the Green Paper which were, of course, unacceptable as a basis for discussion for the ramblers' groups. They gave provision for gamekeepers to turn walkers off grousemoors when they thought that the walker had broken a bye-law.

Caught in the centre of this disagreement, the Countryside Commission drafted a statement to ministers in September 1988, which, as a compromise between the views of the Moorland Association and the Ramblers' groups, had the agreement of neither. The Open Spaces Society tried to propose legislative arrangements similar to access agreements where restrictions on grouse moors would have to be specially negotiated and be made part of the bye-laws. This reflected one of the recommendations of the Centre of Leisure Research (1986) for common land, the other being for special-access legislation for commons.

In November 1988, however, the Moorland Association issued a further statement about what it would like to see, which was essentially access to grouse moor commons on rights of way and a few other paths only. This, the Open Spaces Society felt, would set an unacceptable precedent for landowners to seek special dispensations, and would

Grouse moors idea under fire

By John Harlow

THE LATEST attempt to unite grouse moor owners and ramblers behind a Parliamentary Bill to open the moors and commons to the public was shot down by both sides yesterday.

Grouse moor owners said a proposed compromise gave too much public access to the moors, especially during the birds' nesting and rearing times, and the Ramblers Association predicted violent clashes if gamekeepers were given more powers to eject walkers.

The Countryside Commission had said it would ask the Government to give moor managers the power to bar the public from grouse moors during the peak shooting season between Aug 12 and Sept 30.

It said this was a compromise between the Ramblers Association, which wanted the freedom for people to walk where they wanted, and the Moorland Association, which wanted the general public entirely restricted to an expanded network of paths and other rights of way.

Mr Martin Gillibrand, secretary of the Moorland Association which represents owners and managers of 90 per cent of British heather grouse moors, rejected the six-week veto as inadequate.

"There is a real need to keep wanderers away during nesting and rearing periods too, which goes back into the spring.

"But we fundamentally do not believe that 95 per cent of people are interested in wandering all over the moors and would prefer to have a good network of paths where they won't get lost."

A spokesman for the Game Conservancy Council said it was waiting to read the fine print, but in principal it believed that unrestricted access remained "a difficult issue".

Mr Alan Mattingly, director of the Ramblers Assocation, said there was serious concern about the commission's proposal to allow gamekeepers to enforce bylaws more rigorously and eject ramblers "where they legally didn't feel strong enough to do it before."

"That could lead to violent clashes between ramblers asserting their rights and these men policing the bylaws and a return to the staged mass trespasses of the 1930s which first re-opened the commons."

"The commission has leaned too far towards the moor owners," he said.

At present the situation varies from moor to moor, and leads to confusion among walkers, who can find themselves regarded as welcome visitors on some moors and commons and trespassers on others.

Figure 3.5 Conflicts in common: conflicts over access to common land typify the strength of feeling over public access to private land that remains one of the cornerstone controversies of public provision for rural leisure (Source: *Daily Telegraph*).

affect 150 000 hectares of grouse moor commons, which is a third of all commons in England (Open Spaces Society, 1988b).

By the end of 1989, Virginia Bottomley, a then junior environment minister, said that comprehensive legislation for common land was still a firm government commitment as it had been since 1986, but 'a little further work and agreement' was necessary, particularly relating to the controversy about public access over grouse moor commons (Country-side Commission News, 1989). Today, because of the intractable positions of the two groups in the fight for access, this time conducted around the committee table rather than on open moorland as it was in the 1930s, the issue of common land remains unresolved.

Indeed, considerable tensions exist in all cases – public rights of way, access agreements, common land and so on – where the legal rights of access over land are asserted. As the Centre for Leisure Research (1986, p. 108) expresses it:

> whenever recreation enters the legal forum . . . it is in a relatively weak position and recreation requirements often are marginalised.

3.7 PUBLIC PROVISION AND MARKET PROVISION AT THE CUSP

Much of the tension relating to public access over private land generally, then, relates to the lack of any real comprehensive legislation relating to public rights. The landowning interest in Parliament has ensured the repression of this. Thus as Bonyhady (1987), cited in Lowe, Clark and Cox (1991, pp. 18–19) states:

> Public enjoyment in the countryside still depends on a fragile combination of rights and the tolerance of landowners. . . . The public rights at common law are clearly only a few. . . . *De facto* rights are therefore likely to remain critical as a means of ameliorating the public's lack of express rights.

But the danger in the 1990s is that strong legislation for *de jure* access that might contribute to a resolution of the conflicts and controversies described above becomes less likely as the reassessment of access to the countryside as a market commodity takes on greater significance. This has already happened for public recreation facilities, an increasing number of which, as has been noted in the first part of this chapter, are being operated on market principles. Farm diversification and an increasing market orientation of government have served to commoditize access in a number of respects, shifting it away from the notion of access as a custom based on historic freedoms.

3.7.1 Privatization of access rights

In some instances, such as for shooting and fishing, the 'privatization' of access rights has had a long history, and cash payments for access agreements – and indeed the opportunity to charge for access to areas secured by agreement under the 1949 Act – contain many of the hallmarks of treating access as a private good. But in the 1990s it has become more controversial. As Lowe, Clark and Cox (1991) point out, discussions have taken place in a number of areas about the possibility of charging for access to beaches.

In addition, an increasing number of reparian owners are claiming payment for access for things such as water skiing, canoeing, trials riding and scrambling. Furthermore, much informal access to existing Forestry Commission and water lands is under threat from privatization under the 1981 Forestry Act and the 1990 Water Act.

Between 1981 and 1991 150 000 hectares of public woodlands, most of which had informal access provisions bestowed upon them by the Forestry Commission, had been sold into the private sector with no formal provision for the retention of access rights (Redmond, 1991). The Commission was, up to 1991, unwilling to dedicate permissive routes or insist on public access as a condition of sale in case this depressed the market value of disposable land. It was the sale of many urban fringe woodlands where this loss of access became critical, and continuing debate about the complete privatization of the Forestry Commission invariably embraces the dramatic impact that this could have on public access.

A ten-minute rule Bill was introduced in the House of Commons by Martin Redmond in April 1991 to protect these access rights in forests for 'air and exercise', but it never became law. The Department of the Environment (1992g), however, does give a mandate to local authorities to continue to secure access to woodlands, particularly those owned by the Forestry Commission, in the absence of any legal compulsion for the Commission to sustain access opportunities.

By October 1991 the Forestry Commission had agreed to seek a management agreement with the relevant local planning authority to preserve access before the sale of any further land. The initial indications are, though, that this system is not working at all well because of the reluctance on the part of local authorities to involve themselves in such work as it is often considered a low priority.

For the water sector, clause 7 of the 1990 Act allows the new water companies to charge for what used to be customary access to their lands and as an alternative, of course, they can always bar customary access altogether. The 1991 Water Resource Act, however, does go some way towards prohibiting absolute restrictions of access on water company land. In truth, this commoditization of access opportunities has met with some favour on the part of both recreationists and planners. It can act as a means of catering for increased demands for specific activities and it also gave a greater security of access since it is provided on a contractual basis. Shoard (1989), too, feels that paying for access might be the only way to safeguard both the quantity and quality of sites that have historically existed if the only alternative is the termination of rights altogether.

Less surprisingly, perhaps, treating access as a market commodity has also been encouraged by farmers and landowners in the context of agricultural diversification. As well as an additional income, financial arrangements serve to legitimate their legal rights of ownership, often in dispute, and allow a greater degree of regulation.

On the negative side of commoditizing access, it runs the risk of destroying access rights and denying access opportunities to those who cannot afford it. Further, it might encourage landowners who traditionally have allowed *de facto* access to reduce this through access for payment only, thus actually reducing the supply of access that traditionally had been free. It could also severely slow down the process of registering *bona fide* rights of access on the definitive map.

In some cases, too, some recreationists may purchase access rights as a means of excluding others, as was noted by the Centre for Leisure Research (1986) where anglers were paying for access as a means of excluding canoeists. Overall, however, it appears in all of these developments in the commoditization or privatization of access the market is seeking to provide opportunities principally because legislation to rationalize customary freedoms into *de jure* rights has failed.

3.7.2 Public and private access in joint consumption

One step removed from this overt privatization of access is the use of private access in conjunction with existing public-access rights. A good example of this is the introduction of the notion of bridleway tolls. The British Horse Society recently welcomed an initiative from the Groundwork Trust for farmers and landowners to set up permissive bridleways on their own land for which they would charge (Lowe, Clark and Cox, 1991). They have been introduced, for example, in Essex, Berkshire and Cheshire and link up public bridleways avoiding roads, to create more comprehensive systems of access on horseback. This can lead to a reduction in trespass and allows field boundaries through which these 'private' bridleways pass to remain uncultivated. They also generate income for the diversifying farmer through annual membership subscriptions.

In using these tolled bridleways in this way, the potential for more comprehensive bridleway systems increases, but many feel that this runs against the spirit or principle of public access. In addition, there is a danger of the erosion of public rights in terms of the quality of public bridleways and the diminution of their usability, unless consumed jointly with private products. This kind of erosion of rights was much publicized when Peter de Savery purchased Land's End in Cornwall and proceeded to charge for access to developed facilities, restricting the use of public rights of way.

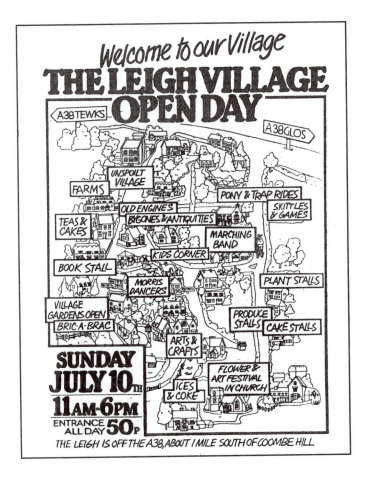

Figure 3.6 The 'privatization' of a village: charging access to the village of Leigh in Gloucestershire, despite the facilities within it, calls into question the abuse of traditional access rights. (Source: *Gloucestershire Echo*)

3.7.3 Privatizing the village

This move to privatize customary rights has even extended to whole villages as the community jumps on to the 'revenue raising' bandwagon. As Figure 3.6 illustrates, a village in Gloucestershire actually charges for access to it on certain days, stressing those facilities within it that may be consumed for leisure purposes. This is made possible, because Leigh is on a loop road with only one access point from the main road. Non-payers therefore can be excluded. The facilities themselves are perhaps uncontroversially market commodities, but access charges to the village *per se*, severely threaten rights of access.

3.8 PRIVATE PROVISION

Private provision for countryside recreation is on the increase, therefore, either through the opening of new facilities, or the internalization of traditional rights and customs into the market place. Examples of private countryside facilities from one county, Gloucestershire, include a butterfly park, a birds of prey centre, a farm and wildfowl park, a rare breeds centre, a bird garden, a vineyard, potteries, a woollen weavers centre, a glass-blowing centre, a puzzlewood, caves and various private gardens, arboreta, museums and collections.

One of the principal interests in relation to such facilities for public policy centres around planning policy and the extent to which planning permissions for them will be granted. Thus, controversies range about the appropriateness, particularly of large-scale developments such as Alton Towers, Centre Parcs, Thorpe Park and so on, to their countryside setting. This controversy is particularly acute in national parks. The Council for the Protection of Rural England (1990) expresses concern about the increasing number of such planning applications in national parks in the late 1980s, that are seemingly unrelated to the essential qualities of parks.

MacEwen and MacEwen (1987) question the appropriateness of such developments as the Langdale Centre in the Lake District National Park, with its timeshares, hotels, pubs, restaurants and so on, owing more to the image of a holiday in the Caribbean than remoter upland Britain. The National Parks Review Panel (Edwards,1991) raises the same issue, disputing whether such large-scale developments constitute the 'green' tourism for which national parks are well suited. Furthermore, they express concerns about whether the expenditure at such centres is effectively retained in the local economy and put forward the notion that where they have been allowed there should be some kind of tourism tax to help fund non-market aspects of recreation provision, such as the maintenance of footpaths.

The Council for National Parks (1990), too, is firmly opposed to such developments. It believes that such large-scale proposals should be forced out of national parks. It feels that recreation in the parks should be restricted to those forms that have their root in spiritual fulfilment and experience of the wilder countryside. Their objections extend to all intensive facilities, particularly air-borne, water-borne and land-based motorized sports, and they call for all national park authorities to develop policies of decisive exclusion. Where these activities have developed within parks, park authorities have tended to adopt policies of land-use zoning to concentrate them in specific limited areas.

In places where developments have been achieved outside of national parks, such as the leisure village in the Cotswold Water Park in Gloucestershire, they have been accompanied by expensive environmental statements (Cobham Resource Consultants, 1988) and lengthy and heated public enquiries. It is interesting to speculate on whether Euro Disney would have received planning permission anywhere in Britain, given the scale of objections in France, and Britain's tighter planning laws. Indeed, the leisure spa towns such as Cheltenham and Leamington and the development of 'inland' seaside resorts such as was conceived, for example, at Malvern in the late nineteenth century in what is now an Area of Outstanding Natural Beauty, may well have had difficulties in securing planning permission as leisure developments if they were conceived today.

These problems, of course, raise issues as to whether many of these larger scale facilities in the countryside actually constitute rural recreation or access at all. Certainly a day at Euro Disney or Alton Towers would generate little in the way of 'rural refreshment'. It is perhaps the more traditional, smaller scale and often impermanent 'activities' that provide a more acceptable notion of private-sector provision, such as village fêtes, horse fairs, country fairs, agricultural shows, and so on. But these often owe more to tradition and community spirit than to any overarching sense of entrepreneurship.

A second area of public policy that impacts on private-sector recreation provision is farm diversification. Farm parks, open days, horsey culture, farm trails, 'pick your own' and so on now have some established tradition and these, in most cases, can be conducted successfully without recourse to planning law. These kinds of developments often represent a more formalized means of 'charging' for recreation and access that has often taken place traditionally without the farmer's permission even outside the rights of way network. In the Centre for Leisure Research (1986) survey of farmers, 71% of them claimed that people used their land without permission, often regularly, for walking, picnicking, picking fruit and poaching, although the overall intensity of these kinds of activity was considered to be quite modest.

But the formalization of farm diversification under the 1986 Agriculture Act is now proposing larger-scale developments based on agriculture that may more commonly require planning consents. This has caused great animosity, for example in the Brecon Beacons National Park (Curry and Edwards, 1991), where a 1600-signature petition was given to the national park authority, calling for a relaxation of planning controls for farm diversification purposes.

Ilbury (1989) considers that farm-based recreation, as opposed to tourism which is considered fully elsewhere by a number of authors (see for example, Slee, 1989), offers considerable potential for increasing farm incomes. This is principally because of the relationship between recreation supply (much of which is in remoter Britain) and demand (the largest expression of which comes from lowland England), which offers 'heartland' farmers the opportunity to fill gaps in provision. In detailing different types of opportunity he distinguishes between resource-based activities and day-visitor enterprises and cites a number of examples where leisure parks have essentially provided the principal source of farm income.

In the development of such enterprises, location, farm type, objectives and market research are all important, as too are the attitudes of farmers and the development of marketing skills. Tenancy restrictions have to be given special consideration where they are appropriate, but it also remains totally unknown as to when any local market for recreation provision will become saturated.

Diversification into recreation gives farmers some advantages over other private entrepreneurs in the availability of grant aid under the Farm Diversification Scheme, both for capital grants and for market research, and the Farm Woodlands Scheme, which has access provisions associated with grant aid. From the examples cited by Ilbury (1989) grant aid has also been attracted from the Rural Development Commission, the regional tourist boards, in Wales, the Welsh Development Agency, and other public bodies.

This availability of grant aid, together with declining incomes from farm production, will undoubtedly lead to a growth in the private provision of recreation opportunities from the farming community. But here again, the legitimacy of some farm-based recreation initiatives as a means of bolstering farm incomes constantly runs the danger of abusing public rights. By 1990 the Countryside Commission was experimenting with ways of paying farmers to manage public rights of way (*Farming News*, 1990a) and in the same year, Devon County Council made £200 000 available for farmers to 'sell' access to their land and woodland under the Country Landowners' Association's Environmental

Land Management Scheme (*Big Farm Weekly*, 1990). One farmer on the Pennine Way, has also placed 'honesty boxes' on the route (*Daily Telegraph*, 1990).

The potential of private farm-based recreation activities is undoubtedly enhanced by the existence of private woodland. In fact, two-thirds of the area of woodland in England and Wales is privately owned, a majority of which is in lowland England. Even before the sale of Forestry Commission lands, some 82% of woodland in the South East of England conservancy of the Commission was privately owned in 1980 (Forestry Commission, 1983). Traditionally, representatives of the private forestry sector, such as the Timber Growers' Association, have seen recreation and access as a residual function in these areas and principally have been concerned with the enduring tensions associated with public rights of way. In tandem with agricultural diversification, however, increasing interest has been shown in the 'commercialization' of private woodland, either through the issuing of licenses and permits (often in association with shooting) or with the provision of specific customer-orientated facilities.

3.9 WHERE DO PEOPLE GO?

In investigating the second proposition of this book, then, the provision of facilities and opportunities for countryside recreation can be seen to be unco-ordinated, fraught with legal difficulties in relation to public access rights and confused in respect of the responsibilities of the public sector on the one hand and the market place on the other. A clear distinction can be drawn within this provision between facilities and the rights of access. Facilities are provided by both the public and the private sectors although for various reasons public facilities are increasingly being operated along market lines. The access rights of the citizen, on the other hand, provide clear responsibilities for the state but because of the uncertainties of the law, and landowning interests, these remain uncertain, ambiguous and of course controversial. Such a situation has led to a number of incursions by the market into traditional access rights, which must be viewed with caution, and suggest a stronger response to classifying access rights on the part of government.

But what is the relative importance of these two types of recreation opportunity – facilities and access rights – to the public at large? Evidence from the 1990 National Survey of Countryside Recreation (Countryside Commission, 1992b) suggests that facilities are very much a minority interest for the countryside recreationist. Historic buildings account for only 6% of trips, country parks 4%, 'pick your own' destinations 2% and visits to all managed countryside account for only 25% of

Percentage of visits

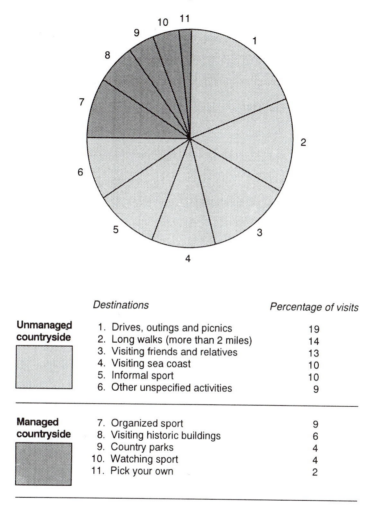

	Destinations	Percentage of visits
Unmanaged countryside	1. Drives, outings and picnics	19
	2. Long walks (more than 2 miles)	14
	3. Visiting friends and relatives	13
	4. Visiting sea coast	10
	5. Informal sport	10
	6. Other unspecified activities	9
Managed countryside	7. Organized sport	9
	8. Visiting historic buildings	6
	9. Country parks	4
	10. Watching sport	4
	11. Pick your own	2

Figure 3.7 Where do people go in the countryside? In 1990 trips to the managed coiuntryside accounted for only 25% of recreation trips. The remaining 75% of destinations suggest that it is the citizen's rights of access that provide the biggest challenges for public policy. (Source: Countryside Commission, 1991b.)

all recreation trips. It is the 75% of visits to the wider unmanaged countryside that provide the focus of the citizen's rights of access and therefore the principle challenge for public policy in relation to provision.

4

Participation in recreation and access

4.1 PROBLEMS OF DATA COLLECTION

The evidence presented at the end of the previous chapter on where people go for countryside recreation trips, suggests that a more general understanding of people's participation patterns provides a crucial input to policy formulation for countryside recreation and access. This being the case, it is important to begin any consideration of the characteristics of participation with a cautionary note on the limitations of empirical data collection which must be borne in mind in the interpretation of any ensuing results.

Broadly speaking, two types of survey have been deployed in discerning information about recreation participation. **Household surveys** give information about recreation behaviour and characteristics of the whole population, through some form of sampling technique, and are used for informing policy decisions. Importantly, they allow information about non-participation to be collected.

Site surveys, on the other hand, are restricted to collecting information about, and from, participating recreationists at individual sites and as such should, and commonly are, restricted to informing management decisions about the sites for which they are collected. Unfortunately, they have also been used to infer patterns and characteristics about the whole population, notably in the 1970s by structure planning authorities (Curry and Comley, 1985), a context in which they can be misleading, since they only take account of the views of people who are already 'recreation active'.

4.1.1 Household surveys: characteristics and problems

Household surveys, then, provide information about recreation behaviour (and therefore the place of countryside recreation in people's general leisure patterns), general attitudes to recreation destinations and population characteristics. The first household surveys that were to inform policy-making in Britain were the British Travel/University of Keele survey (Rogers, 1968), which was based on a national survey of 3187 people in 1965, 328 of whom were younger than 16, in Great Britain. Sillitoe's (1969) work was based on a national survey of 2682 people, aged 15 and over, between 1965 and 1966, but for England and Wales only. Young and Willmot's (1973) work was conducted using a cross-sectional sample of 3000 people in nine London Metropolitan areas from the 1966 Census.

From the 1970s surveys containing questions on countryside recreation have been contained in the General Household Survey in 1973, 1977, 1980, 1983, 1986, 1987 and 1990 (Office of Population Censuses and Surveys, 1976, 1979, 1982, 1985, 1988, 1991 and 1992) all for Great Britain, with varying sample structures, and sizes ranging from nearly 12 000 to over 15 000 (Countryside Commission 1979a; 1987d).

From 1977 the National Surveys of Countryside Recreation have been conducted in 1977, 1980, 1984 and 1990 (Countryside Commission, 1979c, 1982b, 1985b, 1992a) which have been stratified samples for England and Wales only of between 5000 and 6500 people. Again, the sampling frames have changed. The 1977 and 1980 surveys, for example, were summer surveys only, with people between the ages of 16 and 69, whereas the 1984 survey was a year-round survey of people between the ages of 12 and 75.

In parallel with these, the Leisure Day Visits Survey has been conducted by the Central Statistical Office (1985), the United Kingdom Tourism Survey has been conducted by the British Tourist Authority (1990), and the British Airways Tourism Survey has been conducted throughout the 1980s.

All of these surveys point to the first limitation of household data which is that different sample structures and sizes have been used by different organizations and this, together with varying definitions of rural leisure and even of a trip, have tended to yield quite divergent results about various characteristics of countryside recreation. In terms of visits to the countryside, for example, Broom (1991) has noted that the United Kingdom Tourism Survey identified 60 million British tourists staying in the countryside in 1990, the Leisure Day Trips Survey identified 170 million day visits of three hours or more to countryside destinations in a twelve month period over 1989 and 1990, but the National Survey of Countryside Recreation found that there were nearly ten times as many visits by English people to the English countryside in 1990 – 1640 million!

These limitations mean that any data relating to recreation behaviour has to be treated with some caution. The sizes of samples also makes data disaggregation difficult (for example, by region, season or social group) because once the data becomes disaggregated, it also becomes less reliable. Developing a picture of changing recreation patterns over time is also limited for these reasons, but even within individual surveys that are repeated over time, the questions often have been different (particularly in the General Household Survey) or the sample structure has changed (National Survey of Countryside Recreation).

4.1.2 Site surveys: characteristics and problems

Site surveys are restricted to information about attitudes to specific sites, population characteristics of only participating recreationists, and other recreation behaviour of recreationists away from the site. Site surveys are widely available. Elson (1977) estimated that some 750 individual site studies had been undertaken between 1965 and 1975 and there is little to suggest that they have abated to any considerable extent since 1975. They are mainly conducted for local authority or voluntary-sector sites, although Applied Leisure Marketing (1985) did survey 103 separate 'commercial' facilities during September 1985, conducting 1540 interviews with people over 15.

The principal shortcoming of this type of data is, of course, that it is restricted to individual sites and active participants. Inferences about any other people or any other places, therefore, can be misleading, although they are not infrequently made. In particular, they take into account the views only of active participants, and therefore information obtained from them, even if used only for the formulation of management proposals, is likely to reinforce existing recreation patterns. There tends to be a high degree of satisfaction among recreationists at individual sites, particularly if they are regular users, because their very presence implies that they are reasonably satisfied with what they are doing. Site surveys, therefore, should not be used to inform policy, but should simply be concerned with the development of site management plans.

Such surveys are also more difficult to conduct for linear routes, such as public rights of way, because of problems in capturing respondents. This is a limitation, since such routes are more commonly used than sites, and the issues surrounding them are certainly more controversial. Nevertheless, surveys of walkers have been conducted, for example by the Centre for Leisure Research (1986) and the Countryside Commission (1990e).

The Countryside Commission (1991b) is currently proposing to improve the basis upon which surveys are being carried out, and is contemplating the development of a national countryside recreation initiative to assemble and co-ordinate individual site surveys. This has met with favourable responses from practitioners and other interested bodies (Curry, 1991a).

Undoubtedly, the assembly of information about countryside recreation is essential if public policy is to be fully informed about people's behaviour and attitudes. It is useful, however, to be aware of the shortcomings of such data in its use. The attitudes of non-participants are particularly important in this respect, and these are considered more fully below. The preface to the 1978 Countryside Recreation Research Advisory Group conference, reviewing the use that people make of the countryside for recreation, did stress that the many surveys that had been undertaken to that date at national, regional and local levels provided little more than a partial view of the true picture of participation. As the Centre for Leisure Research (1986, p. 32) states:

> there is a great danger of trying to over-simplify the many dimensions of recreation participation, particularly with statistical information.

4.2 RECREATION TRENDS AND INFLUENCES OVER PARTICIPATION

It was noted in Chapter 1 that much of the 'fear of the recreation explosion' in Britain was based on speculation about the influences over recreation participation, rather than any hard evidence *per se*. Much of this speculation was informed by the American 28 Volume report by the Outdoor Recreation Resources Review Commission (1962) which laid stress on income, education and the growth of the population as the principal triggers for outdoor recreation participation. By 1967 the Bureau of Outdoor Recreation (1967) was able to show an increase of 50% in outdoor recreation activities in America between 1960 and 1965, with 'walking for pleasure' having increased by nearly 100%. Further, the study showed that for countryside recreation, supply creates its own demand: providing facilities was itself a strong influence over participation.

In Britain, early work by Burton and Wibberley (1965) considered the principal influences over participation to be: increasing car ownership, increasing total population, reductions in the standard working week, the increasing length of annual holidays, the growth in real incomes per head and the increase in the number of full-time students in higher education. By extrapolating all of these factors, they predicted a doubling in countryside recreation participation between 1960 and 1985, an estimate that Rubenstein and Speakman (1969) considered to be low. By the late 1970s, however, Shoard (1978) was able to state that the 1960s projections of future recreation pressure on the countryside had proved wildly wrong. Population and car ownership simply had not grown as had been anticipated.

By 1967 (Rogers, 1968), the first national survey of leisure patterns and attitudes in Britain had been undertaken. In a sample of over 3000 people the British Travel Association/Keele survey was able to show a close association between income, car ownership, higher education and available leisure time on the one hand, with increasing leisure participation on the other. Most of the growth areas in leisure activity, including sailing, golf, climbing, pony trekking, camping and motoring for pleasure, were space-extensive and inextricably associated with the countryside.

At the same time, Sillitoe (1969) in his national survey was able to point to the importance of the motor car in triggering participation and concluded, from statistical evidence for the first time, that upper social groups were much more likely to make recreation trips to the countryside than lower social groups.

The late 1960s and early 1970s also saw a period of the production of a number of regional surveys for countryside recreation, concerned to identify both participation patterns and levels of provision. These, however, were to have limited impact on the plan-making process for which they were designed in that little evidence that was collected was comprehensively acted upon, a point that is considered further in Chapter 7.

During the 1960s and early 1970s, then, some increases in recreation demands were evident despite an economy moving into stagnation. Although there was still no comprehensive national data in the early 1970s on trends in recreation participation, Harrison (1991) suggests that estimates of participation by Patmore and Rogers (1973) of around 9 million day trips on a summer Sunday had doubled by the time the 1977 National Survey of Countryside Recreation (Countryside Commission, 1979c) was undertaken.

Stoakes (1979), too, indicated an increase in the number of paying visitors to National Trust properties of around 7% per annum between 1955 and 1974. For Department of the Environment properties in the period 1968 to 1972, annual growth in admissions was around 10% per annum. It was, however, the growth in outdoor sports that was most significant during this period (Harrison, 1991).

The principal factors that were considered to influence recreation demand at this time, similar to those that had been perceived in the 1960s – increasing car ownership, affluence leisure time and education (Department of the Environment, 1972) – were growing. Real disposable income grew by 40% between 1970 and 1980 and there were four million more cars on the road at the end of the decade than at the beginning. Although the average working week had declined little, 15% of male manual workers had four or more weeks of paid annual leave by 1980, contrasting with less than 10% in 1970.

There were during the 1970s, however, factors beginning to inhibit participation. The economic recession was having some impact particularly in relation to significant increases in petrol prices (Stoakes and Champion, 1982; Shucksmith, 1979a) and as a direct result of this, there was a marked decline in general recreation participation in 1974, relative to 1973 (Benson and Willis, 1990). Indeed, by 1980 visits to Department of the Environment properties were lower than in 1973, due possibly in part to increases in admission prices, and visits to National Trust properties had become very variable.

By the 1977 National Survey of Countryside Recreation (Countryside Commission, 1979c), the first comprehensive survey of its kind, there were shown to be 101 million trips to the countryside on an average summer month in England and Wales. This compares with an estimate of about 125 million trips for the whole year in the early 1970s (Grayson, Sidaway and Thompson, 1973), although the reliability of this estimate, because it was not based on any extensive survey work, must remain questionable. The principal popular countryside pursuits by 1977 were seen to be a day out in the countryside, usually by car, to a pleasant area where families could picnic and play. Rather fewer people were concerned with serious walking or hiking, but here the coast and cliff scenery proved particularly popular (Veal, 1979).

But this level of participation in 1977 has been seen since (for example by Patmore, 1989) to have been the peak in recreation participation levels. Within the limitations of different types of survey methods, by the second full National Survey of Countryside Recreation (Countryside Commission, 1982b) in 1980, a clear decline in visits to the countryside was apparent. Only 81 million visits per average summer month were recorded, compared with the same survey's figure of 101 million three years before. Day trips from home had declined by 5% but day trips taken on holiday had declined by a third. The effects of unemployment were beginning to bite.

Through the 1980s the picture of participation is one of decline rather than growth (Figure 4.1). The proportion of the population making trips in an average summer month (with the exception of the hot summer of 1984) has hovered at around half of the population (Broom, 1991), with some hint of a downward longer trend.

The number of trips that people made, too, has centred around three and a half per summer month, again with the exception of 1984, with a trend that also shows a slight decline (Figure 4.2).

The British Social Attitudes Survey (Social and Community Planning Research, 1992) notes a decline in countryside recreation trip-making in the four weeks prior to its surveys, from 64% of the sampled population

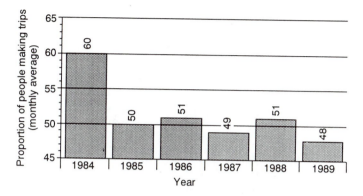

Figure 4.1 The proportion of people making trips per summer month: this has remained static or even declined slightly during the 1980s. (Source: Broom, 1991)

in 1986 to 58.6% in 1987, although their survey period covered only the early spring. Countryside Commission (1992a) figures from the 1990 National Survey of Countryside Recreation also indicate a slight decline in visits to the countryside over the period 1985–90.

Where economic influences have had a significant role to play, they have been most evident in the number of tourism nights in the country-side. Here a clear growth path was evident up to 1987 with the booming economy of the 1980s but since that time there has been a clear decline as the economy moved into recession (Figure 4.3).

A clear growth in the number of visitors at individual sites has been documented for the 1980s by a number of authors but again, set against national trends, these growth patterns must be seen as representing management challenges for those sites rather than implying any wider policy action. Benson and Willis (1990), for example, show more than a

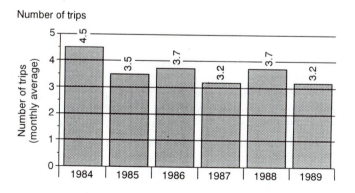

Figure 4.2 The number of trips per participating household: this too has declined slightly during the 1980s. (Source: Broom, 1991)

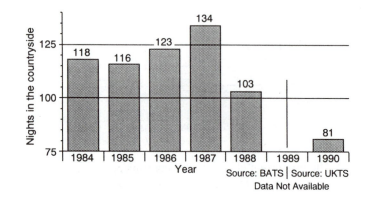

Figure 4.3 British tourism nights in the countryside: these are most susceptible to the state of the economy and they mirror growth and recession. (Source: Broom, 1991)

threefold increase in visits to National Trust properties between 1980 and 1987 and increases in visits to four country parks – Elvaston Castle, Rufford, Rutland Water and Sherwood – of between 300% and 400% between the mid 1970s and 1987. This undoubtedly has much to do with the 'commercialization' and marketing of these parks individually – again supply creating its own demand – since visits to the managed countryside generally, from the National Surveys of Countryside Recreation, have remained a static proportion of a slightly declining overall visit rate to the countryside during the 1980s.

4.2.1 Influences over recreation participation

Given at best an activity plateau during the 1980s, what are now considered to be the principal factors influencing recreation participation? It has been postulated that at the **personal** level a large number of factors may trigger participation. Sidaway (1982) provides a taxonomy of such influences, specifically for the countryside, and a number more generally for leisure as a whole are considered in Torkildsen (1986). Table 4.1 presents a list of such influences, culled from the above two studies.

Apart from personal triggers, many studies of **individual sites** have sought to derive influences over site demand in association with 'travel cost' cost-benefit studies. These can have limitations in identifying demand determinants, however, since they notoriously overstate the importance of some variables (such as distance) and understate the importance of others (such as incomes) by grouping participants in

Table 4.1 Personal influences over countryside recreation participation

Biological	Material	Temporal	Environmental	Predisposition – experience	Predisposition – perception	Opportunity factors
Age	Occupation	Time available	Present residence	Childhood recreation	Attitude to the countryside	Recreation facilities – type available
Stage in life-cycle	Time available	Duties and obligations	Present social environment	Childhood residence	Familiarity with the countryside	Recreation services
Gender	Disposable income	Weekend work	Trends and peer groups	Childhood countryside holiday	Leisure perception	Distribution of facilities
Marital status	Material wealth and goods	Shift work	Social roles and contacts	Will and purpose in life	Interests	Access and location
Skill and ability	Car ownership and mobility	Overtime		Culture born into		Choice of activities
Personality	Dependants	Holiday entitlement		Upbringing		Transport network
				Education		Cost of participation
						Management, policy and support
						Marketing/ programming

Source: Curry and Comley (1986).

various ways (Curry, 1980). Nevertheless, it has been suggested (Kerry-Smith, 1976) that price, income, occupation and age have been the principal determinants to participation at individual sites.

For **the nation as a whole,** it is now more difficult statistically to model these influences over participation, because many of the factors that are considered to trigger it are growing and yet participation is not. No studies since Burton and Wibberley's (1965) work pertaining to the early 1960s have sought to model the long-term statistical influences over recreation participation at the national level.

Despite this problem, Roberts (1979), in analysing the 1977 National Survey of Countryside Recreation, showed a statistical relationship between participation in countryside recreation and, in loose order of influence, car ownership, income, educational attainment, childhood socialization to the countryside and holiday entitlement. Certainly, projecting these influences forward into the 1980s, the number of households with more than one car grew from 57% to 66% between 1977 and 1987, and the proportion of trips made by car is considered to be around 82% in England, 77% in Scotland and 72% in Wales (Benson and Willis, 1990). The growth in real disposable income, too, grew by nearly 30% in real terms for the nation as a whole between 1977 and 1987.

Unemployment is also considered to have an influence over participation, but this is difficult to attribute, however, since it increases, albeit enforced, leisure time likely to stimulate participation, but on the other hand it generates a lack of disposable income likely to thwart it. Certainly, registered unemployment grew from 1.1 million in 1976 to around 3 million ten years later.

Underlying all of these personal and socio-economic influences, the inherent attractiveness, or otherwise, of the countryside undoubtedly has a role to play, as well as the weather. The 1984 National Survey of Countryside Recreation indicated that nearly two-thirds of all countryside recreation trip-making took place when it was sunny and warm, but only 10% when it was wet, cloudy and misty. The hot summer of 1984 undoubtedly accounts for the high level of overall participation in that year, relative to the slight decline in participation in successive years during the 1980s.

Some commentators (Broom, 1991; Glyptis, 1991) have also stressed the importance of the membership of formal recreation clubs and associations as an influence over participation. Social and Community Planning Research's (1992) British Attitudes Survey indicated a slight decline in the overall membership of sport and leisure organizations from 8.3% of the sampled population in 1985 to 6.6% in 1986. This grew to 6.7% in 1987, however.

For specific countryside sport and recreation bodies, membership changes have been variable. Membership of the National Federation of Anglers declined between 1980 and 1990 by nearly a half, and membership of the Pony Club by about 30%. Membership of the Cyclists' Touring Club during this period remained static, but for most of the others, a clear growth can be discerned. Thus membership of the Camping and Caravaning Club grew by 7%, the Royal Yachting Association by 8%, the British Cycling Federation by 17%, the British Orienteering Federation by 42%, the British Canoe Union by 46%, the British Horse Society by 61%, the Ramblers' Association by 127% and the Clay Pigeon Shooting Association by 155% (Broom, 1991).

This growth in memberships may give a clue to the growth in individual activities in the countryside, but it is also indicative of what the economist calls 'option demand': people join such clubs because of an interest in such activities and are essentially expressing an 'option' to consume them some time in the future, rather than necessarily on a regular basis. Even so, club memberships of all types represent only a very small proportion of countryside recreation participants.

But all these influences over participation fail to explain adequately why overall levels of participation have declined during the 1980s. The reason for this is probably less due to the factors that trigger participation in countryside recreation and more to people's longer term structural changes in leisure lifestyles (Curry *et al.*, 1986).

A major and continuing trend since the Second World War has been towards the enrichment of home-based leisure. Homes are the places where most leisure time is spent, and home centredness has increased. The spread of owner-occupation in housing has been partly responsible. Tending homes and gardens has become the nation's main hobby. Televisions, video recorders, hi-fi, CD and cassette players, domestic computers and other items of leisure equipment, plus the installation of central heating now in two-thirds of all homes, have further enhanced homes as leisure environments. It has become more difficult to tempt people out, except by offering clearly different experiences. Cinema and spectator sport audiences have collapsed. Lifestyles have become privatized. Civic participation in religious, political, occupational and community organizations has declined.

As far as countryside recreation is concerned, two growth areas have been evident during the 1980s. First, sports participation has increased. Public facilities have been provided while health and fitness have become sufficiently fashionable to turn marathons into mass events. The fashionable nature of sport and fitness has extended into countryside sports in general, and many of them (such as hang gliding and windsurfing) have grown, because of changing technology, from very low levels at the beginning of the 1980s. The second growth area is option demand, evidenced by the growth in countryside recreation club memberships. This is important because it suggests that an interest in the countryside is not synonymous with participation.

Thus in charting trends in recreation participation and their influences, it is important to note that factors relating to material affluence, while possibly increasing over time in the economy as a whole, are no longer inextricably linked with increasing participation in countryside recreation. Increasing affluence also makes available increasing leisure opportunities in general and these may displace an active interest in the countryside. The fashion for computer games rather than countryside games may herald a longer term structural decline in active recreation participation in rural areas. In turn, this has significant implications for recreation policies that are still based on presumptions of a recreation 'explosion', considered further in Chapter 7, and lends weight to proposition 4 of this book (p. xi).

4.3 RECREATION ACTIVITIES AND PATTERNS

4.3.1 Activities

From the 1986 General Household Survey (Office of Population Censuses and Surveys, 1988) walking in the countryside is by far the most popular specific countryside recreation 'active' pursuit, being 25% more popular than all other classified activities put together. In the main, walkers tend to be frequent users of the countryside, walking over short distances and familiar territory. About 40% of people who participate in walking do so throughout the year, rather than only during the summer period.

On average, from the General Household Survey, nearly 38 trips to the countryside for walking were registered per adult active in any form of countryside recreation in the year, the next most popular being cycling, where only just over 11 trips were recorded per participant. Clearly, this indicates the crucial importance of the public rights of way network as a leisure destination. Swimming, running and playing golf were the next most popular trips in order, and for fishing, water sports, motor sports, sailing, field sports and climbing, fewer than one trip per participating adult on average during the year was recorded.

Despite, and possibly because of, these generally low levels of participation in sports in the countryside, they are, as has been noted above, the fastest growing sectors of participation. Between the 1977 and the 1984 National Surveys of Countryside Recreation, participation in active sports, excluding walking, grew from 7% to 25% of the participating population. Not surprisingly, the newest sports such as hang gliding and wind surfing appear to be the fastest growing activities, starting as they did in 1977 from such a low base of participation.

Placed in the context of more general leisure activities in the countryside, however, these specific active pursuits are still not as popular as general sightseeing and more casual visits. Of those visiting the countryside in 1986 (Table 4.2) over half undertook general sightseeing activities and many visits to attractions were more popular than the specific active pursuits mentioned above. However, as part of people's total leisure trip portfolios, these were all minority activities, with general sightseeing comprising only 10% of all leisure trips by 1989.

Within these overall activities, relatively few people are, in fact, regular users of the countryside for recreation purposes. From the 1984 National Survey of Countryside Recreation, nearly 70% of all trips to the countryside were made by just over 15% of the participating population.

Table 4.2 Leisure activities in the countryside

	% taking part in countryside 1986	% of all leisure trips 1988–9
General sightseeing	54	10
Visiting attractions		
sea coast	36	–
'pick your own'	21	–
historic buildings and museums	40	5
zoos and wildlife attractions	20	2
country parks	27	–
theme parks	–	1
farms and events	–	3
Undertaking activities		
long walks/rambling	34	3
informal sport participation	25	5
organized sport participation	16	4
watching outdoor sport	18	3
nature reserves	14	–
Social and informal activities		
picnicking	–	1
visits to pubs and restaurants	–	–
leisure shopping	–	10
visits to friends and relatives	38	23

Source: Broom (1991)

4.3.2 Patterns of participation

Unsurprisingly, there are quite significant seasonal variations in participation. The 1984 National Survey of Countryside Recreation indicates
that there were more than twice as many countryside recreation trips on
weekdays during the summer holiday season than during the winter
months. Seasonal variations are less for recreation trips made on
Sundays with around 12 million trips being made on a winter Sunday
compared with 18 million on a summer Sunday. On Saturdays, the
volume of trip-making, however, is substantially the same throughout
the year.

4.4 ATTITUDES TOWARDS RECREATION AND ACCESS

As well as those factors that are held to influence or trigger recreation
participation, the attitudes of various people are important for informing
public policy in the development of recreation and access opportunities.
These attitudes are complex and divergent and can be considered in at
least six categories.

4.4.1 General attitudes of the public

The general attitudes of the public, both participants and non-
participants, to countryside recreation can best be viewed in the context
of attitudes to the countryside generally. Information about such attitudes can be considered both quantitatively, through social surveys of
households, or in a more fine-grained qualitative way. Quantified attitudes towards the countryside have been reviewed by Social and
Community Planning Research (1986, 1987, 1988) for the three years
1985, 1986 and 1987, in sample sizes of 1700, 1800 and 3100 individuals
over 18 years of age, representative of the population as a whole,
respectively. In their samples, the number of people who felt that the
countryside had changed a lot over the previous 20 years grew to over
50% in the three survey years, this change being principally perceived to
be as a result of increasing urbanization and changing agricultural
patterns. The countryside was considered to be less attractive as a result
and therefore a less desirable destination for countryside recreation
activities, than it had been in the past.

This tends to support Worth's (1984) findings that the public generally
values landscape and scenery more highly than farming as a benefit of
the countryside. In pursuit of this benefit, Social and Community
Planning Research (1988) found that the popular perception of the
countryside was one of a destination for mass leisure activity, rather
than one of the pursuit of solitude. In this respect, there were percep-

tions of greater opportunities to visit the countryside in the mid-1980s than there had been previously, principally through better roads and a greater number of available facilities, and that this was essentially to be welcomed. Opportunities for access on public rights of way were felt to have declined only marginally during the previous 20 years.

A personal concern for countryside issues grew noticeably during the three years of the survey, with 30% being very concerned in 1985, 40% in 1986 and 44% in 1987. Over three-quarters of the survey respondents were either concerned or very concerned about countryside issues in 1987. Those with the greatest concern were regular users of the countryside, but they also tended to be the more affluent and educated members of society, a point that is considered further in the following section.

Increases in recreation participation were not considered to be an important threat to the countryside in the three surveys. New developments in rural areas and changing farming practices, in that order, were considered to be much more threatening. Very few people felt that casual users to the countryside damaged or spoilt it in any way, a point that is considered more fully in Chapter 8.

As for new policy directions for the countryside, the general public seem much more concerned to protect the countryside for its landscape and amenity values than for any economic or residential considerations. The most popular policy change, more popular than any controls over development or agriculture, was considered to be the provision of new facilities for countryside recreation, such as picnic areas and camping sites. There was a clear demand from all three surveys for greater access to rural Britain on the part of the population at large.

These broad statistical findings tend to support more detailed qualitative surveys of households in Greenwich, conducted by Harrison (1991) who found that the countryside does provide enormous pleasure to the majority of people, even though most people may not actually visit the countryside very often. This research shows a great diversity of values to be derived from visiting the countryside and people seek very different physical settings and social contexts in which to enjoy themselves.

In the detailed analysis of these values (Harrison, Burgess and Lumb, 1986) it is possible to distinguish distinct but closely related types. Some people express 'therapy' values, where getting out into the countryside simply makes them feel better. 'Spiritual' values portray the countryside as a backcloth that allows people to be quiet and reflective. 'Freedom' values allow children in particular to enjoy themselves without the rules and regulations of the town. 'Solitude' values simply allow people to be alone in what is considered to be an environment of great temporal constancy. 'Nostalgic' values can often invoke happy childhood memories.

Enduring among all of these values was the fact that the social meaning of the countryside was found to be one of the strongest determinants of participation. The countryside represents for many the image of a better way of life even though this was invariably considered to be an historic or even a nostalgic one. Harrison (1991) is able to conclude that the social and cultural significance of the countryside has an enduring personal meaning for most people and because of this the statistical representation of countryside recreation participation – through car ownership, income, education, social class and so on – provides a poor indicator of the real value of countryside recreation to most people.

Nevertheless, Harrison (1991) was able to distinguish from her household interviews of the public at large clear differences in the attitudes towards the countryside of different people. Working-class people, for example, had a clear preference in countryside activities for particular facilities such as villages, pubs and 'pick your own' farms. Middle-class people, on the other hand, tended to be disposed towards wilderness areas, solitude activities and so on. And importantly, an interest in the countryside was not universal. A significant minority of people had no particular disposition towards the countryside at all.

These findings have a number of policy implications. First, it would appear that the historic development of public policy for countryside recreation, in introducing national parks, Areas of Outstanding Natural Beauty and even to an extent country parks, has essentially perpetuated the middle-class interest in countryside recreation that was noted in Chapter 1 as being instrumental in the promulgation of these policies in the first place.

Second, general public interest in the countryside seems to be stimulated principally by people's social meanings and connotations of the countryside as a places representing a 'better way of life'. This would suggest that people's enjoyment of the countryside, whether they visit it or not, is possibly best served by more general countryside policies – towards environmentally sensitive agriculture and forestry, and policies for conservation – rather than recreation *per se*. Care should be taken, however, that such policies do not themselves occlude the recreation interest, a point that is considered more fully in respect of conservation policies in Chapter 8.

Third, the attitudes of those who do not have an interest in the countryside for recreation purposes must be considered with some care if for no other reason than that there is a danger that socially based recreation policies designed to encourage non-participants into the countryside might be misdirected. This issue is considered further in Chapter 5.

4.4.2 Attitudes of recreationists

Turning now to active participants in countryside recreation, rather than the public at large, one of the few studies of recreationists relating to their attitudes towards recreation and access as opposed to facilities at individual sites comes from the Centre for Leisure Research (1986). This survey, relating specifically to the unmanaged countryside, suggests that 80% of respondents found that a trip to the countryside allowed them to gain pleasure from natural surroundings. Some 77% felt that it provided them with an opportunity to be with friends, 76% found the countryside relaxing and 65% found it a change from everyday life.

These attitudes did not vary significantly by social class, but there was sufficient distinctiveness between various groupings of recreationists to allow a kind of market segmentation, by varying attitude, to be derived. This was seen by the researchers to be valuable in informing provision, although it does presuppose that all recreation participation is driven by market demands rather than social needs, something that is a principal concern of the following chapter.

Three categories of recreationist were distinguished in the Centre for Leisure Research (1986) survey. It was considered that those who hold **aesthetic** attitudes see the countryside as having scenic value, tranquillity and so forth and therefore might often wish to limit access in some way. Conservation and amenity groups often hold this attitude. Those who hold **instrumental** attitudes see the countryside as a means to an end – a context in which recreation is undertaken. These people have a less restrictive viewpoint except where different recreation activities are in conflict. Those who hold **social** attitudes see the countryside as being a convenient place to spend time with the family and friends. They may be happy with more intensively managed facilities, such as country parks.

Not surprisingly, these three different groups tend to have different views about priorities for improved provision although the need for more information about where to go and what to do, followed by the need to improve the maintenance of public rights of way, were the most commonly stated suggestions across all groups. Significantly, these differing views among unorganized recreationists were seen as one of their enduring characteristics by the researchers. Relative to interest groups of all types, their diversity of attitudes and lack of organization ensured that they were in a relatively weak bargaining position in the securing of access and recreation rights in general.

4.4.3 Attitudes of recreation interest groups

The attitudes of interest groups towards access in particular tend to reinforce the conflicts outlined in Chapter 3. Again, surveys by the Centre for Leisure Research (1986) are instructive of these.

As well as classifying general recreationists into three types, the Centre for Leisure Research also distinguishes between **recreationists**, **casual sporting activists** and **competitive sporting activists**. It is this third category that tend to be members of specific interest groups, both traditional and novel, the memberships of which have grown consider-ably during the 1980s as was noted above. These 'sporting' organiz-ations, termed by the researchers 'interest' organizations, are distinct from the longer-standing access groups such as the Ramblers' Association and the Open Spaces Society (termed 'principle' organiz-ations), but like them, have technical, promotional and political roles, including making claims on recreational resources.

But there is often a conflict between the casual sporting activists, who frequently create access conflicts in the countryside through a lack of organization and legitimacy, and the competitive sporting interest groups , who commonly seek to pursue their interests through formal agreement. Where participation in these activities greatly exceeds orga-nizational membership, such as, for example, in canoeing, this distinc-tion can cause particular problems.

There is also a problem in this respect in terms of who actually 'represents' particular sports, with casual and competitive sporting activities often at variance in their access claims. Between interest groups, there is often perceived to be a noticeable 'power struggle' with each seeking to preserve their own interests. In this context, new interest groups often representing new types of sports activities in the countryside have to seek a place in this power hierarchy. Many recrea-tional interest groups tend to have exclusionary attitudes towards other forms of recreation than their own, partly from self interest, but also from a sense of seeking to defend the quality of the recreation resource.

There is thus often a conflict of attitude between different recreation and sport interest groups, particularly in respect of the 'proper' use of the countryside, which can generally weaken the case for increased access to the countryside for recreation and sporting activities as a whole.

4.4.4 Attitudes of conservation interest groups

The wide range of pressure groups with an interest in the countryside ensures a lack of unity over attitudes towards recreation and access. The Centre for Leisure Research (1986) groups them into either **exclusionary**

groups (such as the Royal Society for the Protection of Birds and some county wildlife trusts) who wish to restrict access in some way, often to particular areas of countryside, or **participatory groups** who wish to increase access (such as the Ramblers' Association and the Open Spaces Society).

At the local level, exclusionary conservation groups might successfully practise exclusion through the ownership and management of land. Participatory groups on the other hand often use the process of public involvement in planning – making representations, lobbying councillors and so on – to further their cause.

Both sets of group are often able to use expertise greater than that available to the local authority in pursuing their cause. Local authorities, in turn, can often use this expertise to their advantage in pursuing, severally, their conservation and recreation responsibilities. These conservation groups, then, when added to those with a recreation interest in the countryside, serve further to diffuse a common attitude towards access and therefore weaken the case for its enhancement.

4.4.5 Attitudes of farmers and landowners

Farmers, as a recreation interest group, tend to have varying views towards access according to their experiences and inherent attitudes, but nevertheless the prevailing view among them is that access is a problem. In the Centre for Leisure Research (1986) survey, 36% of farmers said that recreation and access problems were either severe or very severe.

The main influences over these attitudes tend to be the volume of visitors or type of farming tenure but are more readily attributable to education and age – more educated and younger farmers tend to have more favourable attitudes towards access. Even so, the majority of these more receptive groups were generally not in favour of further provision except where it could be shown clearly to be in their economic interest. These survey results contrast quite markedly with the Country Landowners Association (1984) survey which claimed a high degree of receptivity by farmers to increased opportunities, although again farmers may have perceived these as offering potential increases in income.

The principal problem groups for farmers in the Centre for Leisure Research (1986) survey were felt to be 'local residents' and 'new residents' rather than more generally the 'urban hoards'. It was their ignorance of farming methods and systems that constituted the principal problem. Again these findings contrast with the views of both the National Farmers' Union (1990) and the Country Landowners

Association (1984) who feel that the principal problems relating to access over farmland centre on the urban population rather than local people.

These findings have significant implications for recreational management since it has traditionally been considered to have its principal focus in ameliorating the impacts of migrant urban recreationists. If the problem, as farmers perceive it, is more local, then the potential for a 'community-based' approach to access issues becomes greater.

4.4.6 Attitudes of countryside managers

The Centre for Leisure Research (1986) study found the attitudes of countryside planners and managers towards access to be very variable both between and within local authorities. In Snowdonia National Park, for example, it was considered by planning staff that access should be concentrated on particular recreational footpaths, but in the Peak District National Park there was a much broader 'freedom to roam' philosophy.

Within local authorities it was also found that 'countryside' sections in planning departments were often progressive in making improvements to access in specific targeted areas, while at the same time highways authorities were faced with a backlog of public rights of way objections and an incomplete definitive map. Limited resources were common inhibitors to the development of more positive access policies in this respect. The study notes a significant change in emphasis in the priorities of countryside managers between the mid-1970s and the mid-1980s away from general facility provision towards information and interpretation projects, as a recognition of the importance of smaller scale projects in the totality of provision. But as has been noted in Chapter 2, these may have had a limited impact on the public.

4.4.7 The implications of attitudes for policy

One of the hallmarks of the attitudes of those actively involved in countryside recreation is that they are disparate, competitive and even conflicting. This leads in general terms to a weakening of their case for securing access. The success in gaining access thus appears to be related to the extent to which groups organize themselves and openly negotiate with farmers, landowners and public authorities. But this seems inherently at variance with the general public's inclination to indulge in informal and unorganized public enjoyment in the satiation of cultural, social and personal desires (Harrison, 1991).

There would therefore appear to be a case for public policy to respond to these aspirations of the public at large by improving access opportunities to the wider countryside, if not to specific managed facilities.

Yet Harrison (1991) contends that the Countryside Commission appeared, historically at least, to be working within existing statutory access mechanisms and the Common Land Forum has been disbanded. This status quo can really only perpetuate the access conflicts examined in Chapter 3.

4.5 THE SOCIAL STRUCTURE OF PARTICIPATION

In addition to these general attitudes and behaviour, an understanding of the social structure of participation is important for informing the functions and purposes of social policies for countryside recreation. It has been noted in the previous section that an interest in countryside recreation is not universal, and the implications of this for public policy need to be examined more closely.

Undoubtedly, some leisure activities are spread fairly evenly across all sectors of the population. Young and Willmot (1973), for example, found very little difference indeed in home-based leisure activities across different social groups, apart from reading and gardening. For countryside recreation, Fitton (1979) concludes from the Countryside Commission's 1977 National Survey of Countryside Recreation that participation is spread across all classes of the population. Of importance for public policy, however, is that this spread is uneven – a pattern that is in fact reflected in most types of leisure behaviour (Torkildsen, 1983).

Groups in society may be distinguished in a large number of ways, for example, by age, education and gender. To examine the social structure of participation, however, it is important to distinguish one or more of three types of grouping – income groups, social groups and occupational groups. The latter two of these may relate very closely since Reid (1977) has maintained that 'social class can be regarded as the grouping of people into categories on the basis of occupation'.

Information on the structure of recreation participation is less abundant than on participation patterns as a whole. From earlier household surveys relating to the 1960s, Rogers (1968) found that generally executives had a much wider recreation experience than manual workers and that recreation participation increased very strongly with increases in income. Specifically for countryside recreation, Sillitoe (1969) found that lower social groups, defined by either occupational status or social class, were only half as likely to visit the countryside than the average visit rate for the population as a whole.

Results from Young and Willmot's (1973) survey (of a similar size to the other two, but based within nine London Metropolitan areas in 1966) confirmed this picture. Generally, they concurred that richer, more educated, higher status people tended to participate more in all types of leisure activity, although for countryside recreation, this was not quite so strong. Table 4.3 indicates differing levels of activity by occupational group for four identified countryside pursuits. For certain types of recreation activity, particularly going for a walk of a mile or more, there were a greater proportion of higher social groups than lower social groups participating at that time.

Into the 1970s, this picture for countryside recreation as a whole became more marked (Fitton, 1976). The General Household Survey has had questions relating to leisure that distinguish social groups in 1970, 1977, 1980 and 1983. Although, as Sidaway (1982) notes, the survey doesn't give a particularly accurate picture of unstructured informal recreation activity, it does show for all years a much clearer gradation of participation by occupational group than was evident from the Young and Willmot study.

Apart from watching sports and fishing, there is a greater level of countryside recreation activity as occupational status increases in all four years. Fitton (1978) has been able to manipulate the General Household Survey data to derive estimates of participation levels in all countryside recreation by occupational group for the years 1973 and 1977. This does provide limited time-series information and in fact shows very little change in the amount different occupational groups recreated in the countryside between these two years. Table 4.4 shows that higher socio-

Table 4.3 Countryside recreational participation by occupational status in 1966

	Proportion in each occupational class doing activity 12 times or more in previous year				
	Professional and managerial	*Clerical*	*Skilled*	*Semi-skilled and unskilled*	*All*
	%	%	%	%	%
Going for a drive in a car for pleasure	62	51	62	49	58
Going for a walk of a mile or more	56	63	41	36	47
Caravanning	2	1	5	3	4
Camping	2	1	3	0	2

Source: Young and Willmot (1973).

economic groups were consistently recreating in the countryside in greater proportion than lower socio-economic groups.

This structure is reinforced into the 1980s. Participation can be compared using social class with the National Surveys of Countryside Recreation for 1977, 1980 and 1984 (Table 4.5). Here again, there is a higher degree of participation in higher social groups. Variations across the three years are more likely to be due to factors unrelated to social group characteristics, for example, the weather. Commenting on the 1977 National Survey, Fitton (1978) emphasizes the clear relationship between the degree of participation by social group and the incidence of car ownership. He does note, however, that as incomes increase, trips to the countryside increase irrespective of car ownership.

All of these national surveys, then, indicate a positive relationship between social or occupational group and participation in countryside recreation. This is a broad conclusion confirmed in other studies (for example, Hillman and Whalley (1978)), and reflects the social structure of participation into the 1990s in Northern Ireland (McConaghy, Ogle and Stott, 1992). It must be emphasized, however, that although as social class rises countryside recreation participation is more likely to occur, because there are actually more people in lower status groups, in fact just under half of all trips made to the countryside are made by manual workers (Fitton, 1978).

In addition to this broad trend, there is also evidence that the **frequency** of recreational trips correlates closely with occupational status. Again from the 1984 National Survey of Countryside Recreation, higher social groups make more trips to the countryside than lower social groups (Table 4.6).

This social structure of the frequency of visits was instrumental in allowing the Countryside Commission (1987a) to classify users by their frequency of use. Of those participating in countryside recreation at all, 25% were considered to be **frequent** users. These tended to be young males in professional occupations living in or near the countryside in good-quality housing. They were car owners, often also owning a boat, caravan or horse and frequently would be a member of some countryside recreation organization.

Occasional visitors to the countryside, comprising 50% of all visitors, tended to be under 60 and equally likely to be male of female. They were in clerical or skilled-manual employment, living within three miles of the countryside, with a car and young children. The final 25%, **rare** users, were more likely to be from low income groups and either unskilled or unemployed. They tended to live in poor housing, several miles from the countryside and dependent on public transport. Many were over 70, or from an ethnic minority background, or both.

Table 4.4 Countryside recreation by socio-economic group in 1973 and 1977

	% participating at least once in the previous summer month	
	1973	1977
Employers and managers	55.8	55.2
Professionals	57.1	54.1
Intermediate and junior non-manual	48.7	49.3
Foremen and skilled	41.7	45.4
Semi-skilled manual	35.6	34.5
Unskilled manual	32.2	31.6
Total participating population	44.1	43.1

Source: Fitton (1978).

Table 4.5 Countryside recreation participation by social class in 1977, 1980 and 1984

	Percentage participating in the four weeks prior to the survey		
Social class	1977	1980	1984
A,B	67	58	75
C1	55	50	69
C2	55	39	61
D,E	38	29	43

A higher managerial, administrative or professional staff;
B intermediate managerial, administrative or professional staff;
C1 supervisory, clerical, junior managers and administrative staff;
C2 skilled manual workers;
D semi-skilled workers;
E state pensioners, widows, casual and lowest paid workers.

Source: Curry and Comley (1986).

The same pattern of this general social structure of participation holds good for individual recreation sites. Elson (1977) reviewed a wide range of site surveys up to 1976, and grouping them into regions to reduce the variation in the social structure of the base populations, similar profiles for different regions emerge. Table 4.7 compares the social structure of participation in three regional sets of site surveys with that of the most

Table 4.6 Social class and frequency of participation in 1984

| | *Number of trips in the previous four weeks by social class[a] (%)* | | | | | | |
	A	B	C1	C2	D	E	Unemployed
More than 9 trips	23	26	20	18	12	7	7
No trips	26	23	32	40	52	57	60

[a] social classes are defined in Table 4.5.

Source: Curry and Comley (1986).

affluent south east region as a whole. In all cases, there is an over-representation of managerial and professional workers, similar proportions of skilled and manual workers, and fewer semi-skilled and unskilled workers compared with the south east region as a whole. All of these sites provided informal passive recreation.

In the late 1970s and 1980s a similar pattern emerges from a compilation of six site surveys compared with the social profile of Great Britain as a whole (Curry and Comley, 1986) indicated in Table 4.8. This confirms the broad over-representation of managerial and professional workers and the underrepresentation of semi-skilled and unskilled workers.

All of these distributions refer to countryside recreation as a whole. According to the Countryside Commission (1982b), however, it is when particular recreation activities are considered that social stratification becomes a key determinant of participation. Rogers (1968), for example, found perhaps not surprisingly that golf was most markedly skewed towards high income groups. Young and Willmot (1973) indicated that a greater proportion of skilled manual workers participated in caravaning and camping than any other social group. Evidence from the General Household Survey too (Office of Population Censuses and Surveys, 1976, 1985) suggests that fishing might be the most popular among skilled manual workers. These observations clearly suggest that the social class/recreation participation relationships that pertain for countryside recreation as a whole do not hold for all individual recreation activities.

A number of other writers also have noted that specific countryside recreation activities might generate different levels of participation across classes. Pearson (1977), for example, considers that working-class people have a tendency to use more intensive commercialized rather than public facilities, reinforcing Harrison's (1991) findings from qualitative research, noted above. Fitton (1978), too, suggests that lower-

Participation in recreation and access

Table 4.7 Site surveys and participation by occupational group, 1965–75

Forest of Dean day visitors[a]	%	West Midlands[b]	%
Managerial	15	Managerial	16
Professional	8	Professional	9
Clerical	25	Clerical	16
Supervisory	8	Supervisory	6
Skilled	27	Skilled	26
Semi-skilled	8	Semi-skilled	13
Unskilled	2	Unskilled	6
Self-employed	2	Self-employed	2
Others	5	Others	8
(n = 811)		(n = 797)	

South East[c]	%	Region in 1966	%
Managerial ⎫ Professional ⎬	24	Managerial ⎫ Professional ⎬	11
Clerical	34	Clerical	27
Supervisory	7	Supervisory	6
Skilled	19	Skilled	24
Semi-skilled	10	Semi-skilled	22
Unskilled	5	Unskilled	9
Others	1	Others	1
(n = 3977)			

[a]   14 site surveys between June and September 1968
[b]   6 site surveys between June and September 1973
[c]   31 site surveys between June and September 1973

Source: Elson (1977).

status occupations tend to use more intensive recreation areas such as rivers, canals, country pubs and safari parks, possibly because of a tendency towards group rather than solitude activity (Curry, 1985b). This type of assertion is reinforced by the House of Lords (1973) who considered that lower occupational groups were using the countryside not so much for a natural experience, but for something more akin to a town park in the countryside. In a household survey of recreation activities and attitudes, the Centre for Leisure Research (1986), too, found that active walkers and sports participants were likely to be of a higher social group than other informal recreationists.

Relative preferences for different types of activity also have been identified from the 1984 National Survey of Countryside Recreation

Table 4.8 Site surveys and participation by occupational group: 1975 onwards

All figures in percentages

	Clent Country Park	Waseley Country Park	Lickey Country Park	Exmoor National Park	Rufford/ Sherwood Country Park	Stover Country Park	Great Britain
	(1979)	(1979)	(1979)	(1980)	(1982)	(1984)	(1981)
Professional	18	24	17	33	9	7	16
Managerial					20	35	
Clerical	33	31	30	25	33		20
Supervisory	29	23	28	14	28	38	8
Skilled				17			23
Semi-skilled	10	11	12	9	5	7	14
Unskilled	3	4	2	3	1	3	6
Others	8	6	10	–	3	10	13

Source: Curry and Comley (1986).

(Curry and Comley, 1986). Initially, occupational groups were ranked according to the percentage of those people in each group participating in each of a number of different activities. This process indicated that there was again a close positive correlation between social group and recreation participation. The exceptions to this were visits to country parks and visits to zoos, safari parks and wildlife parks. In these cases, Fitton's (1978) views tend to have some support in that they are relatively more popular with clerical (and to an extent skilled manual) workers, than higher social groups. Statistical testing showed a particularly strong relationship between higher social groups and higher participation for visits to historic buildings and nature reserves. The same statistical tests showed a disproportionately high level of visits to zoos and safari parks from social groups C1 and C2, and a particularly high number of visits for fishing purposes from social groups D, E and E unemployed, with a lower representation from social groups A and B.

In terms of countryside recreation patterns both generally and for individual sites, then, it appears that both the likelihood of participation and the frequency of visits are likely to increase as social or occupational group increases. For individual activities too there is not an even spread of participation, with some evidence to suggest that among middle and lower social groups commercial and facility-orientated activities are the most popular.

Of themselves, these data may hide more subtle underlying characteristics relating to the social structure of participation. Indeed, as Roberts (1979) maintains, sociology has a contempt for research that naively treats statistical manipulation of occupational and class variables as exhausting the possibilities of class analysis. Because of the need to examine these underlying characteristics more closely, the following chapter assesses in more detail the consequence of this social structure of participation for the development of recreation and access policies with social goals. It is in the area of social policy formulation that the social structure of participation has its principal significance.

5

Social policies for countryside recreation and access

5.1 SOCIAL OR MARKET POLICIES?

In Chapter 4 it has been argued that there is a clear skew in the social structure of recreation participation towards the more affluent. This chapter explores the consequences of this uneven distribution in the social structure of participation, for public recreation and access policy.

The starting point for this exploration is to consider the extent to which public policy for countryside recreation access actually has, historically, catered for social needs on the one hand, or market demands on the other. Undoubtedly, there has always been the **intention** of a social element to public leisure policies. Early social policies, for example, centred on securing paid holidays for the mass of the working population. The Government Committee on Holidays with Pay, which reported in 1938, could find no examples of paid holidays for wage earners earlier than 1884 and indeed there was little interest in the phenomenon, possibly through fear of unemployment, before 1914. It was not until 1911 that the first resolution in favour of universal annual paid holidays was passed by the Trades Union Congress and by 1925 about one and a half million manual workers were included in collective agreements providing paid holidays (Rubenstein and Speakman, 1969).

By 1936 this figure had risen to about three million, and the Committee recommended at least one week's paid holiday for all workers, something that found its way into the 1938 Holidays with Pay Act. About 80% of wage earners achieved this position by 1945 and clearly since then it has become effectively universal, even though, as Harrison (1991) notes, it has benefited white-collar workers much more than the working class.

Social considerations specifically in countryside recreation policy can be traced back at least to Dower (1945) and Hobhouse (1947a). Both were concerned that recreation and access to the countryside, specifically national parks, should be 'for all people and especially the young of every class and kind . . . and not just some privileged section of the community'. From this time, social policies for rural leisure have tended to be targeted more directly at disadvantaged groups. It has been noted in Chapter 2 that the 1970s was a period during which attempts were made to put social leisure on the political agenda. Thus, the House of Lords Select Committee in 1973 recommended a 'recreation for all' role for the Countryside Commission, with 'recreation priority areas' to be targeted at the less well-off. The Government's Countryside Review Committee (1977), too, found favour with the development of country-side recreation facilities for social purposes.

In the late 1970s and early 1980s, the Town and Country Planning Association (1979) launched a campaign for recreation among the car-less and the English Tourist Board and Trades Union Congress (1976) developed the notion of 'social tourism' for the physically and mentally handicapped, the low paid and the elderly. The Chairman's Policy Group (1983) similarly stressed the importance of social policies for rural leisure. But the hallmark of all these proposals was that very few of them ever found their way into implementable policies.

The Sports Council stood distinct in being allowed to pursue 'sport for all' policies, but these would have their dominant impact in urban areas, and further, it has been argued, they actually exacerbated inequalities in participation (McIntosh and Charlton, 1985) a point which is considered further in the concluding chapter of this book. By the beginning of the 1980s, the market orientation of the new Conservative government ensured that the social function of rural leisure would remain subservient to notions of cost-effectiveness.

In the local authority sector, too, lip service has continually been paid, in the policies of structure plans and countryside strategies, to the social need for countryside recreation. This has remained of minor importance, however, relative to the perceived need to respond to market demands, and has been considered, more often than not, in the context of some form of material deprivation – an issue that is considered further below. Again, the means of implementing such strategic policies for social need have remained vague.

Even in the context of implementation, there has been a confusion over whether public recreation facilities are designed to cater for social needs or market demands, or both. The Countryside Commission's (1974a) advisory notes on country park plans, for example, permitted both of these objectives, in allowing parks to be considered either as a 'social service' or to maximize income. On the other hand, the Commission's (1977) more general guidelines for considering grant aid included 'need' (which they would measure in terms of consumption levels, base populations and available supply), but neither the demand for, nor any potential income to be derived from, recreation provision. It would seem that these policy guidelines for implementation, even if they can be interpreted as taking both need and demand into account, say little about the circumstances in which it is more appropriate to consider social need objectives than those of market demand.

Although lip service has thus been paid to the social importance of countryside recreation and access in policies at all levels, there does appear to be some confusion about the situations in which they might be most appropriately applied. Despite this, some social policies for countryside recreation actually have been instituted during the 1970s and 1980s, often on an experimental basis, and a number of these are considered below. There is evidence to suggest, however, that the overwhelming impact of policies for the pubic provision of countryside recreation and access, whatever their intent, has been to cater for market demands rather than social needs.

5.2 SOCIAL NEEDS OR MARKET DEMANDS?

In the context of countryside recreation, social need arises in situations where people do not have the means to pay for recreation consumption, but nevertheless have a desire to participate. Market demand is evident where people have both the willingness and ability to pay for recreation consumption. From this distinction, a simple understanding of levels of recreation participation, which is a principal preoccupation among collectors of recreation data, provides little information to distinguish between demands and needs since some participants may be 'needers' taking part in recreation activities as a result of some social policy, but others may be 'demanders' triggered into participation by a willingness and ability to pay.

A better means of examining this distinction between social needs and market demands among recreation participants is by making reference to the factors that influence participation. Both individual site studies and market studies for countryside recreation give a clear indication that it is demand factors that have had the most significant influence over recreation participation, rather than any satiation of social needs.

The derivation of site demand curves for public recreation facilities has formed a common preoccupation among researchers since the late 1960s, usually in the context of cost-benefit studies (Curry, 1980). In these studies, the price of recreation (often expressed in terms of the cost of getting to the site) has invariably has been found to be the most significant determinant in recreation participation, despite some of the computational problems associated with the grouping of recreation participants.

In addition, a number of researchers have found that several other demand factors have had a significant influence on consumption levels at individual sites. It has been postulated that, in order of importance, price, income, occupation and age have been the strongest influences over participation (Kerry-Smith, 1976). Thus, it is those variables that affect both the willingness and, particularly, the ability to consume recreation (demand factors) that provide the clearest influences over recreation consumption at individual sites.

Factors influencing overall participation levels in countryside recreation have been less closely researched than those for individual facilities. Nevertheless, Burton and Wibberley's (1965) work in the 1960s did identify car ownership, the growth in real incomes and increasing leisure time as the principal triggers to participation. In the 1980s the National Surveys of Countryside Recreation in 1977 and 1984 (Countryside Commission, 1979c, 1985b) confirmed these factors as the strongest determinants of recreation trips, adding to them occupational status and age.

The significance of all of these factors is that they suggest that participation is triggered by factors that exhibit a willingness to pay rather than any expression of social need. Furthermore, evidence on the social structure of participation, skewed towards the more affluent, presented in Chapter 4, supports this notion.

Thus almost irrespective of any policy option to cater for market demands or social needs, the overwhelming outcome of public countryside recreation policy appears to be the satisfaction of some form of effective demand. Indeed, in its analysis of countryside recreationists, the Centre for Leisure Research (1986) actually distinguishes one from another through a process of what it terms 'market segmentation', into **aesthetic, instrumental** and **social** consumers. The Countryside Commission (1992a) also proposes assessing people's needs for countryside recreation, through a process of 'market research'.

This market orientation of public provision has been exacerbated by public policies born of a 'fear of a recreation explosion' which have often **constrained** public authorities to cater for market demands.

5.3 CONTROL, FACILITATION OR PROMOTION?

In terms of the overall purpose of recreation policy, particularly for public recreation facilities, the 1968 Countryside Act, and subsequent Countryside Commission (1974a, 1977) policy statements, did not require local authorities and other public providers actively to **promote** countryside recreation in any positive way. Rather, the tenor of the Act was that they should **facilitate** it. This meant that for those resorting to the countryside (Dower, 1978) for leisure purposes recreation was to be allowed and catered for. In this sense, policy could be interpreted as attempting to solve a problem of recreational access, rather than exploit an access potential.

In this context, such a remit clearly makes the development of social policies for countryside recreation very difficult. Only if authorities are allowed to **promote** recreation in some way can they begin actively to encourage people into the countryside, by whatever means, rather than simply cater for those who already have expressed a demand. Thus the tenor of the 1968 Act in empowering **facilitation** rather than **promotion** in public-recreation providers, although it was designed simply to temper the 'fear of a recreation explosion', was in practice constraining them to cater for market demands rather than actively developing policies for social need.

Worse still, the questionable assumption of an incessant growth in consumption led local authorities, particularly through their structure plans, to take an unduly restrictive stance in promulgating countryside recreation policies. For the 1970s, Fitton (1979) has argued that such presumptions had often been the cause of 'moral panic' and the preservationist concern for the countryside that was so popular on the part of the public at large. This concern, he suggests, had arisen from the common misconception that recreation was a problem – that people and their associated activities had a negative effect on the ecological and aesthetic balance of the environment and upon other land users.

Misconceptions such as these had often led to local-authority policies actually being more concerned with **control** than with either **facilitation** or **promotion** in the context of public-recreation provision. According to Fitton, phrases such as 'over-visitation' and 'people pollution' had led to structure plan policies being designed to provide alternative facilities such as country parks and picnic sites close to urban centres to stop the 'unnecessary' use of more vulnerable areas. Ironically, it has been shown that in the provision of new facilities such as these, supply often creates its own demand (Seckler, 1966) and therefore developing new sites as a means of controlling recreation may in itself generate additional consumption, which in turn will require further control.

Fitton (1979) also notes instances of policies that were even more negative than these policies of control:

> At the extreme in some local authority planning documents (notably of the shire counties adjacent to conurbations), policies are clearly for exclusion (p. 58).

He goes on to discuss the types of words that were used at the time in some structure plans in relation to countryside recreation – 'destroy', 'contain', 'filter', 'explode' and 'intercept' – and parallels them with:

activity at some set piece battle rather than a description of people seeking to enjoy themselves (p. 59).

Certainly, such plans represented a very different attitude towards countryside recreation from that expressed in the 1966 White Paper (Ministry of Land and Natural Resources, 1966) which spawned the notion of specific recreation facilities such as country parks and picnic sites. The White Paper envisaged these as having a positive role in provision.

During the 1970s, at least then, policies for control rather than facilitation or promotion dominated public-recreation provision in the local-authority sector. In this context it became almost impossible to develop positive policies for social provision and therefore participation was clearly exerted through market demands. The extent to which structure plan policies have remained restrictive during the 1980s and into the 1990s is considered more fully in Chapter 7.

Despite some mention of social policies for countryside recreation, then, the way in which policies have developed has led them, in fact, to cater for existing market demands and not social needs. Often they have even, through control-based structure plan policies, actually had the effect of constraining market demands. This evidence would appear, at first glance, to suggest that social policies should now have a much higher priority for countryside recreation, relative to their historical catering for market demands, to redress the imbalance in the social structure of participation. Indeed this may now be made possible, since Section 17 of the 1986 Agriculture Act requires agriculture ministers, at least, to **promote** the enjoyment of the countryside by the public, and recent Countryside Commission (1992a) policies have adopted a perceptively more promotional stance.

But the advisability of this depends on one crucial factor. Do non-participants in countryside recreation not participate because of some form of material deprivation, or do they simply choose not to? If the former is the case, then the development of social policies is entirely appropriate. If the latter is true, then the development of social policies is, at best, likely to be ineffectual and, at worst, runs the risk of being socially regressive. The efficacy of social policies thus hinges on people's preferences for, or constraints on, countryside recreation participation.

5.4 PREFERENCES OR CONSTRAINTS?

5.4.1 Disinterest in the countryside

As has been noted in Chapter 4, an interest in the countryside is not universal. Ashley (1978), cited in Fitton (1979, p. 71), for example, stresses that certain sections of the population have little interest in participating at all:

> the assumption that most people wish to enjoy the use of the countryside on foot is a nonsensical myth. Very few people either wish to walk, or intend to. The pastoral idyll of communing with nature is an anathema to most of the population.

Fitton's (1979) own analysis of the 1977 National Survey of Countryside Recreation indicates that certain people do not like the countryside because there is a perception that there is nothing for them to do there or because it has bad memories for them (for example, as a result of being evacuated to the country during the war). Other researches have found negative evaluations of the countryside, based on the difficulty of access and perceived overcrowding (Centre for Leisure Research, 1986). Rather than pointing to a dislike of the countryside, Ryan (1978) maintains that other forms of leisure pursuit may simply have a stronger pull. He asserts that countryside recreation is still a minority activity in people's leisure time, relative to watching television, and indulging in a variety of forms of urban recreation.

A study by the Qualitative Consultancy (1986) has indicated in general terms what motivates people to visit the countryside. Almost universally, good weather triggers an interest in participation and commonly visits are made as a means of entertaining others. For many, however, there is apathy and inertia towards the countryside: this type of recreation is simply not at the top of people's minds. Further, visits are often inhibited by a lack of consensus within the family, particularly among children and husbands.

5.4.2 Aspirations for participation

The Countryside Commission's 1984 National Survey of Countryside Recreation asked questions about people's preferences for visiting the countryside as well as their levels of interest in the countryside and the ease with which access to the countryside was achieved. Within the limitations of direct questions of this nature (some people will overstate their case for fear of a loss of access, others will understate it for fear of being asked to pay), this information does shed some light on people's preferences.

Table 5.1 indicates people's preferences for how much they would like to visit the countryside. Irrespective of social group, about 50% of the population would like to visit the countryside more. This, of course, may be due to a lack of time or a lack of priority, rather than material deprivation, but the survey provides no information on causal factors. The table indicates, though, that lower social groups do not wish to go to the countryside noticeably any more than higher social groups do. In this sense, there would appear to be no greater degree of constraint from one social group to another in terms of people's wishes to visit the countryside.

Table 5.1 Social class and attitudes towards visiting the countryside

Attitude towards how much people visit the countryside	Social group[a]						
	A	B	C1	C2	D	E	Unemployed
Quite happy	48	47	42	46	40	42	36
Would like to go more	48	47	51	46	48	48	53
Would like to go less/ Don't know	4	6	7	8	12	10	11

[a] social classes are defined in Table 4.5.

Source: 1984 National Survey of Countryside Recreation, Countryside Commission (1985b).

The table does indicate that the proportion of people who would like to go to the countryside less, or who have no particular views on the matter declines, as social group declines.

5.4.3 Interest and social class

As well as people's aspirations for participation, there is evidence that an interest in countryside recreation might be less strong among lower occupational groups. Fitton (1978, 1979) finds an association between the image of the countryside as 'boring' and the semi- skilled and the unskilled worker. These occupational groups are also likely to be culturally less attuned to the idea of spending leisure time in the countryside. Evidence from the 1977 National Survey also indicates a stronger preference among lower social groups for urban leisure pursuits. This is shown in Table 5.2.

Some evidence also exists about different levels of interest among different social groups, for particular types of facility. In Margam Country Park in South Wales, for example, the social profile of visitors shifts to lower occupational groups when more 'performance' or 'show-man' activities are put on, and higher occupational groups are more evident when only passive or solitary activities are offered (Curry, 1985c). Perversely, perhaps, admission fees are higher for the former type of activity, indicating that it is not material constraints that reduce participation by lower social groups to the latter type of activity. It has also been noted by the park that the social structure of participation

Table 5.2 Preferences for urban recreation by occupational group in 1977

	Percentage agreeing that they 'preferred to spend their leisure time in the town rather than the country'
Employers and managers	10.0
Professionals	10.0
Intermediate non-manual	10.5
Junior non-manual	18.5
Self-employed non-professional	10.5
Foremen and supervisors	13.4
Skilled workers	21.1
Personal service workers	18.4
Semi-skilled workers	25.5
Unskilled workers	31.0

Source: Fitton (1978).

changes with weather conditions: lower social groups are proportionately more evident in warmer weather.

As has been noted in Chapter 2, Prince (1980) has also observed differing levels of interest across social groups in the use of countryside interpretation facilities. Even among those people participating in informal activity within the North York Moors National Park, it was the upper occupational groups that made the most significant use of interpretation facilities. It would seem to be a preference rather than as a result of constraints that other recreationists made less use of such facilities, since there was no material obstacle preventing their use.

Further information about the relative interest in countryside trip making comes from a comparative survey of 'culture' sites, including historic buildings, stately homes and craft workshops, 'nature' sites, including wildlife parks, safari parks and nature reserves, and 'white knuckle' sites, which are basically big thrill rides and theme parks such as at Blackpool Leisure Beach and Alton Towers (Applied Leisure Marketing, 1985). Table 5.3 indicates the relative incidence of visits to each of these types of site by social group.

The first point to note about this table, as with the social structure of participation at individual countryside recreation sites portrayed in Tables 4.7 and 4.8, is that there is again a consistent over-representation of visits to all sites by social groups A and B compared with their representation in the sample (the bottom line in the figure), roughly an

Table 5.3 Recreation participation and social class by recreation type

Recreation type	Numbers of visits	Social class[a]				
		AB	C1	C2	DE	Total
		Figures in percentages				
Any culture site	235	24	33	23	20	100
Any nature site	195	19	26	30	25	100
Any white knuckle site	99	14	24	29	27	100
Base number of visits to all sites	529					
Total of households in sample	**1540**	**11**	**25**	**31**	**33**	**100**

[a] social classes are defined in Table 4.5.

Source: Applied Leisure Marketing (1985).

equal representation in the middle social groups C1 and C2, and an under-representation in the lower social groups D and E.

But what is important is that the **relative** participation levels in the higher social groups A, B and C1 appears to decline as the recreation type becomes more intensive, moving from culture through nature and into white knuckle. The converse is the case for social groups C2, D and E: relative participation increases as the activity becomes more intensive.

Although these data are somewhat tentative, being based on site rather than household surveys, they do seem to confirm the Margam instance in a more generalized way, that interest in recreation tends to increase among lower social groups as the activity becomes more intensive. And in so doing, this interest would appear to owe increasingly less to the inherent attributes of the countryside for recreation purposes.

The most detailed study of the identification of the social needs for countryside recreation is to be found in Roberts (1979) who has undertaken an analysis of the social-class elements of the 1977 National Survey of Countryside Recreation (Countryside Commission, 1979c). In his conclusions he argues that need is a relative term, and questions whether countryside recreation is sufficient a deprivation to require a social policy at all. He also finds that, among semi-skilled and unskilled manual workers, exclusion from countryside recreation is the norm, but notes that they feel less deprived of countryside recreation than people in higher social groups. In other words their preference not to recreate in the countryside is a stronger determinant of non-participation than the constraints of access to the factors influencing demand. People who do not participate in countryside recreation, Roberts notes, have a much higher propensity not to participate in recreation of any sort.

5.4.4 Class and triggers to participation

Related to the differing preferences for countryside recreation by social group are variable preferences according to phases in the life-cycle. Both Sterelitz (1978) and Rapoport and Rapoport (1975) claim that people are much more likely to undertake countryside recreation within the 'establishment' phase of the family lifecycle. Within this phase, though, the upper occupational group propensity is still the strongest. Kelly (1978) notes that it is the middle-class image of parenthood and the corresponding sense of the need to educate children about the countryside that increases participation. Sterelitz (1978) maintains that this activity is also driven by a middle-class interest in complementing the school curriculum. In support of this notion, there is some evidence from the 1977 National Survey that lower-status occupational groups wish to spend less of their time in the family group. Fitton (1979) quotes a manual worker who considers that 'real' leisure time is spent away from the wife and family.

In terms of identifying preferences, too, Sterelitz (1978) notes that some social groupings have no interest in the countryside because of their cultural background. She cites older Afro-Caribbean immigrants who find the English countryside beyond their cultural horizons and who have a tradition of spending leisure time in social and family groupings. These attitudes are likely to be less entrenched, however, among subsequent generations who are exposed to the English school system.

5.4.5 The nature of preferences and constraints

From these characteristics, three principal aspects of the nature of preferences and constraints can be summarized. First, participation in countryside recreation becomes relatively more popular as social or occupational group increases. This pattern is common across most types of recreation. This bias towards higher social groups is less pronounced in certain group activities, often with a commercial flavour, for example, zoos and safari parks (Countryside Commission, 1985b). In one or two of these instances there may even be a bias towards lower social groups. This characteristic of group activities may be related to the lower incidence of car ownership among lower social groups, but it is more likely simply to be triggered by preference.

Second, all social groups appear to suffer some deprivation as far as countryside recreation is concerned although this might be slightly higher among lower social groups. In this respect, it is possible that constraints on higher social groups may relate more to a lack of time and on lower social groups to a lack of material opportunities. Evidence of people's perceptions in this respect, from the 1977 National Survey of Countryside Recreation (Countryside Commission, 1979c), tends to support such a difference. This can be seen in Table 5.4.

Table 5.4 Perceived constraints on visiting the countryside

	Figures in %				
Occupational group	*Temporal*	*Material*			
	Not enough time	*Don't have a car*	*Can't afford to visit the country- side*	*Can't afford public transport*	*Other*
Employers/ managers	64	5	3	0	28
Professionals	73	4	5	0	18
Intermediate non-manual	56	6	6	1	31
Junior non-manual	48	16	4	2	30
Self-employed non- professional	66	2	0	0	32
Foremen and supervisors	50	9	7	2	32
Skilled workers	57	11	6	2	24
Personal service workers	39	29	4	2	26
Semi-skilled workers	45	18	7	3	27
Unskilled workers	37	16	10	1	36

Source: Fitton (1978).

Third, an interest in visiting the countryside tends to decline as social status declines. The exceptions to this pattern mirror those evident in patterns of participation: more commercial activities tend to be of greater interest to lower social groups. Many limitations in interest to an extent may be attributed to 'life-cycle' and cultural factors, which themselves are related to social class.

This evidence, of course, does not suggest that there is no interest in the countryside among certain social groups, nor that certain social groups do not find it hard, materially, to participate in countryside recreation. Indeed, from the evidence in Table 5.1, it may be that all groups face some material constraints in participation. What it does indicate, however, is that policy-makers simply cannot assume that all non-participation arises as a result of material deprivation (Hantias, 1984).

Simply put, if non-participation derives dominantly from factors of constraint, then a growth in recreation activity may be anticipated in line with general economic growth as constraining factors fall away. If non-participation derives from preference, however, changing the economic circumstances of individuals will not provide a spur to participation. Growth in recreation activity will occur in response to people's changing cultural perspectives, and this growth will be much slower. Indeed, as more material opportunities present themselves a range of different leisure opportunities is likely to become available and as a result, as has been suggested in Chapter 4, an interest in countryside recreation may actually decline. In this context, recreation policies targeted at specific social groups and policies based on philanthropic good intent may be less than successful. Three examples of such policies illustrate this.

5.5 SOCIAL POLICIES: RECREATION TRANSPORT

Both the 1977 and 1984 National Surveys of Countryside Recreation (Countryside Commission, 1979c, 1985b, 1989a) indicate the importance of the car in countryside recreation trip-making. Upwards of 70% of all trips were made by this means. For those who do not have immediate access to a car, a wide range of public policies has developed, with specific social goals. These came to prominence in the 1960s when public recreation transport policies were promulgated not just to stem the pervasive influence of the motor car in the countryside, but more specifically to counter the reducing access to rural areas as a result of rail closures (Rubenstein and Speakman, 1969).

Such policies centre on the development of public recreation transport schemes which not only provide an alternative means of transport, particularly for the disadvantaged, but ease traffic congestion, allow people access to the 'wider' countryside and save energy. In certain circumstances, they are also considered to help keep existing rural transport services alive in otherwise marginal situations.

Public recreation transport was thus promoted from the beginning of the 1970s, particularly by the Countryside Commission which set up a series of recreation transport experiments concerned particularly to get people from the larger cities into the open countryside. These types of initiative became adopted by many county and district councils in the structure and local plans of the later 1970s and they were given positive promotion by the Regional Councils for Sport and Recreation in their Regional Recreation Strategies into the early 1980s.

In fact, between 1976 and 1983 around half of the county councils in England and Wales directly supported or promoted recreational transport services. Around two-thirds of these were new, specifically recreation services, rather than enhancements to existing routes. Most of these services were designed, interestingly enough, to take people from urban areas to more distant places rather than the countryside around the towns. Over half of the authorities maintained that such services were predicated on the notion of social considerations (Groome and Tarrant, 1985). Despite this growth in such schemes, Elson (1977) has noted that rarely did the number of people arriving at recreation sites by public recreation transport exceed 4%.

Harrison (1991) has noted some successes in recreation transport experiments, particularly the Wayfairer project in the north-west of England, if they are accompanied by aggressive and targeted marketing. But once marketing was cut back on the Wayfairer project, the use of the schemes declined considerably. It was also difficult to tell, in relation to this project, how many users were doing so solely for recreation purposes. The experimental nature of the project has made it impossible to tell whether it has caused any more permanent structural changes in participation patterns.

More generally, however, in an analysis of a large number of recreation transport schemes to the mid-1980s, Groome and Tarrant (1985) found that there was a principle preoccupation in designing them with where people might like to go, rather than whether they wanted to go in the first place. As a result of this lack of attention to preference, the failure of many recreation services was not unusual. Around a sixth of all those started between 1978 and 1983 had been abandoned. All of the schemes required subsidies (as might be expected for social policies) and around a half of them failed to do as well as the operators themselves had expected, sometimes carrying very few passengers at all.

It was significant, though, that those schemes which were 'added on' to existing rural transport services that served local people or existing tourist areas did better than those set up specifically for recreation purposes. Significant, too, was the invariable absence of marketing studies before the schemes were started. From other evidence in Gloucestershire, a free bus service from one of the poorer parts of a town to the local country park was withdrawn through lack of support after three Sundays in operation (Blunden and Curry, 1988).

Worse, in terms of the fulfilment of social objectives, Groome and Tarrant (1985) found that in individual studies of transport schemes, the social profile of the dominant users reflected that of recreation participants as a whole. The more affluent used the schemes proportionately more than the less affluent and in such cases these policies could actually be considered to be socially regressive.

In the 1990s, the lack of success of recreation transport policies for social purposes has led to a reassessment of their function. They are still promoted by the Countryside Commission (1992a) but their purpose is now unambiguously one of resolving traffic management problems in areas of greatest pressure, rather than for any notion of social benefit. But even in this respect, Groome (1991) has noted opposition to such schemes where they have been used as an integral part of traffic management measures to stem the volume of recreational traffic. In 1990 the Lake District National Park Committee proposed the introduction of public recreation transport in tandem with the restriction of traffic to Borrowdale during peak periods. Local opposition centred on the fear of a reduction in the number of visitors and a consequent loss of income. In addition, the local parish council was convinced that there was no serious traffic problem in Borrowdale, and that the scheme would threaten the existing public bus service.

5.6 SOCIAL POLICIES: THE LOCATION OF FACILITIES AND THE ATTRACTIONS THAT THEY OFFER

The principle thrust of prioritizing the location of countryside recreation close to urban centres came from the House of Lords Select Committee (1973). Dower (1978, p. 16) quotes the report in this respect:

> Where there is a high urban population, the policy should be no longer to divert their recreation towards the deeper countryside, but to provide day-visit facilities close to towns. . . . Many people are not necessarily looking for a truly 'natural' countryside, but something more closely akin to a town park in the countryside.

By the mid-1970s, under the influence of the Regional Councils for Sport and Recreation, the Countryside Commission (1977) in its general guidance on the allocation of grant-aid for recreation purposes, had begun to give priority in the allocation of grants to recreation projects in Green Belts and other areas of the urban fringe. Such policy priorities are sustained into the 1980s and 1990s by Planning Policy Guidance Note (PPG) 2 on green belts (Department of the Environment, 1988b) and by PPG 17 on sport and recreation (Department of the Environment, 1991a).

This policy impetus has been for the explicit social motive of allowing the car-less, and therefore the less well off, increased recreation opportunities. But evidence on the social structure of participation at individual sites, contained in Tables 4.7 and 4.8, indicates that there is in general no significant difference in the social structure of participation at individual sites, irrespective of location.

In some instances (Tourism and Recreation Research Unit, 1980) one or two parks close enough to urban centres to be within walking distance have shown a significant use by local populations, but Harrison's (1991) study of recreation sites in the South London green belt, was able to conclude (p. 115):

> Neither the assumed accessibility of recreation sites in the urban fringe to those people who are dependent on public transport, nor their accessibility to inner-city residents, was substantiated by the study.

This may well be because, as Duffield (1982) notes, people have relatively fixed perceptual maximum and minimum distances that they are prepared to travel for recreation purposes, associated with different modes of transport. Within these limits, the location of individual sites is relatively unimportant. For the majority of recreationists, who travel by car (73% according to the 1977 National Survey of Countryside Recreation (Countryside Commission, 1979c)), nearly 50% of them travel over 20 miles (return journey) and in some cases up to 150 miles. Surveys by Applied Leisure Marketing (1985) have indicated that the distance people travel increases the more intensive or commercial the destination.

Given the number of sites available to most people within these distance ranges, the location of any one of them is probably an insignificant trigger to participation. And even for the car-less, the provision of public-recreation transport has been less than successful, as discussed above.

A further influence on the locational determinants of recreation participation has been shown to be petrol prices. But here again, the location of individual sites does not appear to be particularly important. Rises in the real cost of petrol prices have been shown to reduce the total number of recreation trips, rather than make them shorter in distance (Shucksmith, 1979b).

Thus locational preferences, as part of social policy for countryside recreation, appear to have little impact when observed participation is considered. Indeed, such policies were abandoned by the Countryside Commission for Scotland (1974) in the mid-1970s. As Roberts (1979) has argued, urban fringe locations for recreation are probably less important to poorer sections of society than urban recreation resources themselves.

The Countryside Commission (1987b) has responded to this notion by recognizing that the enjoyment **of** the countryside doesn't necessarily require enjoyment **in** the countryside. In this respect developing urban farms, urban 'countryside' interpretation centres and so on may well assist in bringing enjoyment of the countryside to the town.

In truth, the promulgation of policies for locational preference for countryside recreation facilities close to urban centres might have more to do with the 'control' philosophy in land-use planning, outlined previously, that seeks to limit recreation activities to Green Belts and the urban fringe as a means of protecting the wider countryside from incursion. As has been noted in Chapter 2, such locational preferences also serve to justify the implementation of green belt policies and provide a let-out for many urban areas not achieving open-space standards.

In contrast to locational policies for social purposes, there is little public policy concerning the **content** of sites, in terms of their particular attractions, save for the general desirability of conservation and interpretation provision. In has already been noted in Chapter 2 that these may be of limited value in terms of consumer preferences anyway. Yet if social policies were to be developed, and it is argued in the final chapter that this is inadvisable, it is in the content of sites that the social structure of participation appears to be most sensitive. It has been noted in Chapter 4, for example, that lower social groups exhibit a preference for villages, pubs and pick your own, whereas 'solitude' activities are much more the interest of the middle and upper classes.

To the extent that non-participation in countryside recreation arises as a result of preference, then providing attractions at sites that people want or prefer is more likely to trigger participation, even among lower social groups, than any policies concerned with location. The Margam Country Park case cited above clearly indicated greater participation among lower social groups when summer fairs were provided, compared to when only a sculpture park was on offer.

5.7 SOCIAL POLICIES: THE 'FREE ACCESS' CRITERION

The 1968 Countryside Act and Countryside Commission (1974a) policy guidelines for recreation facilities stipulate that fees should not be charged for access to publicly owned facilities. There is a clear social purpose behind this, since the principle of free access is based on the egalitarian notion of not debarring any potential participants on grounds of cost.

Economists would also argue that free access can be legitimated for countryside recreation since it is one of those goods that exhibit a degree of 'market failure' and as a result would be underprovided if provision was left entirely to the private sector. This arises because the recreation market is considered to have sufficient 'externalities' (important aspects of provision, such as psychological benefits and the inability physically to exclude people from many recreation resources) that they cannot be fully internalized into the market and therefore fully paid for. Given these shortcomings, recreation should be publicly provided, and, in many instances, free.

But information about the observed structure of participation presented in Chapter 4, indicates that in fact recreation provision does actually cater dominantly for a market demand rather than a social need. Such provision is therefore not obviously operating in a situation of market failure and therefore the free-access criterion would seem inappropriate. Worse, if the egalitarian principle is used to justify the free-access criterion, the observed structure of participation, which indicates that those who benefit from countryside recreation most are the already privileged and active, would suggest that the free-access criterion is again, in fact, socially regressive.

In addition, when the factors that are considered to trigger participation as a whole are taken into account, income, occupation, leisure time, car ownership and so on, it could be that people are not even particularly sensitive to whether they pay to enter a recreation site or have free access. This is given credibility by a study of pricing at National Trust properties (Bovaird, Tricker and Stoakes, 1984) where the demand for visits to a large number of properties was seen to be price inelastic. In other words, participants were not particularly sensitive, in terms of their level of participation, to changes in admission prices.

Even when individual site studies are considered, where 'price' is found to be a significant determinant in triggering participation, this is invariably a surrogate measure – the cost of getting to the site – rather than any actual admission charge. From the case of Margam Country Park, again, it could even be that positive admission charges might actually encourage lower social groups to participate in countryside recreation, as long as they are paying for what they want to come and see, and therefore might form a more legitimate part of social policy.

As well as the 'free-access' notion of policy being inappropriate, then, it may be to a large extent also unimportant as far as the recreationist is concerned. It also appears inconsistent to prohibit local authorities from charging for entry to their sites when other public-sector recreation sites, such as Department of the Environment Ancient Monuments, have always commanded an entry fee. Indeed, there are a number of positive advantages in charging at public recreation sites that are considered in Chapter 9.

5.8 THE LIMITATIONS OF SOCIAL POLICIES FOR COUNTRYSIDE RECREATION

It has been argued in this chapter, that social policies have been promulgated in the past by both government agencies and local authorities, but most recreation policies as a whole have, in fact, ended up catering for market demands rather than social needs. This has been exacerbated by the control aspects of recreation policies, but has also, significantly, been influenced by the relationship between people's preferences and constraints for countryside recreation and access.

Undoubtedly, although some non-participation is frustrated by lack of opportunity, the fact that there is a limit to people's interest in and preferences for the countryside as a leisure destination has led to severe shortcomings in the success of social policies for rural leisure when they have been introduced, supporting proposition 3 of this book (p. xi). This has led Roberts (1979, p. 64) to sound a note of caution as to their validity in general:

> channelling more resources into countryside facilities will be less likely to tap latent working-class demand than to benefit the already privileged and active.

The principal limitation of such social policies lies, of course, in using policy instruments that are concerned almost exclusively to adjust the supply of recreation, as a means of attempting to manipulate demand and need factors. The inherent limitations of this kind of approach are considered more fully in the final chapter of this book. It is the nature and potential of these supply-based policies, in relation to land-use planning, that form the focus of interest in the following two chapters.

6

Government advice for rural leisure land-use planning

6.1 THE JURISDICTION OF LAND-USE PLANNING FOR RURAL LEISURE

Land-use planning for rural leisure has a large number of elements. At its core is the local-authority sector which has a statutory responsibility for the strategic planning of recreation through structure plans (by county councils and in two instances national park authorities). This sector is also responsible for the implementation of recreation policies through local plans (produced by county councils and all national parks, but principally district councils) and additionally in national parks, the implementation of policies and the management of recreation and access through national park plans.

As an extension to this statutory basis, a range of informal strategic plans has also been introduced from the late 1980s onwards, principally through county councils, which take the form either of recreation strategies, countryside recreation strategies or of more general countryside strategies that have recreation and access components. Added to this are a large number of non-statutory management plans formulated chiefly by county council planning, highways or leisure departments and by national park authorities, but also by voluntary organizations such as the National Trust and the county wildlife trusts. These are usually concerned to steer change at individual recreation sites, rather than develop strategic policy for rural leisure.

The 1968 Countryside Act also makes provision for the establishment of Joint Advisory Committees for recreation purposes in recognition of the fact that recreation, as a migratory activity, can often be planned more coherently beyond individual local authority boundaries. Although not widespread, these committees also produce planning documents (for example, Cotswold Water Park Joint Advisory Committee, 1983), but they have the greatest force where committees are given delegated powers and a degree of autonomy to implement proposals, as in the Lea Valley Regional Park.

Strategic land-use planning for recreation and access also takes place in the resource sectors. The Forestry Commission, particularly since the White Paper 'Forest Policy' (HMSO, 1972), has been charged with the production of conservancy recreation plans and in the water sector too, strategic planning documents have been produced from time to time on an *ad hoc* basis. Since the privatization of the water sector, however, land-use planning appears to be restricted to one or two broad statements of intent in the rolling corporate plan of the National Rivers Authority (1991). Here, the principal emphasis lies in working in collaboration with other organizations, particularly local authorities, in the development of land-use policies. This is often done through the process of consultation on draft structure and local plans. Individually, the new water companies appear currently to be focusing more on a review of recreation activities (Welsh Water, 1991) rather than any coherent forward planning.

The jurisdiction of land-use planning for rural leisure, like the organizational structure of agencies with a general responsibility for recreation and access considered in Chapter 2, is thus diffuse. This immediately poses problems for the coherence of land-use planning and the development and implementation of comprehensive and holistic policies and plans, as proposition 1 of this book suggests. But not only are those agencies that are responsible for the formulation of land-use plans many and varied. Advice in their formulation also comes from a number of different governmental sources. The extent to which the disparate nature of this advice inhibits plan formulation provides the principal focus of this chapter.

6.2 THE NATURE OF GOVERNMENT ADVICE

Government advice on the production of land-use plans for rural leisure comes from a number of sources and in a variety of forms. It is targeted principally at the local-authority sector, since little published advice is available relating to the development of recreation plans by the resource sectors. The principal advisory documents are summarized in Table 6.1 and their rural leisure components are fully evaluated elsewhere (Curry and Pack, 1992).

Guidance on the production of statutory plans originated in the Development Plans Manual (Ministry of Housing and Local Government, 1970a) and was modified up to 1988 through a series of government Circulars. Specifically for rural leisure, Circular 47/76 (Department of the Environment, 1976b) established Regional Councils for Sport and

Recreation, and Circular 73/77 (Department of the Environment, 1977) empowered these councils to produce regional recreation strategies. Other salient leisure Circulars have included 4/76 (Department of the Environment, 1976a) which considered a number of issues relating to recreation and access in national parks, including the policy that conservation should take precedence over recreation where the two are seen to be in unavoidable conflict.

Circular 13/79 (Department of the Environment, 1979) considered the role that local authorities should play in tourism. Circular 1/83 (Department of the Environment, 1983a) contained provision in relation to public rights of way and the completion of the definitive map. Circular 23/83 (Department of the Environment, 1983b) outlined regulations relating to the control of caravans and caravan sites, and Circular 14/84 (Department of the Environment, 1984) on green belts, contained guidance on the sensitive development of recreation in these areas.

From 1988, the Department of the Environment introduced a series of Planning Policy Guidance Notes (PPGs) for statutory planning, designed to 'provide clearer, more accessible and more systematic policy guidance' (Department of the Environment, 1992a). Different PPGs now provide guidance on different topics of relevance to development plans, representing a move away from the comprehensive approach of the Development Plans Manual. PPGs are supplemented by Regional Planning Guidance Notes (RPGs) for different parts of the country.

Planning Policy Guidance Note 12 (Department of the Environment, 1992a) identifies rural leisure as a concern for structure plans and indicates in broad terms those geographical areas in which facilities for recreation, tourism and leisure will be provided. PPG 7 *The Countryside and the Rural Economy* (Department of the Environment, 1992b) identifies leisure as a prime means of rural diversification and PPG 2, *Green Belts* (Department of the Environment, 1988b) requires that green belts have a positive role in providing access to the countryside for the urban population.

The principal PPGs that provide advice for rural leisure in the development plan process, however, are PPG 17 *Sport and Recreation* (Department of the Environment, 1991a) and PPG 21 on *Tourism* (Department of the Environment, 1992f). PPG 17 bases its policies on a presumption of continuing recreation growth which, as has been noted in Chapter 4, is questionable, and contains policies for the urban fringe, the wider countryside and individual activities. The PPG 21 on tourism encourages the growth of tourism in response to market demands, subject to environmental considerations.

In general, the land-use planning policy guidance for rural leisure contained in these PPGs has four main strands. First, policies should be restricted to land-use considerations. Recreation should be for everyone and specific social groups should not be targeted within a land-use planning framework. Second, recreation and sport should be contained in areas of low quality environment and where developments do take place, they should be in tandem with farm diversification. This inevitably makes the urban fringe a developmental priority area. Third, all rural leisure objectives should be subservient to environmental conservation goals. Finally, the public rights of way network should be maintained and enhanced wherever possible.

A number of regional planning guidance notes also contain policies for rural leisure, for example, for East Anglia (Department of the Environment, 1991b), Merseyside (Department of the Environment, 1988d) and the West Midlands (Department of the Environment, 1988c) and in general terms these are noticeably more positive than PPGs. In contrast to PPGs they see the principal potentials for recreation as both stimulating public enjoyment and assisting the rural economy.

A growth of interest in rural tourism, particularly in the context of agricultural diversification, has spawned further policy statements from governmental organizations. This advice has come from the Department of Employment (1991) and its agencies. The English Tourist Board's (1988) national policy statement on visitors to the countryside embraces policies for both day-visitors and tourists and has been extended into a series of environmentally sensitive principles for rural tourism agreed jointly with the Countryside Commission (English Tourist Board/ Countryside Commission, 1989).

These principles have been widely adopted in the tourism strategies of regional tourist boards (for example, the Heart of England Tourist Board, 1989) which themselves are cited in a number of structure plans. These are supplemented by rural tourism advice from the Ministry of Agriculture, Fisheries and Food and the Rural Development Commission (1991a), sponsored by the Department of the Environment, all of which are cited in development plans.

For countryside recreation, access and sport, the Countryside Commission (for example, 1987a, 1992a), the Countryside Policy Review Panel (Countryside Commission, 1987a) and the Sports Council (1988, 1992) all have provided advisory documents which have a direct bearing on both statutory and non-statutory local authority rural leisure land-use planning. The Regional Councils for Sport and Recreation too, produce regional sport and recreation strategies designed specifically to co-ordinate the statutory and non-statutory planning functions, at a regional level, of the various agencies concerned with sport and recreation. They are therefore intended as a regional 'benchmark' for local authority land-use planning. Voluntary organizations too, produce policy statements designed to inform, among others, the local authority

Table 6.1 Advisory policies for rural leisure land-use planning

Principal government advice containing elements relating to the preparation of countryside recreation, access, sport and tourism components of: structure plans (SP); local plans (LP); unitary development plans (UDP); national park plans (NP); countryside, countryside recreation or recreation strategies (CS)

Date	Ministerial	Government agency
1970	Ministry of Housing and Local Government, 'Development Plans, a Manual of Form and Content' (SP, LP)	
1974	Department of the Environment, 'Structure Plans', Circular 98/74 (SP)	Countryside Commission, 'Advisory Notes on National Park Plans' (NP)
1976	Department of the Environment 'Regional Councils for Sport and Recreation', Circular 47/76 (SP, LP)	English Tourist Board and the Trades Union Congress, 'Holidays: the Social Need' (SP, LP, NP).
	Department of the Environment, 'Report – National Parks Review Committee', Circular 4/76 (NP)	
1977	Department of the Environment, 'Regional Recreation Strategies', Circular 73/77 (SP, LP)	
1979	Department of the Environment, 'Local Government and Tourism', Circular 13/79 (SP)	
1980	Department of the Environment, 'Development Control – Policy and Practice', Circular 22/80	
1981	Department of the Environment, 'Local Government Planning and Land Act, 1980: Town and Country Planning: Development Plans', Circular 23/81 (SP, LP)	

Table 6.1 *continued*

Date	Ministerial	Government agency
1982		Sports Council, 'Sport in the Community: the Next 10 years', (SP, LP, NP)
1983	Department of the Environment, 'Public Rights of Way', Circular 1/83 (SP, LP)	
	Department of the Environment, 'Caravan Sites and Control of Development Act 1960', Circular 23/83, (LP)	
1984	Department of the Environment, 'Green Belts', Circular 14/84, (SP, LP)	
1985	Cabinet Office 'Pleasure, Leisure and Jobs: the Business of Tourism' (SP)	
1987		Countryside Commission, 'Policies for Enjoying the Countryside' (SP, CS)
		Countryside Commission, 'Enjoying the Countryside: Priorities for Action' (SP, CS)
		Countryside Policy Review Panel, 'New Opportunities for the Countryside' (SP, LP, LS)
		Sports Council, 'Which Way Forward?', (SP, LP, NP, UDP)

Table 6.1 *continued*

Date	Ministerial	Government agency
1988	Department of the Environment, 'Unitary Development Plans and the Town and Country Planning (Unitary Development Plans) Regulations' Circular 3/88 (UDP)	English Tourist Board, 'Visitors to the Countryside', (SP, LP, NP)
	Department of the Environment, 'Green Belts', Planning Policy Guidance Note PPG 2, (SP, LP)	Sports Council, 'Sport in the Community: into the 1990s', (SP, LP, UDP, NP)
	Department of the Environment, 'Strategic Planning for the West Midlands', Planning Policy Guidance Note PPG 10, (UDP)	
	Department of the Environment, 'Strategic Guidance for Merseyside', Planning Policy Guidance Note PPG 11, (UDP)	
1989	Department of the Environment, 'The Future of Development Plans', White Paper, (SP, LP, NP, UDP)	English Tourist Board and the Countryside Commission, 'Principles for Tourism in the Countryside', (SP, LP, NP)
1990	Department of the Environment, 'This Common Inheritance', White Paper, (SP, LP, NP, UDP, CS)	
	Department of the Environment, 'Regional Policy Guidance, Structure Plans, and the Content of Development Plans', Planning Policy Guidance Note PPG 15, (SP, LP, UDP)	
1991	Department of Employment, 'Tourism and the Environment: Maintaining the Balance' (SP, UDP)	English Nature, 'Rural Strategies', internal memorandum, (CS)
	Department of the Environment, 'Regional Guidance for East Anglia', Regional Planning Guidance Note RPG 6, (SP, LP)	Sports Council, 'Sport and Recreation Content of Unitary Development Plans (U.D.P.s) in London', (UDP)
	Department of the Environment, 'Sport and Recreation', Planning Policy Guidance Note PPG 17, (SP, LP, UDP)	

Table 6.1 *continued*

Date	Ministerial	Government agency
1991		Sports Council, 'District Sport and Recreation Strategies: A Guide', (LP)
		National Rivers Authority, 'Corporate Plan 1991/1992', (SP, LP, UDP, NP)
		Rural Development Commission, 'Tourism in the Countryside: A Strategy for Rural England', (SP, NP)
		Rural Development Commission, 'Meeting the Challenge of Agricultural Adjustment, A New Rural Development Commission Initiative', (SP, NP, CS)
		Rural Development Commission, 'Rural Development Strategies', internal memorandum, (CS)
		Countryside Commission, 'Enjoying the Countryside: Policies for People' (CS)
		Sports Council, 'A Countryside for Sport: A Policy for Sport and Recreation', (SP, LP, UDP)
1992	Department of the Environment, 'Development Plans and Regional Guidance', Planning Policy Guidance Note PPG 12, (SP, LP, UDP)	
	Department of the Environment, 'General Policy and Principles', Planning Policy Guidance Note PPG1, (SP, LP, UDP, NP)	
	Department of the Environment, 'The Countryside and the Rural Economy', Planning Policy Guidance Note PPG 7, (SP, LP, NP)	
	Department of the Environment, 'Tourism', Planning Policy Guidance Note PPG 21 (SP, LP, UDP, NP)	
	Department of the Environment, 'Nature Conservation', draft PPG, (SP, LP, UDP, NP)	

sector, an example of which is *Sport and Recreation in the Countryside* (Central Council for Physical Recreation, 1991).

The complex nature of this guidance documentation has been articulated in response to the Sports Council's (1987) consultation paper, *Which Way Forward?* A significant number of people responding to this paper felt that the whole land-use planning framework for countryside recreation and sport needed to be rationalized. There was felt to be a need for a clearer hierarchy of planning functions from national and regional guidance, through structure plans to local plans, and the relationships between these plans and the agencies responsible for their formulation needed to be formalized. In the light of this concern about the fragmentary nature of government advice for rural leisure land-use planning, the remainder of this chapter evaluates some of the principal limitations in its adoption in plan formulation in practice.

6.3 LIMITATIONS IN REGIONAL SPORT AND RECREATION STRATEGIES

One of the principal sets of advisory documents designed to assist the local-authority sector and others in the formulation of plans for countryside recreation, and one which the Sports Council (1992) sees as being increasingly important in informing the land-use planning process, has been the regional sport and recreation strategies produced by the Regional Councils for Sport and Recreation. The first round of these strategies was characterized by a considerable variation in the time taken to produce them, with the first being produced in 1977 (West Midlands, South West) and the last in 1982 (North, South East and Greater London).

These strategies were also produced with a great diversity of planning methods, subject coverage and presentational styles, with many topic papers appearing at different times to the strategies themselves. This early diversity has been attributed to the absence (apart from Circular 73/77 (Department of the Environment, 1977) which introduced them) of any nationally agreed policy framework for their production. By 1988 the Sports Council (1988) had recognized that in no sense did they add up to a coherent and consistent national picture. Responses to the Sports Council's (1987) consultation document also provided a common view that the strategies left much to be desired and needed to be considerably improved.

In response, the Sports Council (1988) undertook to pay particular attention to regional strategies to ensure that they became better co-ordinated, particularly in respect of their approach and their timescales. A similar format for each strategy was to be adopted, since strategy compatibility would provide leverage for central government funds for the Regional Councils for Sport and Recreation, and would allow the development of a clearer national planning framework.

Strategies in the main have therefore been reviewed since 1988, with those for four of the regions being produced as second-round strategies in 1989 and a further one in 1990. This review has been justified on the basis of the time that has elapsed since the production of the first-round strategies, changes in participation trends and local demographic factors, and changing criteria for Sports Council grant aid to the Regional Councils. In addition, there have been changes in the structure of Regional Councils in the south-east since the abolition of the Greater London Council. A number of Regional Councils felt that the format of strategies might change again with the mooted reorganization of the Sports Council at the national level in 1993.

Despite the realignment of strategies in 1988, they still have significant limitations in informing rural land-use planning for sport and recreation. The format of strategies still varies greatly: some have substantial background information in supporting documents, some rely on surveys conducted as part of the previous round of strategy production, but others focus almost entirely prospectively on policies. The coverage of countryside issues is also very variable, from over half the document (Yorkshire and Humberside Regional Council for Sport and Recreation, 1989) to a very marginal presence (North West Regional Council for Sport and Recreation, 1989, Southern Regional Council for Sport and Recreation, 1990).

Further, the overall aims of strategies generally are not explicitly stated, except in the Yorkshire and Humberside (1989) strategy. A number of them, too, recognize that it is not feasible to implement all of the policies that they have put forward within the time period of the strategy. In these cases, they have been prioritized. As advisory documents for land-use planning, their function is not always totally clear. Strategies are seen as a 'basic reference point' (North West, 1989) during the preparation of structure and local plans, but many Regional Councils see their role as consultees when these plans have reached their first draft stage. The Southern (1990) strategy, for example, seeks:

> to encourage all local planning authorities to consult the Southern Council for Sport and Recreation on matters relating to sport and recreation. (p. 14).

Overall, the strategies contain few explicit recommendations relating to land uses. Those that do refer principally to the desirability of increasing recreation opportunities over water areas, lowland forests, green belts and the urban fringe. Some general encouragement is also given to improving the public rights of way network.

A review of all structure plans, recreation strategies and countryside strategies up to 1992, considered fully in Chapter 7, together with telephone interviews with officers of the regional councils for sport and recreation, suggests that the influence of regional recreation strategies on land-use planning has been slight. Some officers feel that topic reports have had more impact than the strategies themselves, despite PPG 17 (Department of the Environment, 1991a), which now requires regional strategies to be given particular attention in the production of development plans. The renewed emphasis to be given to them by the Sports Council (1992) might prove, perhaps, a little optimistic.

The South East Regional Council has conducted an informal analysis of the uptake of regional recreation strategy policies in structure plans and has found their use to be limited. Principal reasons for this lack of success of these advisory documents are seen to be their variability in both form and content, their lack of consistency with Sports Council national policy and their lack of achievable measurable targets, being restricted in most cases to less specific general exhortation.

Overall, these strategies are limited by having no direct powers and are therefore dependent upon the good offices of the constituent Regional Council members. Most policies in them are recommended for bodies other than the Regional Councils to implement, but the Councils have no sanctions over constituent members' actions. Further, the Councils have no resource base with which to implement strategies, nor any direct ownership of, or control over, recreation resources. In the last resort, they are able actually to do very little.

The Centre for Leisure Research (1986) has added to these limitations. It suggests that the Regional Councils are neither directly elected nor politically accountable, and because they are consensus bodies of a number of organizations, they tend to be restricted to the consideration of consensus or establishment issues and skirt more radical ones such as the promotion of *de jure* access rights. Because they are representative of recreation organizations, too, they often do not reflect the interest of the casual non-affiliated recreationist very well.

6.4 VARIABILITY IN DEVELOPMENT PLANS

A second limitation in the adoption of advice for rural leisure planning from government agencies, specifically within development plans, is that these plans themselves have faced a number of changes and uncertainties during the 1980s and early 1990s.

Development plans have three components: structure plans, local plans and unitary development plans which perform the functions of both structure and local plans in metropolitan areas. Policy guidance on their formulation in respect of recreation policies has been distinct. The first two were introduced in the Town and Country Planning Acts of

1968 and 1971 and their functions have been modified by Circulars and statutes since that time. Unitary development plans were introduced after the abolition of the metropolitan counties in 1986.

The detailed process and objectives of structure plan formulation generally are considered in a number of documents (Cross and Bristow, 1983; Curry and Comley, 1985), but their purpose has been to provide both an interpretation of national and regional policies in terms of physical and environmental planning for their area and the framework in which the more detailed proposals of local plans are developed (Department of the Environment, 1984). They are normally to be reviewed at least every five years and are to work to a 15-year time horizon from the base date of the plan.

For local plans, a critical evaluation of their functions, objectives and performance generally, may be found in, for example, Healey (1983) and Bruton and Nicholson (1987). Their original functions were to apply structure plan strategies, provide a detailed basis for development control, provide a basis for co-ordinating development and bring local and detailed issues before the public. They were also to be reviewed every five years (Ministry of Housing and Local Government, 1970a). They could relate to whole districts (district plans), areas requiring particular attention (action area plans), or subjects requiring particular attention (subject plans).

Guidance on the production of local plans again originally came from the Development Plans Manual. This allowed district, action area and subject plans to be produced for the countryside but the clear priority for all of these was to secure conservation objectives for both the built and natural environment. As with structure plans, guidance on the recreation content of local plans is now contained in planning policy guidance notes.

The disbanding of metropolitan county authorities in the mid-1980s has led to a single-tier planning system in metropolitan areas. Some of the county functions for the countryside have been sustained by 'independent' units (such as the Greater Manchester Countryside Unit) which have had an advisory input into unitary development plans. General guidance in the preparation of these plans was contained in Circular 3/88 (Department of the Environment, 1988a). Specifically for recreation and access policies in these plans, guidance has been somewhat *ad hoc*.

In London, for example, guidance has been produced by the London Council for Sport and Recreation (Sports Council, 1991a). This stresses the importance of strategic links to green space, such as the Colne Valley and the Lea Valley, the maintenance and enhancement of public rights of way and the sensitive use of the green belt for countryside recreation and sport. Exploiting the potential of London's water areas is also given specific attention. Other guidance is offered in London by the London Planning Advisory Committee, although for recreation their guidance is based on the Regional Council's recreation strategy.

A significant limitation in the adoption of government advisory policies for rural leisure land-use planning during the 1980s in all of these statutory plans has been the erosion of the importance of the development planning process itself. Circular 22/80 (Department of the Environment, 1980) moved the whole of the planning system away from plan-led decision-making towards one of negotiation between planner and developer with a general presumption in favour of development unless there were clear reasons for refusal. This declining importance of structure, local and more latterly unitary development plans has generally curbed the energies and resources disposed towards plan formulation as a whole.

In this context, structure plans have been exceptionally vulnerable, with proposals for their abolition in a 1989 White Paper (Department of the Environment, 1989), a reaffirmation of their existence in the 1990 Town and Country Planning Act and Planning Policy Guidance Note (PPG) 15 (Department of the Environment, 1990a) and a strengthening of their powers in the 1991 Planning and Compensation Act. Under this Act, planning decisions must accord with structure plans unless material considerations dictate otherwise. One of the general purposes of the 1991 Act has been to rekindle a plan-led planning system.

Clearly, the vulnerability of this principal statutory plank of strategic planning has created significant uncertainties for plan formulation. Even within this context, to 1985 at least (Curry and Comley, 1985), countryside recreation has been considered an issue of 'second order' importance in all structure plans except that of South West Hampshire, which covers the New Forest. The results of strategic countryside recreation planning in structure plans under these uncertainties is reviewed fully in Chapter 7.

Variability in local plan formulation relates more to geographical coverage. Guidance on where local plans needed to be produced, provided in Circular 23/81 (Department of the Environment, 1981) has ensured that the vast majority of them have been urban. Indeed, McNab (1985) has suggested that the continuum from urban to rural has almost defined local plan preparation priorities. Local plans concerned with rural leisure have therefore been geographically patchy and those with a significant rural leisure component have often been produced by county councils (Cornwall County Council, 1983) rather than, as is more usual, district authorities.

Again, significant changes in the role of local plans came in the 1990 Town and Country Planning Act. They are now to be singular district-wide local plans, which means that many parts of the countryside are to receive local plan coverage for the first time presenting new challenges to the formulation of countryside recreation policies by district authorities. This new role also brings into question the relationship between structure plans and local plans where some districts, such as the Cotswolds, are producing local plans covering a larger geographical area than many county structure plans. In this context, local plans are likely to contain significant strategic elements for issues such as countryside recreation as well as policies for implementation. These local plans have enhanced powers under the 1991 Act, commensurate with structure plans. The adoption of government advice for rural leisure in local plans, then, has been inhibited historically by the geographical extent of such plans and more recently has been made uncertain by their changing geographical jurisdiction, to cover the whole of each district for the first time.

These limitations are compounded by the fact that government advice in the preparation of rural leisure policies in structure and local plans is itself somewhat contradictory. The Development Plans Manual (Ministry of Housing and Local Government, 1970a), which remained the principal guidance for the preparation of development plans up to 1988, allowed structure plans to be both positive and comprehensive (Curry and Comley, 1985). For local plans, however, recreation policies were to be more restrictive since they were 'to reconcile recreation pressures where there is a need to channel and control the demands of nearby towns' (p. 50). Because local plans are to apply structure plan strategies to provide a basis for development control, there has always been a tension in this advice, where structure plans have been anything other than restrictive.

The variability in plan formulation in metropolitan areas has come from a complete change to the development plan system. This is significant in that before their abolition, metropolitan structure plans had distinctively more positive, promotional and socially orientated countryside recreation policies than all of the shire counties (Curry and Comley, 1985) and although unitary development plans do embrace strategic issues, the change in planning style has rendered the force of countryside recreation policies less clear cut (Curry and Pack, 1992). The perceived success of unitary planning in these areas, together with the introduction of district-wide local plans of complete geographical coverage that may well increasingly contain strategic policies, also has implications for the importance of non-metropolitan structure plans into the future. The prospect of single-tier local authorities may elevate the importance of local plans to one of mimicking unitary development plans, again bringing into question the need for county-led structure plans at all. This is likely to create further uncertainties for the role of government advice in development plans, for rural leisure planning in the future.

6.5 THE ENFORCEABILITY OF ADVISORY STATEMENTS

The enforceability of advisory statements provides a further problem in the adoption of advice from government agencies in rural leisure land-use planning. Guidance from PPGs and RPGs has a certain degree of compulsion since the Secretary of State may intervene in the formulation of structure plans and must approve district-wide local plans under the 1991 Planning and Compensation Act. Through this mechanism, conformity to PPGs and regional planning guidance can be (though is often not) ensured.

For other forms of advice, however, there is no mechanism to ensure that it is heeded. In interviews with Regional Council for Sport and Recreation officers, one of the principal tasks was seen as being to 'market' regional strategies to local authorities to 'try and promote them, and get them to adhere to policies therein'. Clearly, there may be little incentive on the part of local authorities to adopt such advice, beyond conscience and goodwill.

At the national level, too, there is little to persuade local authorities to adopt Sports Council and Countryside Commission advice, beyond possible enhanced chances of grant-aid provision, a point considered more fully in relation to countryside recreation strategies in Chapter 7. Its adoption is made particularly difficult where advice, especially between these two agencies, is contradictory and where it relates to issues that are, strictly, not land-use planning matters. PPG 12 (Department of the Environment, 1992c) places renewed stress on the jurisdiction of development plans being land-use plans only.

6.6 A CHANGING POLICY EMPHASIS OVER TIME

A further limitation in the adoption of government advice for rural leisure land-use planning, common to many other components of development and informal plans, relates to the time lag between the issue of guidance and plan production. When development plans historically have taken a considerable time to produce and review they can often be out of date relative to contemporary guidance, as soon as they are approved. In the formulation of structure and local plans, for example, the comprehensive approach of the Development Plans Manual giving way to sector-based guidance of PPGs and RPGs from 1988 inevitably involved a time lag in PPG guidance filtering into development plans. A number of extant development plans were produced before the issue of the first PPG in 1988, and the four PPGs and one draft PPG produced in 1992, all of which are relevant to rural leisure, clearly post-date nearly all development plans produced by the end of that year.

In addition, the production of some 26 county-based rural recreation strategies or countryside recreation strategies to mid-1992, exhibits no clear phasing with structure plan production, into which many country-side strategies are designed to have an input. The production of regional recreation strategies, at the other extreme, has, even at the admission of the Sports Council (1988), often lagged behind the production of struc-ture plans for which they were designed to have an input. More than 50 structure plans had been produced and approved by the Secretary of State even before the first of the regional strategies appeared, for example.

Over time, the Countryside Commission has moved from a position, prior to 1981, of producing no strategic guidance for countryside recrea-tion planning, being constrained by its civil-service status. From 1981, with its new grant-in-aid status under the 1981 Wildlife and Countryside Act, an orchestrated range of policies for 'Enjoying the Countryside' (Countryside Commission, 1987b, 1987c) has been designed to have a significant input to the development plan process. Local authorities received this information only after all first-round structure plans had been completed.

In the wake of the completion of a majority of structure plan reviews, the Sports Council (1992), too, has produced its first comprehensive national 'Countryside for Sport' policy, again with significant impli-cations for structure and local plans. Being perceptibly more promo-tional than policies for 'Enjoying the Countryside', it is difficult for local authorities to distinguish between these two policy positions as being a temporal shift on the one hand or simply a different agency stance on the other.

Perhaps the most significant changing policy emphasis over time in the rural leisure sphere, however, lies in the realm of policy advice for rural tourism. To the mid-1980s, this was squarely concerned with commercial exploitation within existing planning powers, often associ-ated with job creation. Thus, for example, the Heart of England Tourist Board's (1976) *Tourism in Rural Areas*, stressed the economic potential of tourism, particularly in relation to agriculture, and the associated mul-tiplier effects. By the mid-1980s the Cabinet Office (1985) was champion-ing the deregulation of the planning system as a means of creating jobs through the business of tourism. In the local authority sector, too (Morrisey, 1986), the principal objective was seen as supporting a frag-mented industry to help it compete for changing patterns and levels of visitor spending.

By the late 1980s, however, policy guidance had shifted to the message that the environment is the essential infrastructure of the industry. The English Tourist Board/Countryside Commission (1989) *Principles of Tourism in the Countryside* stresses the importance of the enhancement of historic and attractive buildings, the countryside, townscapes and cultural activity. It proposes a growth in activity holidays and farm-based tourism but that these should be encouraged in lesser known rather than congested rural areas. They should be used to extend the holiday season and should be developed in tandem with environmental quality and increased opportunities for access.

The principles call for tourism to be an additive rather than extractive force for rural communities, supporting village shops and local craft and food producers as well as linking support to social facilities such as rural churches and events. These principles have been developed into a more comprehensive package for 'sustainable tourism' by the Department of Employment (1991) which stresses the intrinsic value of the environment and the rural community as a tourism resource. Tourism developments should respect the scale, nature and character of their location and local authorities and other agencies should adopt such an ethos in their strategic planning and implementation processes. These are very much the sentiments expressed in the PPG 21 on Tourism (Department of the Environment, 1992f).

The Rural Development Commission's (1991a) strategy for rural tourism replicates these principles but in a further policy statement (Rural Development Commission, 1991b), the Commission sees rural tourism as a central force in arresting the decline in agricultural employment and proposes the introduction of a new rural development initiative run along the integrated development lines of Rural Development Areas, the Countryside Employment Programme, for those areas most severely affected by agricultural decline. This policy runs in parallel with a range of initiatives introduced by the Agricultural Development Advisory Service and the Ministry of Agriculture, Fisheries and Food under the 1986 'Alternative Land Uses in Rural England' package, a number of which provide specific grant assistance for farmers seeking to diversify into rural tourism.

Much of the implementation of these policies and strategies falls to local authorities, through the planning process, working in collaboration with other government bodies. To rationalize this diverse bureaucratic interest, a number of joint working parties have been set up for specific rural areas, for example, 'Herefordshire Tourism' and 'Gloucestershire Tourism' to help co-ordinate different policy interests and to market the tourism potential of the area (Curry, Gaskell and Turner, 1992).

Thus, there have been three distinct policy phases for rural tourism since the start of the 1980s. It had shifted from an economic mechanism *par excellence* for rural areas, through to one of environmental sustainability and thence to one of agricultural diversification. This often has meant that extant guidance in development plans, particularly for developers in relation to stimulating economic development, runs contrary to most recent central government advice. Policies towards agricultural diversification and 'surplus' agricultural land emanating from the 1986 Agriculture Act, disposable for leisure purposes, have also taken time to filter into development plans. Many adopted structure plans, even into the 1990s, consider agricultural land 'sacrosanct' in the rural leisure context, a point that is considered further in Chapter 7.

Clearly, any good development planning process is a dynamic one, but with continually changing policy guidance over time, there is a danger of promoting built-in obsolescence to the rural leisure component of statutory plans as soon as they are produced.

6.7 LACK OF CONSISTENCY IN POLICY GUIDANCE

A further and perhaps most important characteristic of policy guidance from government and its agencies that serves to nullify its adoption in development plans is, of course, that such guidance is commonly not consistent across different originators. A common view in relation to access, provides an exception to this. PPG 7 (Department of the Environment, 1992b) and PPG 17 (Department of the Environment, 1991a) as well as PPG 10 (Department of the Environment, 1988c) all call for improved maintenance of public rights of way and the extension of the network wherever possible. Leisure developments must not compromise this network.

These views are echoed by the Countryside Commission (1987b, 1987c) and the National Parks Review Panel (Edwards, 1991) all of which call for an increased use of access agreements to secure further access, particularly over common land. The Sports Council (1982, 1988, 1991b, 1992), too, has consistently called for improved access via public rights of way. This consistency of view has led to a greater degree of enforcement of rights of way maintenance, if not the creation of new public paths, particularly in the wake of the 1990 Rights of Way Act.

The consensus relating to guidance on access dissipates somewhat when views on the overall aims of recreation policies for development plans are considered. Differing views on these aims already have been noted in respect of structure plans and local plans, from the Development Plans Manual (Ministry of Housing and Local Government, 1970a). There is also a different ethos in PPGs relative to regional planning guidance (RPGs) in respect of the general purpose of recreation policies. Advice on the overall aims of recreation policies also varies between different government agencies.

Countryside Commission (1987b, 1987c) advice suggests that recreation should be viewed, in part at least, as a pressure on the countryside, but the Sports Council (1982, 1988, 1992) is less ambiguously concerned to see the promotion of active recreation and sport in the countryside. The goal of the Sports Council is to increase participation and it claims that restrictive approaches to provision are based largely on unfounded presumptions about recreation damage in the absence of any long-term comprehensive data on environmental impact.

Conflicts in policy guidance arise, too, in relation to the importance of environmental considerations. PPG 12 (Department of the Environment, 1992c) now requires environmental factors to be 'taken into account' in all aspects of development plans, but the extent of its overriding importance for rural leisure varies in different advisory statements. PPG 17 (Department of the Environment, 1991a) and the Countryside Commission (1987c) claim that recreation must be ubiquitously subservient to conservation objectives in national parks, AONBs and heritage coasts, although both claim the importance of extending the rights of way network in these areas. The National Parks Review panel, too (Edwards, 1991) sees recreation as a secondary objective to conservation in national parks, yet access to open country must be improved.

In contrast, the Sports Council (1988, 1992), although it calls for due regard to be given to agriculture and nature conservation in the development of sport and recreation in the countryside, takes perhaps a less reverential view of environmental considerations because of the lack of evidence of environmental damage from recreation. It calls not for constraints on development in areas that are environmentally sensitive, but promulgates the notion of 'sustainable promotion'. This is echoed in PPG 17 (Department of the Environment, 1991a) where it is claimed that good management should allow sustainable recreation development. In extreme cases, where development cannot take place for environmental reasons, the Sports Council (1992) calls for compensation to be made through active provision in other areas.

The relationship of tourism to the environment is also ambiguous in policy advice. PPG 7 (Department of the Environment 1992b), for example, suggests that tourism should be allowed to grow in response to demand, but in so doing, the environment should be taken into account. Environmental priorities are of a higher order in other government guidance, especially from the Department of Employment (1991) and this itself represents a swiftly changing position from the Cabinet Office's (1985) view that the deregulation of the planning system provided excellent opportunities for the exploitation of tourism as an employment generator.

Policy guidance in relation to the types of land that might appropriately be developed in rural areas is also not concordant. The

Sports Council (1992) favours the use of all areas, with the proviso of 'sustainable promotion' where necessary. In particular it calls for new areas to be identified and developed for noisy and intrusive sports.

Other policy guidance prioritizes in a more restrictive way water areas and areas close to towns. Here there is some interplay between the use of the term green belts on the one hand, and the urban fringe on the other. PPG 17 (Department of the Environment, 1991a) sees the urban fringe as a priority area for recreational developments, to act as a buffer to the wider countryside. Degraded sites, disused mineral workings and setaside land are particularly important in this respect. The Countryside Commission (1987b) concurs with this priority and further promotes (Countryside Commission, 1987c) the use of urban fringe forests, because of their ability to absorb capacity.

PPG 2 (Department of the Environment, 1988b) extends this priority to green belts, originally designated as 'no development' areas to restrict urban expansion. This PPG proposes their increasing use for both active and passive recreation, suggesting that favourable planning considerations should be given to the development of sports facilities as an exception to generally restrictive development control policies. Apart from the views of the Sports Council, there is no positive guidance for the exploitation of other parts of the countryside for recreation purposes. Indeed, designated areas, including Sites of Special Scientific Interest (SSSIs), are to develop increasingly restrictive policies towards recreation.

There are also discrepancies in policy guidance in relation to facility provision. Elements of policy guidance do encourage the development of facilities for recreation purposes. PPG 12 (Department of the Environment, 1992c) suggests that proposals for the development of specific facilities should be made in structure plans and the Sports Council (1992) prioritizes the development of new facilities for sport, stressing the need for positive development control policies in this respect. The Countryside Commission (1992a) also emphasizes the use of positive development control powers in the development of countryside recreation facilities generally, to encourage the maximum access to facilities for all.

The Commission's (1987c) statement on facilities, however, is somewhat at variance with the tenor of these proposals. In claiming that facilities are only a minority interest for the participating population, it proposes that their development should be undertaken only selectively, and in cases where a clear market demand for such facilities can be perceived.

6.8 THE ADOPTION OF POLICY GUIDANCE IN THE LAND-USE PLANNING PROCESS

From this range of inherent limitations in the adoptability of government advice, a survey of all current structure plans, countryside and recreation strategies to mid-1992 has been conducted to explore advice adoption. This has some difficulties for three principal reasons. First, structure plan policies might resemble elements of advice, but may not derive from it. Many structure plans, for example, are in accordance with advice that post-dates plan production and here it is likely that both have been arrived at independently, probably being informed by the same sources. Second, associated with this, much advice simply post-dates most current plans. Finally, many structure plans embrace rural leisure in more general chapters (on, for example, 'the Countryside' or 'Leisure') the structures of which do not lend themselves to the incorporation of advice in the way that it has been expressed.

Within these limitations, relatively few structure plans actually cite guidance documents. Only 25% cite sport and recreation strategies, 25% central government advice (mainly PPGs) and 10% any Countryside Commission documentation (only four cite 'Enjoying the Countryside' policies explicitly). There are few mentions of any Sports Council advice and no mention of regional planning guidance at all. The most consistent acknowledgement of advice relates to public rights of way. It is perhaps no coincidence that this is the one area of consensus across all advice. The most consistent departure from advice relates to green belts, where most structure plans favour restrictions on opportunities for leisure, but much advice, particularly in PPGs, favours exploitation.

Two examples of policies in structure plans serve to indicate that where policies are concordant with some advice, they inevitably conflict with other advice. In respect of overall aims, structure plans are by and large concerned with controlling and minimizing the effects of recreation on the environment, particularly in designated areas, in line with the advice of the Countryside Commission and PPGs. Few hold with the more promotional position of the Sports Council, a position that considers that environmental damage caused by countryside recreation remains unproven.

As a second example, the review of structure plans in 1992, compared with an earlier study conducted in 1985 (Curry and Comley, 1985) shows a greater concern in plans for targeting specific social groups (the carless, the unemployed). This is consistent with Sports Council advice, but contrasts strongly with PPG 12 (Department of the Environment, 1992c) that reasserts that structure plans should embrace land-use considerations only.

In contrast to structure plans, nearly all countryside strategies and all countryside recreation strategies make explicit reference to the Countryside Commission's 'Enjoying the Countryside' policies, and a third of them cite regional sport and recreation strategies. Many countryside recreation strategies take the form of an overt response to 'Enjoying the Countryside', some openly stating that this is deliberately to enhance grant-aid bids to the Commission.

Thus, the impact of advice for government leisure land-use planning has been limited in the formulation of both structure plans and countryside strategies. There is undoubtedly a case for the simplification and unification of advice if it is to be more successful in steering plan formulation. But it is unlikely to come about unless the organizational structures that generate, and are required to adopt, such advice are themselves rationalized. The fragmentary nature of these organizational structures, discussed in Chapter 2, is both a cause and a consequence of the ineffective use of advice in strategic land-use planning. The resultant content of both formal and informal strategic plans for rural leisure forms the focus of the following chapter.

7

Recreation and access in structure plans and countryside strategies

7.1 THE STRATEGIC PLANNING CONTEXT

As has been noted in Chapter 6, strategic planning for countryside recreation at the local-authority level has two principal forms. Within the development plan process, all structure plans in England and Wales contain policies for countryside recreation, although their form and content vary considerably. Since 1988 a series of countryside strategies and countryside recreation strategies has also been produced at the county level, in response to a number of stimuli such as agricultural change, and the Countryside Commission's 'Enjoying the Countryside' (1987b, 1987c) policies. These provide an informal strategic planning counterpart to development plans (Curry, 1992a), and allow the consideration of non-land-use issues.

In producing Structure Plans, the Development Plans Manual (Ministry of Housing and Local Government, 1970a) outlined the 'scope of material that the Minister would normally expect to see in association with the plan, in order to satisfy himself that the plans are soundly based'. For countryside recreation, this 'scope of material' required surveys to be conducted for recreation 'demands' and current usage, future changes in demand and consumption, future 'needs', an analysis of the likely influences on changes in demand for countryside recreation over time, and estimates of the quantity of land to be allocated for recreation provision. Subsequent to this manual, up to 1988, structure planning for rural leisure was informed by a series of Circulars outlined in the previous chapter.

Structure plans were produced originally quite slowly (only four were submitted in the first five years after the 1968 Act and none were approved). This led to the suggestion of some selectivity of topics, designed to speed up the process, contained in Circular 44/71 (Department of the Environment, 1971). The further confusion stemming from the new two-tier system of local government introduced in 1974, brought about the evolution of the 'key issues' concept in some local authorities. This was endorsed by the Department of the Environment in Circular 98/74 (Department of the Environment, 1974), in which the focus of structure plans was to be on 'issues of key structural importance to the area concerned'. The Circular also suggested that 'in some cases this might also include the extent of provision in recreation and tourism', but except in south-west Hampshire, recreation has never been accorded key issue status in structure plans.

From 1988 PPG 12 (Department of the Environment, 1992c) no longer distinguishes principal issues from other matters, but defines leisure and recreation as one of the nine relevant topics for consideration in structure plans. This represents, *de facto*, an elevated status for the importance of recreation in structure plans, and various PPGs have provided advice on the nature of recreation policies since that time.

From the original structure plans, the last of which was produced by Avon in 1985, county planning authorities (and in two cases, national park authorities, although the Lake District National Park produces its structure plan with Cumbria County Council jointly) have produced structure plan reviews, which either take the form of alterations to the original plan, or a complete replacement plan. Historically, these have required Secretary of State approval, although this is no longer the case under the 1991 Planning and Compensation Act. Under this regime, counties often worked to both approved and submitted plans.

In the past, too, many county authorities produced more than one structure plan, each for different parts of the county, although PPG 12 (Department of the Environment, 1992c) no longer allows this. To mid-1992, however, the 47 counties in England and Wales, and the Peak District National Park, had produced 54 extant structure plans, three counties – Hampshire, Dorset and Wiltshire – having multiple plans.

The changing fortunes of structure plans during the 1980s, noted in Chapter 6, have acted as a stimulus to a growth in the production of informal countryside strategies at the county level for countryside recreation, since 1988, for a number of reasons. First, the threatened abolition of structure plans in 1989 provided a particular impetus for the development of non-statutory surrogates. Second, the need for Secretary of State approval for structure plans encouraged the development of less formal planning mechanisms that were not so constrained. Even though the 1991 Act no longer requires Secretary of State approval for structure plans, the Secretary may still intervene 'where necessary' in their production, threatening the same loss of local autonomy.

Third, PPG 15 reasserts the 'land-use planning only' jurisdiction of structure plans, encouraging the development of informal plans that go beyond land-use matters. Finally, the historical non-'key issue' status accorded to recreation in structure plans could be rectified through the production of informal plans, focusing more clearly on rural leisure. As a result of these factors, informal strategies for countryside recreation have been produced that take one of two forms – countryside strategies with recreation components or countryside recreation strategies.

Because these plans have no statutory basis, their number cannot be definitively ascertained but a survey of all county councils in mid-1992 suggests that 15 countryside strategies with recreation components had been produced to that time (all of which were in England), and a further 11 countryside recreation strategies (five of which were in Wales) had also been produced. These are presented in Table 7.1. Over half of the counties in England and Wales had therefore produced one or other of these strategies to mid-1992, but none had produced both. Sutcliffe (1992), suggests that a further 16 strategies of either type were in preparation in mid-1992 and where they were not yet being produced or had not yet been completed, lack of officer time, lack of finance and lack of authority commitment were the principal inhibiting factors.

7.2 UNDERLYING PRESUMPTIONS IN POLICY FORMULATION

In developing policies for rural leisure in both of these types of strategic planning document, a clear empirical basis for policy formulation has been proposed by government. Yet, from Chapter 4, the fragmentary nature of various elements of data relating to countryside recreation participation has undoubtedly inhibited this. This section explores the empirical basis upon which structure plans and countryside strategies are founded, establishes that policies are based on assumptions about recreation behaviour rather than empirical evidence, and considers some of the consequences of this planning on presumption.

It has been noted above that the Development Plans Manual (Ministry of Housing and Local Government, 1970a) required structure plans to collect comprehensive empirical information about recreation demands, needs and supply. Circular 44/71 (Department of the Environment, 1971), however, in defining countryside recreation largely not as a 'principal issue', but as an 'other matter' for consideration in structure plans, gave local authorities discretion over whether surveys were conducted or not. This led, as Palmer (1975) and Fitton (1979) have both noted, to the vast majority of counties failing to carry out any survey work at all in the formulation of countryside recreation policies during the 1970s. This failure was attributed both to a lack of staff time available for the consideration of recreation subjects (Fitton, 1979) and an expertise in, and experience of, countryside recreation among planning staff that 'often left much to be desired' (Veal and Travis, 1979).

Table 7.1 The production of county countryside strategies and countryside recreation strategies in England and Wales

COUNTRYSIDE STRATEGIES

England

Bedfordshire	'The Bedfordshire Countryside – a Strategy for Action'	1990
Cambridgeshire	'The Cambridgeshire Rural Strategy'	1988
Cheshire	'A Rural Strategy for Cheshire'	1989
Cumbria	'Cumbria Countryside Strategy, 1989–92'	1988
Derbyshire	'Countryside Strategy'	1991
Essex	'Enjoying the Countryside – a Strategy'	1988
Hampshire	'Rural Development Strategy'	1991
Kent	'Kent Countryside Strategy'	1990
Leicestershire	'Countryside 2000: Planning for Change in the Leicestershire Countryside: Action Strategy'	1989
Northamptonshire	'A Rural Strategy for Northamptonshire'	1990
Northumberland	'Northumberland Countryside strategy' (consultation draft)	1990
Shropshire	'A Countryside Strategy for Shropshire' (consultation draft)	1991
Suffolk	'Suffolk Countryside Strategy: Issues Discussion Paper'	1992
Surrey	'Surrey Countryside Strategy: Key Issues and Proposals' (consultation report)	1990
Wiltshire	'A Rural Strategy for Wiltshire'	1989

COUNTRYSIDE RECREATION STRATEGIES

England

Buckinghamshire	'Bucks Countryside Strategy (Countryside Recreation)' (one of five topic volumes)	1989
Cleveland	'Opening the Gateway: a Countryside Recreation Strategy for Cleveland'	1991
Durham	'Countryside Recreation Strategy 1989–93'	1989
Gloucestershire	'Strategy for Enjoying the Countryside in Gloucestershire' (Report to Recreation and Leisure Sub Committee)	1988
Hereford and Worcester	'Countryside Recreation Strategy 1991–2001'	1991
Lancashire	'Countryside Recreation Strategy for Lancashire'	1988

Wales

Clwyd	'Recreation in the Countryside: a Strategy for Clwyd'	1990
Dyfed	'Countryside Recreation and Access Strategy'	1989
Gwent	'Enjoying the Gwent Countryside 1990–94. A Joint Countryside Recreation Strategy'	1989
Gwynedd	'Recreation in Gwynedd: a 5 Year Strategy for Countryside Recreation'	1989
South Glamorgan	'Countryside Recreation Strategy'	1990

From 1988, guidance on the empirical requirements for recreation policy formulation in structure plans has been less specific. PPG 12 (Department of the Environment, 1992c) maintains that for the relevant topics in structure plans surveys are still to be conducted, and made readily available to the public. For countryside recreation in particular, PPG 17 (Department of the Environment, 1991a, para. 36) states:

> in the context of an anticipated growth in pressure on the country-side, the planning system should ensure the adequate provision of land and water resources for informal recreation. This should be done by assessing recreational needs against current provision.

7.2.1 Strategic planning for countryside recreation: evidence of survey work

Given this enduring requirement to produce survey work in structure plan policy formulation for countryside recreation, has empirical data collection for this purpose improved since the 1970s? A survey of all 80 extant structure plans in 1985 (Curry and Comley, 1985) shows that only five structure planning authorities (Durham, 1981; Avon, 1982; Cheshire, 1979; Greater Manchester, 1981; and Greater London, 1976) provided any direct evidence of having undertaken comprehensive recreation participation surveys in structure plan formulation. A further four authorities made use of a number of individual site surveys to inform plans but for the remainder, assertions about recreation behaviour were based on informal observations and the broad national trends that have been outlined in Chapter 4. It was commonly recognized in plans to this time that the paucity of empirical work did provide a limitation in plan formulation, and surveys were to become a priority in structure plan reviews.

A re-survey of all 54 structure plans current in the summer of 1992 indicated that this situation had not improved (Curry and Pack, 1993). Only eleven of these plans made any reference at all to empirical surveys of the population, only four of which made reference to local surveys. The remaining seven again cited national statistics on participation, principally the Countryside Commission's 1984 National Survey of Countryside Recreation (Countryside Commission, 1985b), but also in one instance, summary statistics from the Sports Council (1982). A number of plans restated their intention to undertake surveys in the future.

Countryside strategies with recreation components and countryside recreation strategies have no formal requirement to produce empirical data in policy formulation, since they are not statutory planning documents. Despite this, their approach to survey work has been more reverential and more fully considered than in structure plans. Over a third of the 15 countryside strategies with recreation components produced by mid-1992 made reference to local site studies or other local studies to provide background information for countryside recreation proposals. Two-thirds of these strategies also cited the 1984 National Survey of Countryside Recreation and one strategy referred to Regional Council for Sport and Recreation data. Where such information was used, though, it was extrapolated directly to the county level without modification.

Explicit recognition was given in most strategies to the paucity of empirical information to aid planning. Derbyshire (1991), for example, admitted a lack of recent material – their most recent site survey was conducted in 1982 – and recognized the need to update information. The Kent (1990a) strategy included as one of its objectives 'to improve information on the public's needs for countryside recreation', and intended to fulfil this by carrying out market research on consumer preferences.

Some strategies simply confessed a lack of data, as in Shropshire (1991, p. 45):

> precise figures do not exist for measuring the scale of recreational use in the countryside.

Others argued that such data were not informative in policy-making, as in Leicestershire (1989, p. 7):

> the numerical quantification of demand for organised sport and leisure needs in the countryside is an inadequate guide for provision.

Countryside recreation strategies paid closest attention to the importance of empirical data. Of the 11 such strategies produced to mid-1992, two undertook specific local household surveys and a further two cited existing site surveys. Frequent reference was made to both the 1977 and 1984 National Surveys of Countryside Recreation and the 1986 General Household Survey was also referred to. Nearly all strategies contained a brief resume of whatever surveys had been used, summarizing the principal characteristics of both participants and non-participants in countryside recreation.

In addition, three strategies discussed the significant shortcoming of a lack of knowledge of demand and participation at the local level, and the difficulties of applying national statistics to the county and sub-county level. They all commented on their intent (and the need) to carry out some form of monitoring or survey work to provide more accurate information at the local level.

Strategic planning for countryside recreation has thus been characterized by a very low level of empirical information about recreation participation as an input to plan formulation. Evidence from the 1985 and 1992 surveys of structure plans suggests that empirical surveys have been carried out even less frequently in more recent plans. This information deficiency has been recognized more overtly in informal plans than in structure plans, and it is through these informal channels that empirical databases appear most likely to improve (Curry and Pack, 1993). In the light of this paucity of information, what, then, are the principal presumptions about recreation behaviour in strategic plans upon which such planning is based?

7.2.2 Trends and forecasting

Structure plans have set the context for countryside recreation policies by some form of forecasting procedures to establish trends in participation. However, forecasting recreation behaviour has to date proved highly speculative, since nearly all the work undertaken on identifying factors affecting participation has been based on statistical association, rather than on direct cause and effect, as has been noted in Chapter 4.

These problems are recognized by many county councils. In the 1985 survey (Curry and Comley, 1985), for example, forecasting recreation behaviour was considered in several plans to be difficult and unreliable. A majority of plans made use of Countryside Commission estimates of the growth of recreation. One county, Gloucestershire (1979), had made forecasts simply on the basis of historical patterns, while another, Devon (1981), had made forecasts based on anticipated changes in the factors presumed to influence demand, particularly age and gender profiles.

As a result of these processes, all counties formulated countryside recreation policies on the presumption of a growth in recreation participation. Some (for example, North Yorkshire, 1981) considered this growth to be accelerating, but others (Northumberland, 1980) considered it to be slowing down.

In the 1992 re-survey of structure plans, the plans still contained information on forecasting. One in ten plans again explicitly discussed difficulties in forecasting, recognizing in the main that simply projecting past participation patterns was no guide to future consumption. It is changes in those factors that influence demand that were a more reliable guide. Because of the difficulties in quantifying these, a number of plans reverted to the consideration of growth in recreation pressures rather than recreation consumption, allowing them to focus policies on particular 'pressured' areas.

Despite these difficulties, all plans asserted a continuing growth in countryside recreation participation, usually based on some notion of its inherent importance, rather than any formal projections:

visits to the countryside are the most popular leisure activity throughout Britain' (Clwyd, 1991, p. 42);

informal countryside recreation is the most popular outdoor pursuit in Great Britain (Kent, 1990a, p. 123).

In contrast to structure plans, both countryside strategies and countryside recreation strategies have paid little attention to forecasting either of the influences over demand or participation patterns. Those that have mentioned trends have all assumed a continuing increase in participation. Despite admitted difficulties in forecasting, and evidence of a reducing frequency of its use in more recent plans, therefore, the underlying ethos for all countryside recreation strategic planning, both formal and informal, is one of a continuing growth in participation.

7.2.3 Influences over countryside recreation demand

Most structure plans produced during the 1970s asserted some general influences over demand. These mainly comprised mobility, incomes, leisure time, attitudes and fashion. Some plans produced into the 1980s (for example, Wiltshire, 1983; Surrey, 1980; and Hampshire, 1983) and some plan reviews (Northamptonshire, 1985), however, stressed a changing set of demand influences focusing on unemployment, new technology, early retirement and an ageing society. Some plans also offered local influences over demand, and others, such as Devon (1981), articulated different demand influences for different activities. No plans, however, distinguished the different demand influences of different social groups.

In terms of the structure plan's own ability to influence demand, a number of authorities (for example, Central and North Lancashire (1983) considered that this was limited because of the supply-based nature of structure plan policies. On the other hand, some authorities felt that policies would have a direct influence over demand, since supply itself creates its own demand.

The 1992 re-survey of structure plans indicated that many plans were very detailed in suggesting the factors influencing changes in countryside recreation demand. A third of plans mentioned an increase in leisure time and a further third increasing real incomes or affluence (although one or two acknowledged this was not for all sectors of society). Increases in leisure time were further attributed in about half the plans to changing work patterns such as early retirement, a shorter working week and more holidays. Time and money were therefore seen as the two biggest influences over demand.

Beyond these factors, increasing car ownership and personal mobility were mentioned in a fifth of plans (some included the availability of better roads in this respect), and eight plans suggested that changing attitudes to sport and recreation also had a significant influence (reference is made here to Sports Council campaigns, and the recognition of the importance of exercise to health and well-being).

Further factors articulated included an ageing population structure and increasing environmental or green awareness. Four plans mentioned unemployment as a demand factor increasing time but not money. Increasing tourism was also mentioned as a factor influencing recreation demand more generally, and growing links with Europe were seen as a potential future influence over demand especially in the South East.

A number of plans in the 1992 survey also listed local influences on demand. Most important in this respect was accessibility from large population centres, but possessing large areas of attractive countryside, local population growth and the impacts of local tourism policies were all considered to have an influence.

Greater awareness and provision of, and access to, recreation facilities were themselves again seen as factors influencing demand in some plans. In four plans the existence of latent demand was explicitly mentioned, whereby the provision of new facilities to some extent was creating its own demand:

> much existing demand is latent, and only expresses itself when new facilities become available (Devon, 1989, p. 95);

> to a significant extent, the supply of countryside recreation facilities tends to create additional demand (Shropshire, 1987, p. 107).

All countryside and countryside recreation strategies have mentioned influences over recreation demand. These are similar, and as diverse, as those articulated in structure plans.

There are three principal shortcomings in these analyses of influences over recreation demand in strategic plans. First, such a large range of them is articulated that even if they were empirically verifiable, any precise notion of their influence would be difficult to discern. In this respect, the utility of articulating them as an aid to policy formulation is questionable. Second, they are, of course, only assertions, and no evidence is presented in plans in respect of any causal relationships. As has been noted in Chapter 4, increasing leisure, car ownership, education and so on have been associated during the 1980s, with a **decline** in recreation participation.

Third, and perhaps more importantly, nearly all of the influences articulated are those that have been presumed to trigger increased consumption in the future. Little attention is given to factors, related to economic recessive cycles and declining real incomes, that might lead to reduced participation. For the 1970s, for example, Stoakes (1979) was able to show a relationship between increases in petrol prices and reduced recreation participation. The principal purpose, therefore, of itemizing these influences over demand appears to have been to reinforce the assertion of a continued growth in countryside recreation participation.

7.2.4 Participation, demands and needs

In addition to statements on forecasting and presumed influences over demand, many structure plans have provided information about current and anticipated participation patterns, again with the intention of informing policy formulation. In this respect, terminology has been imprecise and ambiguous, where notions of participation (current consumption levels), demand (an expression of a willingness and ability to incur expenditure) and need (a desire not matched by ability to pay) are used interchangeably.

In the 1992 survey, 17 of the 54 extant structure plans made no mention at all of current levels of participation, demand or need. Of those that did (as they did in the 1985 survey) most suggested that the purpose of recreation provision was to cater for anticipated increases in levels of participation. This has often been couched either in terms of demands:

informal countryside recreation is becoming increasingly popular, and these new demands should be catered for (Cleveland, 1990, p. 58);

or needs:

greater numbers of people will have a greater amount of leisure time in the future to devote to leisure activity and . . . these needs must be met wherever possible (Avon, 1991, p. 74).

or it has been seen simply as being incontrovertible:

recreation is an increasingly essential ingredient to modern life . . . and a failure to make adequate provision in suitable locations will cause it either to take place in locations where it conflicts with other countryside interests, or to be suppressed with undesirable consequences (Kent, 1990b, p. 123).

Although the consideration of needs was less common than either participation or demand in both the 1985 and 1992 structure plan surveys, the use of the term has been particularly ambiguous. Teeside (Cleveland, 1977a) and Staffordshire (1984), for example, both have claimed a need for more golf courses because Sports Council standards have not been met (need here equates to the failure to meet a prescribed level of provision). In Cambridgeshire (1980) the need for a country park was considered to be the greatest around Cambridge (need here equates to unsatisfied demand). In Avon (1982), by contrast, it was considered that the bulk of the need for informal recreation arose from urban areas (here, need could equate either to unsatisfied demand, or some form of deprivation).

In the 1992 survey, approximately a third of structure plans, fewer than in 1985, contained some reference to meeting the recreation needs of certain groups in society, more overtly in the context of some form of deprivation. These references were more common in more recent plans. Although some plans simply mentioned the need to provide for all groups in society, 10 of the 54 plans mentioned specifically both the disabled and non-car owners. Other named groups included the elderly, those deterred for whatever reason from visiting the countryside, and 'disadvantaged' groups generally. Some plans even targeted specific types of recreation facility, particularly public rights of way, to disadvantaged groups.

Countryside strategies and countryside recreation strategies have been more systematic in their consideration of needs in the context of deprivation. A high proportion of all strategies have commented on the importance of catering for the needs of those groups in society that traditionally have rarely visited the countryside. The elderly, the disabled, ethnic minorities and the car-less were a particular focus here and it has been commonly proposed that improvements in public transport and increasing publicity and awareness should be developed for such groups. Two strategies, Durham (1989) and Hereford and Worcester (1991b), have departed from this view somewhat, claiming that efforts are better targeted at 'occasional' users (white-collar workers, skilled manual workers) than those who go to the countryside rarely, if participation rates are to be more effectively increased.

Assertions have also been made from both structure plan surveys about the changing structure of participation patterns for particular countryside recreation activities. East and West Cleveland (Cleveland, 1977b), Gwent (1981) and North Yorkshire (1981), for example, anticipated a move away from team and group activities towards more informal, or as one plan (Shropshire, 1987) terms it 'simple' pursuits, such as walking. Thirteen plans in the 1992 survey focused specifically on the increasing demand for golf and the shortage of provision to meet this demand. Agricultural diversification did provide an opportunity to develop more courses, but these 'still need to be targeted to the main areas of demand' (Devon, 1989).

Particular emphasis was also placed on the increasing demand for water recreation (specifically mentioned as a priority in 12 plans in the 1992 survey) and in many areas there was concern that facility provision was not able to match demand. In countryside strategies, golf and water recreation also have been noted as growth areas, but a number of strategies have also focused on a growth in active and 'noisy' sports. In the Suffolk (1992) strategy, for example, in the context of sports which cause visual or noise intrusion, it was considered that 'the demand for some of these facilities seems almost limitless'.

In the absence of clear empirical evidence, these statements exhibit the confusion noted in Chapter 5 about whether strategic policies for countryside recreation are intended to cater for market demands or social needs or both. This is exemplified in the Kent (1990a) countryside strategy cited above which 'seeks to improve information on the public's needs' by carrying out 'market research'. Again, all assumptions about participation, demands and needs are predicated on a ubiquitous notion that they each will increase into the future.

7.2.5 The consequences of planning on presumption

The sparse use of empirical information as an input to countryside recreation strategic plan formulation thus places great reliance on presumptions about recreation behaviour. On this basis alone, resultant policies can be questioned, depending upon views of the legitimacy of the presumptions made. But there are four more specific problems associated with the observations made in this section about planning on presumption.

The first of these is that even where empirical information is used, serious questions can be raised about its legitimacy. The vast majority of empirical inputs to plan formulation in both structure plans and countryside strategies employ inferences from site surveys and national data and both are seriously flawed for use at the county level.

As has been noted in Chapter 4, site surveys provide information about participation patterns only at individual sites. They say nothing about behaviour elsewhere in the county. More importantly, they say nothing about non-participation in the wider population that the plans and strategies are designed to serve. They thus provide biases in observations about recreation behaviour towards those who are already recreation active, who are atypical of the wider population in recreation terms.

National data, too, may only be of tangential relevance at the county level. The Countryside Commission's (1979c) 1977 National Survey of Countryside Recreation, for example, showed regional variations in participation patterns in excess of 30%, severely reducing the extrapolative power of national data to the regional, let alone county, level.

Furthermore, the most comprehensive data on recreation behaviour by mid-1992 was the 1984 National Survey of Countryside Recreation, which was still being cited in plans, some eight years after it had been carried out. It is quite possible that recreation patterns have experienced some structural shift since that time.

The second and perhaps most significant problem associated with this planning on presumption, in relation to both trends and influences over demands and needs, lies in the supposition of an enduring growth in recreation participation. The data from the Countryside Commission, the General Household Survey, Social and Community Planning Research and the British Tourist Authority, cited in Chapter 4, shows this simply not to be the case, certainly at the national level, which is the level upon which most plans base this assumption.

This inaccurate presumption of an incessant growth in consumption, a legacy, perhaps of Michael Dower's (1965) 'Fourth Wave', has led strategic plans, particularly structure plans, to take an unduly restrictive stance in promulgating countryside recreation policies, supporting the fourth proposition of this book. This, in turn, has derived from concerns that recreation growth will do untold damage to the countryside if it is not controlled in some way, a tenet that is considered further in Chapter 8.

A third problem relates to the presumption, in most plans, of a shifting structure of participation away from more organized activities, and towards more informal pursuits. This appears to contradict the 1984 National Survey of Countryside Recreation data, which indicates a growth in participation in active sports, particularly 'new' ones, relative to less formal activities.

This trend towards active sports is likely to continue, since the Sports Council's (1988, 1992) policies for the countryside are perceptibly more promotional than those of the Countryside Commission for informal recreation (Curry and Pack, 1992), something which may have an increasing effect if the proposed formation of the English Sports Council in 1993, specifically to increase mass participation in sport, ever comes about.

Finally, amidst the confusion between recreation demands and needs portrayed in strategic plans, the notion of targeting recreation policies towards the socially disadvantaged may have considerable limitations not only because of the nature of people's preferences discussed in Chapter 5, but also because, for structure plans at least, of the reassertion in PPG 15 (Department of the Environment, 1990a) of the 'land-use planning only' functions of development plans.

7.3 STRUCTURE PLANS: POLICIES FOR LAND USES AND FACILITIES

Planning on presumption, then, has provided strategic land-use plans with an inaccurate basis for policy formulation – an assumption of continued recreation growth. To explore the extent to which this has actually led to restrictive policies in structure plans, in support of the fourth proposition of this book (p. xi), they can be analysed on a restraint – development continuum. In fact, this is the convention in analysing structure plan policies in general. It has been adopted by White (1981), for example, in the analysis of structure plan tourism policies, May and Green (1980) in the consideration of employment, and Cloke (1983) in assessing settlement policies. Healey (1983) has suggested that recreation policies inevitably will fall at the restraint end of this continuum since it is chiefly a public-sector activity and at time of scarce resources in local authorities, restraint policies minimize financial burdens.

Bracken's (1980) analysis of recreation in structure plans, however, found some variability along this continuum with shire counties generally being more restraint orientated than metropolitan authorities, but he also found an exceptional blandness or even ambiguity in the overall objectives of many recreation policies. Palmer (1975), too, found that in many cases, overall objectives for recreation were often difficult to place on this continuum.

In analysing recreation policies for structure plans along this continuum, it is important to note the particular meaning of 'development' in the recreation context. Whereas structure plan policies in general commonly consider development to be that which requires some form of planning application, this is not the case for recreation. Here, structure plan 'development' proposals embrace a long list of facilities and resources including the public rights of way network, country parks, scenic drives, and facilities for fishing, sailing, cycling, climbing, motor sports and so forth. Whereas development associated with these activities may require planning approval, commonly they do not, and in terms of planning legislation therefore, do not constitute development.

There is an issue as to whether structure plans should consider these activities at all, because they do not constitute development in its legal sense, and it may be legitimate that they are embraced in informal plans. Since this broader definition of development has been used in structure plans, however, this is the one that has been adopted in evaluating planning aims and policies for countryside recreation on the restraint–development continuum.

7.3.1 Overall aims of recreation policies

In the 1985 survey of structure plans (Curry and Comley, 1985), overall aims for recreation policies were in general terms at the restraint end of this continuum, with Cumbria and the Lake District (Cumbria County Council 1983) among the most restrictive; being concerned to minimize social and environmental problems associated with recreation; including policies of restraint. A few plans, however, were more development orientated, notably the metropolitan authorities and Bedfordshire (1980), where overall aims were concerned to improve the range and accessibility of facilities to urban areas where the majority of the population live.

Although the overall aims of these policies embraced both land (or resource) and population (or social) issues, the weight of the policies themselves were generally disposed towards land uses or facilities, reflecting the legitimate policy interest of structure plans. Again, metropolitan authorities generally gave a higher priority to social policies than other areas, although the assumptions made about population characteristics considered in the previous section have provided considerable difficulties in translating such objectives into meaningful policies.

In the 1992 resurvey of structure plans, this general picture was repeated. Most overall aims for countryside recreation were restraint orientated. In a very few cases only, aims were development orientated without any qualification, as in Somerset (1986, p. 71):

policies will provide and encourage the provision of facilities which improve recreational opportunities in the countryside.

There was a greater convergence in 1992 on the justification of restraint policies. Fears of a recreation explosion had given way to the imperative of environmental protection, particularly in plans that postdated the White Paper *This Common Inheritance* (Department of the Environment, 1990b). Thus in Hereford and Worcester (1991a, p. 32):

this alteration (from the earlier structure plan) makes it clear that effects on environment and ecology are significant factors that must be considered in the planning of facilities.

The vast majority of plans thus qualified all overall recreation objectives with environmental safeguards, and a significant number had policies that clearly gave the environment precedence over recreation.

The place of social objectives for recreation in structure plans was less evident in 1992 than in 1985 possibly due in part to the environmental imperative, but also because structure plans were not produced by metropolitan authorities after 1986, when they were abolished.

Overall, the general aims of recreation policies were less precise and defined, as Bracken (1982) and Palmer (1975) both found, than guidance in the Development Plans Manual (Ministry of Housing and Local Government, 1970a) and PPG 12 (Department of the Environment, 1992c) suggests. No plans, for example, undertook land allocation exercises as required by the Development Plans Manual. This generally imprecise nature of overall aims has been noted by Struthers and

Brundell (1983), who maintain that only general recreation policies were included in the draft plan for the West Midlands, in the expectation that they would be revised quickly. The Secretary of State required more detail before approving the plan, and suggested that recreation should be considered further in the plan review.

7.3.2 Policies for land areas

In placing policies for land areas from the 1985 structure plan survey into a restraint–development continuum, land areas where recreation was not to be encouraged, and also where it was to be encouraged, were grouped into six broad types. These are presented in Tables 7.2 and 7.3.

All of the areas where recreation was not to be encouraged were in one sense or another 'valued landscapes'. In contrast, areas where recreation was to be encouraged were generally 'undistinguished' or low-value landscapes. Areas of landscape conservation value were the most restrictive in recreation terms, being mentioned in all some 49 times as places where recreation was not to be encouraged. The productive countryside and threatened areas were the next most commonly mentioned in this respect, with agricultural land – mentioned some 26 times in one form or another – being the most commonly identifiable single land type where recreation was not to be encouraged. Other sensitive areas, areas of nature conservation value and areas with insufficient facilities, were the other groups in this category. All of the areas where recreation was not to be encouraged, then, were concerned with the quality of land (Blunden and Curry, 1988).

This was not exclusively the case where recreation was to be encouraged. The majority of these areas were land-area types, but the most frequently mentioned areas, accessible locations, also embraced a social component. Accessibility in terms of transport and proximity appeared to be the prime concern of recreation provision. Notwithstanding this, the largest item in this category, the urban fringe, distinct from the green belt, was commonly considered to be a low-value landscape, an area of often residual land uses.

Water areas were very commonly proposed for recreation for no consistent reason. In many instances they were cited as areas that had lost their former non-recreational function. Perhaps they were inherently popular, without necessarily being distinguished in physical character. Rivers and canals, in fact, provided the largest single area types where recreation was to be encouraged. These were seen as providing particularly important linear routes out of metropolitan areas. Other popular categories of land were derelict land, and sites that would absorb capacity. Again, both of these categories were concerned to minimize environmental impact.

Table 7.2 Types of recreation area where recreation is not encouraged in the structure plans of England and Wales in 1985[a]

	General activities not encouraged	Specific activities not encouraged
Areas of landscape conservation value	**38**	**11**
AONB	10	6
Heritage coasts (and other coastal areas)	10	0
Areas of high landscape value	7	1
Unspecified areas of designated landscape	5	1
National parks	4	3
Sites of archaeological significance	2	0
Productive countryside	**26**	**4**
All agricultural land	20	3
Forestry land	3	1
Higher grades of agricultural land	3	0
Threatened areas	**26**	**1**
Areas of excess or low capacity	10	1
Environmentally sensitive areas	10	0
Vulnerable or fragile areas	5	0
Areas of conflict	1	0
Other sensitive areas	**18**	**4**
Inland water areas	7	2
Deeper or remoter countryside	5	1
Open countryside	2	1
Quiet areas	2	0
Attractive or high amenity areas	2	0
Areas of Nature Conservation Value	**15**	**3**
'Natural' environments (including those of wildlife and ecological significance)	8	2
Statutory nature conservation areas (National Nature Reserves, SSSIs)	6	1
Conservation priority areas	1	0
Areas with insufficient facilities	**3**	**0**
Areas with no suitable car parks/access	3	0

[a] The figures in this table represent the *number* of structure plans in which the land area or type is mentioned in the context of the non-encouragement of recreation. This may be either in the form of a general statement, or for specific activities only.

Source: Curry and Comley, 1985.

Table 7.3 Types of recreation area where recreation is encouraged in the structure plans of England and Wales in 1985[a]

	Generally activities encouraged	Specific activities encouraged
Accessible locations	**72**	**12**
The urban fringe	36	11
Accessible sites	13	0
Sites near to main roads	12	1
Sites near to public transport routes	8	0
Sites within walking distance of users	3	0
Water areas	**70**	**16**
Rivers and canals	48	5
Inland water area (not linear)	13	2
Coasts and beaches	9	9
Areas of derelict land	**64**	**5**
Disused mineral workings/gravel pits	23	1
Derelict, disused or damaged land	20	0
Disused railway lines	14	4
Low value land	5	0
Areas of land reclamation	2	0
Sites to absorb capacity	**42**	**9**
Forest and woodland	12	3
Areas which can absorb capacity	10	2
Recreation priority areas/intensive recreation areas	9	2
Where conflict is minimized or diversion takes place	6	2
Historic houses	2	0
Lowland areas	1	0
Linear open space	1	0
Buffer zones	1	0
Areas of high need or poor provision	**14**	**0**
Areas of high need or poor provision	14	0
High value landscapes	**9**	**13**
Green belts/green wedges	6	0
Attractive areas	2	0
Deeper open countryside	1	4
AONBs	0	4
Upland areas	0	2
National parks	0	2
Heritage coasts	0	1

[a] The figures in this table represent the *number* of structure plans in which the land area or type is mentioned in the context of the encouragement of countryside recreation. This may be in the form of a general statement or for specific activities only

Source: Curry and Comley, 1985.

Areas of high need and poor provision again reflected a 'social' element in land-use allocation policies and were mentioned 14 times. The final classification, high-value landscapes, was a small one and exhibited a caution within plans about the encouragement of recreation in these areas. Here, proposals for specific activities only, outnumbered the instances were general encouragement was given to recreation.

All of these observations relating to the spatial priorities for recreation provision in structure plans tend to reflect a perceived need to minimize recreational impact, rather than maximize recreation opportunity. It appears that recreation was to be developed in lower value physical environments, and a majority of structure plans sought to divert recreation pressures to less environmentally sensitive areas.

By 1992, policies for land areas in structure plans had become less easy to quantify. The overall style had become much more one of placing environmental qualifications on all land uses and making any development conditional upon this. In very general terms, however, the same pattern of encouragement and non-encouragement was evident. Derelict and damaged land was most commonly seen to be where recreation development potential was greatest. Water areas were considered to be the next most significant area of recreation potential, particularly where this could be combined with a new use for derelict land associated with mineral workings.

Recreation was also encouraged in sites to absorb capacity, particularly in relation to woodland. Accessible locations, however, were much less frequently cited in the plans reviewed in 1992 compared to those in 1985, as areas offering recreation potential. This reflects the diminished interest in 'social' considerations in the more recent review, and possibly some acceptance of the relative insignificance of location as a factor determining participation, considered in Chapter 5. Overall, recreation was encouraged in any areas that offered the potential to minimize environmental damage.

Reflecting this environmental concern, in the 1992 survey, recreation was not to be encouraged generally speaking where any detrimental impacts were a possibility. By far the most commonly cited areas for restraint in this respect were Areas of Outstanding Natural Beauty, heritage coasts, national parks and Areas of Great Landscape Value. These were accorded a greater prominence than in the 1985 survey. In exceptional cases, where recreation was to be permitted, it was in Areas of Outstanding Natural Beauty rather than national parks, despite the fact that the former has no recreation objectives in its designation, but the latter does.

Curiously, in the context of policies for agricultural diversification in the wake of the 1986 Agriculture Act, the non-encouragement of recreation on agricultural land was as important in 1992 as it was in 1985. Only three of the 54 plans reviewed made any distinction in this respect between lower and higher grades of agricultural land. Threatened areas outside of designated areas had little significance in the 1992 survey, as places where recreation was not to be encouraged.

In general terms, then, land area policies for recreation tend to be at the restraint end of the restraint – development continuum in structure plans, with land areas susceptible to provision being generally of the poorest environmental quality. Three criticisms may be levelled at this policy orientation of diverting recreation to ordinary or low-value landscapes. First, these landscapes clearly do not maximize consumer satisfactions from countryside recreation in the way that the ethos of Dower (1945) and Hobhouse (1947a), for national parks, had intended. Policies that were more development than restraint orientated would seek to provide the recreationist with more gratifying landscapes wherever possible.

Second, various categories of derelict land are commonly proposed, as areas of recreation potential, as a means of minimizing environmental impact. These areas, however, are increasingly seen as areas or emerging environmental significance, particularly in the light of the impoverishment of ecological values in the agricultural countryside as a result of modern farming practice (Bradshaw, 1979; Spray, 1984). Recreation policies in structure plans often underestimate the ecological value of derelict land.

Third, as Fitton (1979) maintains, this policy orientation is often borne out of a fear of the ecological problems that might have been expected as a result of the 'recreation explosion'. There is evidence to suggest, however, that this fear is largely overstated. As Sidaway and O'Connor (1978, pp. 120–1) conclude in their study of recreation pressures in the countryside:

> Pressure on the countryside is often inferred. . . . We would not deny that such pressures existed (or indeed still exist), but question whether the limited evidence quoted is symptomatic of conditions in general.

This issue is considered more fully in the following chapter.

7.3.3 Policies for facilities and activities

As for land areas, policies for facilities or activities were placed on a restraint–development continuum in the 1985 survey, by classifying them into those that would be restricted, and those that would not. Those facilities or activities that were actually identified with an intention to restrict them were not commonly noted in plans, but where they were, they were done so as to minimize detrimental impacts. They related to noise, congestion and visual disamenity, as well as to a lack of infrastructure.

In respect of activities and facilities that were not to be restricted, mentioned more commonly in plans, it was generally the case that the more passive the activity, the more likely it was to be proposed for development. These more passive activities were also more likely to be provided directly by the public sector than more active and sports-orientated pursuits. They were also the ones that were more likely to attract grant-aid from the Countryside Commission. Commonly, encouragement was given to the development and rationalization of the rights of way network.

In the 1992 survey, again greater environmental qualification was given to the consideration of all recreation facilities, but the same pattern emerged as in 1985. Greater prominence, however, was given to activities that actively would be restricted, particularly in relation to water sports and noisy pursuits. In a number of plans, restraint policies appeared to pertain for all facilities, as in Humberside (1988, p. 76):

> Recreation facilities will normally be permitted in built-up areas; . . . if there are no suitable sites there . . . they will normally be considered favourably in urban fringe locations; . . . facilities which cannot reasonably be located in or on the fringes of built up areas will be considered favourably elsewhere, if they are acceptable in terms of their effect on the environment.

In terms of those facilities that were to be encouraged, a much greater focus was placed on the public rights of way network, with the majority of authorities asserting their responsibility for maintenance, and the updating of the definitive map. Many authorities proposed defining new recreational routes, of all lengths, and the creation of circular routes. Of particular importance, here, was the expressed intention to liaise with farmers and landowners, as well as district authorities and parish councils.

Correspondingly less prominence was given to the development of country parks and other site-based facilities, reflecting both the policies of the Countryside Commission, and the attitudes of the general public articulated in Chapter 4. Where they were proposed, country parks were principally to act as diversionary facilities, but were less likely actually to be provided by the public sector. A significant increase in prominence was also given to the permissibility of developing golf courses, both in response to increasing demand and agricultural diversification, despite the fact that farmland was a land area where recreation generally was not to be encouraged. Again, such proposals were commonly accompanied by environmental qualifications.

7.4 STRUCTURE PLANS: OTHER PLANNING ISSUES

7.4.1 Major influences over policy formulation

From the 1985 survey of structure plans, it was possible to discern from policy statements some of the principal influences over policy formulation. Minimizing resource costs was the most important of these, in line with Healey's (1983) contention. In this respect, principal consideration was given to the provision of facilities that would attract grant aid, especially country parks and picnic sites. Elsewhere, the promotion of facilities was most positive, where they were likely actually to be provided by the private or voluntary sectors.

By 1992, minimizing resource costs had become a clearer priority still. A number of authorities suggested that investment in countryside recreation could not be sustained at historic levels, but most stressed the increasing need to work in partnership both with other public authorities and the private sector. Unlike in 1985, these more recent plans commonly prioritized policies for execution if, and when, resources became available.

Of other major influences, minimizing environmental impact was considered to be important, alongside making use of underutilized land. Recreation was commonly seen as offering the potential to solve other land-use problems. Simple opportunism was also evident in a number of plans where recreation provision would be undertaken as appropriate sites became available.

Some use was also made of planning standards in policy formulation. The most common of these related to golf courses, where the Sports Council standard of one 18-hole golf course to 30 000 population was used. Occasionally, as in Essex (1982), for example, reference was rather curiously made to an unattributed 'countryside open space' standard of 8 acres per 100000 population within the county. A number of coastal counties, too, made reference to space standards for harbours, and mooring densities for boats. Lincolnshire (1979) stood alone in applying design and layout standards to facilities. Here, picnic sites were to be greater than 0.5 hectares, but less than 10 hectares. Inland dingy sailing should have a minimum of 6 hectares of water at a depth of not less than 1.5 metres.

In all of these influences, then, the formulation of recreation policies appears to pay scant regard to people's demands and needs, despite an acknowledgement of them in the presumptions upon which policies are based. This may well derive from the difficulties of identifying demands and needs empirically, but it also represents a tradition of planning to standards, a style championed by the Advisory Sports Council in 1965, and other resource and environmental objectives, rather than consumer preferences. The limitations of this are particularly stark in the case of golf, where a considerable growth in the popularity of the game has been evident during the 1980s (Royal and Ancient, 1987) and yet the same standard ratio of courses to population has been the basis of provision during the same period.

7.4.2 Regionalism

Another significant attribute of recreation policies in structure plans lies in a recognition of the importance of adopting a regional perspective in plan formulation. The majority of plans in both the 1985 and 1992 surveys recognized the importance of recreation as a migratory activity and that the recreation destinations of the population were often in different counties than their origins. Thus, North Yorkshire's recreation policies were essentially catering for the needs of the urban Cleveland population. The Peak District National Park, as was the case 50 years before, was catering for the countryside recreation aspirations of the metropolitan areas of Sheffield and Manchester.

In recognition of this, many structure-plan recreation policies promoted liaison between contiguous counties, particularly in respect of policy formulation and the joint use of resources. In many places, this work was to be conducted through a joint committee, permissible under the 1968 Countryside Act, such as the Standing Conference of South Pennine Authorities, and liaison with regional planning agencies such as the Forestry Commission, the Countryside Commission, the Sports Council and the Regional Councils for Sport and Recreation.

A number of problems, however, can be noted with this approach. First, joint committees, because they do not actually belong to any particular authority, tend to be a low priority in the decision-making of county councils. The phasing of plans is also a problem, where individual authorities produce structure plans at different times. Co-ordination also adds a different layer of complexity to decision-making, for a structure plan topic that is already a residual priority for most structure planning authorities. The ineffectual nature of the Regional Councils for Sport and Recreation, too, noted in Chapter 6, has not eased this aspiration for strategic recreation planning at a regional scale.

7.4.3 Local plans

Nearly all of the structure plans in the 1985 survey made reference to the means of implementing strategic policies for recreation through local plans. Of particular importance in this respect, proposed by a number of authorities, was the need to produce local subject plans, often specifically for the countryside. Here, counties commonly proposed their production jointly with district authorities, or in some cases, even contiguous counties.

Although the undertaking to produce local plans was less common in the 1992 survey, there was a perceptible shift away from proposals to produce subject plans to proposals for 'action area' plans for particular pressured recreation areas. These embraced regional parks, heritage coasts and parts of Areas of Outstanding Natural Beauty, as well as non-designated areas.

Unfortunately, this opportunity to produce statutory subject and action area plans for the implementation of recreation policies is now lost. The 1991 Planning and Compensation Act, in allowing the production only of district (or national park) wide local plans removes the facility for the production of statutory recreation or countryside subject and action area plans. The loss of such a planning instrument may have created a vacuum to be filled by informal countryside and countryside recreation strategies. In fact, one of the principal differences between the 1985 and 1992 surveys of structure plans in this respect lies in a reduction of proposals for local plans for recreation and increased reference to the production of countryside strategies.

7.5 COUNTRYSIDE STRATEGIES: FORM AND PURPOSE

Advice from government agencies on the production of countryside and countryside recreation strategies is ambiguous. A number of regional sport and recreation strategies of the Regional Councils for Sport and Recreation advocate that all local authorities (county, district and metropolitan) should produce general recreation strategies for both urban and rural areas (for example Yorkshire and Humberside Regional Council for Sport and Recreation, 1989). The Sports Council (1991b) proposes the production of sport and recreation strategies specifically at the district level.

A number of such strategies have been produced at levels other than the county. Some 14 metropolitan authorities have produced countryside recreation strategies and a further 9 countryside strategies. Ten of the former have been produced in the north-west, possibly inspired by the Greater Manchester Countryside Unit, a vestige of the old metropolitan county, disbanded in the mid-1980s, which advises the metropolitan districts particularly on the strategic components of unitary development plans. There has been a history of joint working in this field both during and after the life of the Greater Manchester Council. There is some evidence, too, that a number of non-metropolitan district authorities are producing both countryside and countryside recreation strategies (Sutcliffe, 1992).

The Countryside Commission (1987b) on the other hand proposes that county authorities produce 'countryside recreation strategies – which might form part of a wider strategy for the countryside, or a rural development strategy'. Other Commission (1989b) documentation, however, suggests the production at a county level of a more general 'policy for the countryside' which might include conservation and development proposals as well as those for countryside recreation.

The purpose of strategies, too, is seen as being different by different organizations. The Countryside Policy Review Panel (Countryside Commission, 1987a) considers that they should contain, among other things 'recreation objectives and policies for the use of rural land'. The Rural Development Commission (1991c) on the other hand sees them as a natural development from their own Tourism Development Action Programmes. English Nature (1991) sees them as a means of implementing policies in the government environmental White Paper *This Common Inheritance* (Department of the Environment, 1990b).

The Countryside Policy Review Panel (Countryside Commission, 1987a) suggests that strategies should not be produced before the issue of Department of the Environment advice. However, this has not been forthcoming, and the Countryside Commission (Stansfield, 1990) is unclear about what kind of lead it should take in issuing advice without guidance from central government. There has thus been no guidance, save from informal advice from Countryside Commission regional offices (Sutcliffe, 1992) on the form and content of any type of strategy, a factor considered by Scott Planning Services (1990) to have inhibited their formulation. Although not directed specifically at countryside or countryside recreation strategies, the Secretary of State, under the 1991 Act, does consider all informal plans an unsatisfactory basis on which to determine development decisions. The issue of what constitutes 'development' in recreation terms is, however, itself ambiguous as has been noted above.

As a result of all of these statements, the form, content, and purpose, particularly of countryside strategies, is very variable. Of all extant countryside strategies to mid-1992, two-thirds of them claimed to have been triggered principally by agricultural change and diversification. The next most common motivation for their production was increasing pressures for recreation and access, and a third related to general environmental concerns.

The motivation for producing countryside recreation strategies was quite different in the survey conducted of all extant strategies to mid-1992. In all cases they were a direct response to the Countryside Commission's (1987b, 1987c) 'Enjoying the Countryside' policy proposals, often overtly recognizing that their production would enhance grant-aid allocations from the Commission. All Welsh counties were contacted directly by the (then) Countryside Commission Committee for Wales in this respect which, perhaps, accounted for their frequent production there. Nearly all resultant countryside recreation strategy proposals reflected those of the Commission, except in one case, Gwent (1989), which, although keen to adopt the Commission's strategic approach to planning, also rather nervously stated that it:

> does not altogether endorse the Commission's policies and pro- posals and hopes that the Commission will take a sympathetic account of the differences of circumstances and opinions within the county (p. 2).

7.5.1 Planning in partnership

A principal planning style of nearly all countryside and countryside recreation strategies, unlike structure plans, was to be **integrative** of a wide number of interests in the countryside and therefore to produce integrated strategic policies to guide action by a wide number of agen- cies and not just county councils. Strategies invariably were initiated by county authorities (Sutcliffe, 1992), and some counties were openly seeking to use strategies to increase their sphere of influence over other organizations, but the essential thrust of strategies was one of partner- ship, although the detail of partnership arrangements varied between strategies. The ethos of this is summarized by Suffolk (1992, p. 8):

> Partnership is fundamental. . . . the county council as an elected authority has a vital enabling role to co-ordinate the efforts of a wide range of individuals and organizations in joint schemes, that include farmers, voluntary groups and district councils. In formu- lating the strategy, consultation will take place with these interest groups.

Co-operative working was proffered in all strategies in four main areas. The first of these was in strategy or policy formulation. A number of strategies had been produced jointly by several organizations (three countryside strategies and four countryside recreation strategies), in- cluding district authorities, national parks, the Forestry Commission and water companies, as well as landowners, voluntary organizations, user groups and several departments within county councils. All others had been produced by county councils, but involved wide consultation with interested parties. South Glamorgan, for example, sent its draft strategy to over 100 national and local groups.

Many countryside recreation strategies were thus seen as on-going documents representing a new trend in collaborative planning. In Hereford and Worcester (1991b, p. 23), for example, the strategy was seen as:

a continuing policy vehicle for all agencies in the county which are involved in countryside recreation.

Second, in respect of implementation, where detailed proposals for implementation were offered, these were universally to be executed in partnership, as in Clwyd (1990, p. 3):

> if the proposals in this document are to take place, positive action is needed from a wide variety of public, private and voluntary bodies. The co-operation of all local authorities, the farming and land managing community and conservation interests must be gained.

District councils, the Countryside Commission, farmers and landowners were most frequently cited in this respect, but also the Forestry Commission, the Sports Council, the British Waterways Board, user groups, parish councils and transport operators were all frequently mentioned. Sutcliffe's (1992) survey suggests that 60% of all strategies had formally constituted implementation groups associated with them.

In respect of implementation, over half of countryside strategies included an integral programme of works, with annual or less frequent reviews proposed. In countryside recreation strategies, there was a greater degree of variation in implementation proposals, with some suggesting that the strategy was not concerned with implementation, as in Surrey (1990, p. 3):

> the strategy does not commit the participating authorities to a rigid work programme or expenditure: instead it provides a framework for action within which new initiatives can emerge, for which it is hoped funding will become available,

but others, as in Buckinghamshire (1989, p. 3), deliberately set out to:

> guide and co-ordinate a programme of action on the ground.

Other countryside recreation strategies proposed leaving the development of detailed programmes of work to participating organizations. As a third element of partnership, countryside strategies in particular commonly proposed the establishment of a countryside forum, as a steering group to monitor and adjust the strategy.

Finally, there were proposals in all strategies for partnership to achieve a more effective use of resources, as in Lancashire (1988, p. 23), where the purpose of the strategy was:

> to continue to attract, and make even greater use of, government grants . . . and capitalise on the extremely good value to budgets of sharing costs.

In countryside strategies, statements about resource partnerships were generally restricted to this efficiency in the sharing and integration of resources. In countryside recreation strategies, on the other hand, an exploration of sources of grant-aid funding was often undertaken, from district councils, the Forestry Commission, tourist boards, the Rural Development Commission and the European Community, but particularly the Countryside Commission. Indeed, a number of these strategies couched proposals in the form of grant-aid applications to the Commission.

Despite these notions of partnership in resourcing, only three countryside strategies proffered an increased level of expenditure in the implementation of proposals. Where this was declared, it was invariably to fund a move from site-based management to area-based work. A number of countryside recreation strategies admitted that resources for the implementation of the strategy were not currently available, as in Lancashire (1988, p. 23):

> [the strategy] represents aspirations for the future; targets towards which the County Council will work as and when resources become available.

Because of this, many felt that local-authority funding could only be pump-priming as a means of attracting other investment for the implementation of the strategy, as in Buckinghamshire (1989, p. 68):

> it is important that public money be used to best effect . . . as a pump primer for drawing other investment into the area as part of a joint funding arrangement to develop projects on private land.

Hereford and Worcester (1991b), however, was less optimistic about securing funds from other, particularly government, sources. Changes in Countryside Commission grant-aid arrangements, as part of the 'Enjoying the Countryside' proposals, towards overall 'packages' rather than individual proposals, and away from core funding, had led it to suggest that:

> the change is fundamental, as it places the onus on local authorities to absorb the continued funding of existing schemes, eventually without grant-aid (p. 23).

Interestingly, perhaps, very few strategies of either type promulgated any partnership with contiguous local authorities. This appears to negate the importance of recreation as a migratory activity.

7.5.2 Countryside strategies, countryside recreation strategies and structure plans

Both types of informal strategy were seen either as providing inputs to the statutory structure planning process or complements to it, or both.

A third of all countryside strategies claimed that they were to feed into structure plan reviews, but the majority of all strategies were designed to offer guidance on matters that fell outside structure planning jurisdiction, as in Hereford and Worcester (1991b, p. 1):

> the scope of policies in structure plans has been circumscribed by Government guidance in PPG15 . . . and is now more narrow than previously. The strategy is therefore devoted to stating and elaborating on (structure plan) policies and supplementing them with other supporting policies, guide-lines, justifications and action.

For countryside recreation, therefore, most strategies focused on non-land-use issues out of statutory jurisdiction, as in Northamptonshire (1990, p. 2):

> such documents [structure plans] cannot address the management, organizational and implementation issues which have such a vital influence on what actually happens in the countryside.

They also focused more clearly on policies of positive action rather than development control, the principal concern of structure plans, as in Cheshire (1991, p. 3):

> The rural strategy is wider in scope and designed to stimulate positive action, rather than set out policies to control development.

Thus strategies were designed to run in tandem with structure plans focusing on non-land-use issues and action agendas not associated with development control decision-making. Despite this, only one strategy – Hereford and Worcester – had been produced in tandem with the structure plan.

7.6 COUNTRYSIDE STRATEGIES: SCOPE AND CONTENT

7.6.1 Overall aims

The recreation content of countryside strategies was very variable, from scant mention in the Northamptonshire (1990) strategy, where it was considered within the umbrella of 'countryside services', to Leicestershire (1989, p. 2), where it resembles a countryside recreation strategy:

> [the strategy] is primarily directed at the way the countryside can meet the recreation and leisure needs of Leicestershire people.

Most overall aims for countryside recreation in countryside strategies were not overtly stated because of the integrative nature of the documents. Most commonly, more holistic aims were put forward, stressing a balance between different rural activities, as in Bedfordshire (1990, p. 2):

> critically important will be the need to ensure that countryside activities can co-exist and complement each other, rather than conflict, as is so often the case.

But some countryside strategies focused more squarely on the concerns of the rural economy, as in Northamptonshire (1990, p. 2):

> the paramount need is for agricultural production and the need to maintain the rural economy.

Where specific recreation objectives were stated, they were positive, but usually restricted to general exhortation, as in Shropshire (1991, p. 23) where the aim for recreation was to:

> improve access, recreational and sporting opportunities for all groups in the community.

The aims of countryside recreation strategies were much more uniform. All but two of these strategies were restricted to a consideration of informal recreation, particularly public rights of way and country parks. Although only half produced explicit overall aims, the key issues in each were almost identical. First, there was seen to be a need to provide a balance between recreation and conservation objectives, as in South Glamorgan (1990, p. 4):

> The philosophy of this strategy has been based on the twin objectives of i) improving access to a range of countryside facilities and reducing conflict, while ii) protecting sensitive areas of the countryside.

Second, there was a keenness to adhere to the Countryside Commission's 'Enjoying the Countryside' or 'Recreation 2000' policies as in Lancashire (1988, p. 5) and Durham (1989, p. 2):

> The fundamental purpose is to respond to the spirit, challenge and philosophy of the Countryside Commission's Recreation 2000 initiative.

> The Commission's objective as explained in Recreation 2000 is therefore adopted in this strategy.

7.6.2 Recreation policies: principal areas of concern

Although the treatment of countryside recreation was very different across countryside strategies, with varying presentational styles and varying levels of detail, it was possible to rank their principal areas of concern. This is done in Table 7.4.

Public rights of way were of principal concern in all countryside strategies. Commonly considered issues here included the completion of the definitive map, the promotion of recreational routes, better access for cyclists and horse-riders, the use of disused railway lines and similar routes, and the whole area of liaison and co-operation. All but one strategy considered promotion and awareness a priority and all but three specific recreation sites. In this respect, sites were seen by a majority of strategies as 'gateways' to the wider countryside.

Countryside recreation strategies exhibited a greater variability in the expression of principal areas of concern. Some remained strategic in their proposals but others contained extensive and detailed management recommendations. The principal areas, too, were wide-ranging, including funding arrangements, impacts on local communities, social issues, legal issues and so on. To the extent that a classification of principal areas of concern did exist, most strategies used the Countryside Commission's (1987b) enumeration 'people', 'places' and 'making things happen'.

Under 'people', over half of the countryside recreation strategies again used the Commission's categories of 'improving awareness', 'promoting understanding' and 'creating confidence and ability'. The others rolled these up into more singular priorities relating to improving information and interpretation facilities. For 'place', public rights of way were a universal priority, although there was great variability in the extent to which different counties would be able to achieve Countryside Commission targets by the year 2000. All but one strategy also prioritized the development and management of country parks although some strategies expressed concern about the adequacy of resources to achieve such priorities, as in Dyfed (1989, p. 5):

> the problem in most cases, however, is that the level of wardening and ranger staff is only barely adequate to cover essential site operations within existing country parks.

Other areas considered under 'place' included the wider countryside, water areas and village communities. For 'making things happen', most strategies echoed the Commission's views in relation to the need for more co-ordinated and cost-effective recreation management. Outside this Commission taxonomy, public transport for improved access to the countryside, and the need to serve the whole of the population and not just specific groups, were articulated in a third of all strategies. The need to provide affordable accommodation and the need to seek a balance between conservation and recreation, particularly in sensitive areas, were mentioned in a smaller number of strategies.

Table 7.4 Countryside strategies: principal areas of concern

Key topic areas and policies in countryside strategies (number of strategies in which topics occurred, out of a total of 15 strategies)

Predominant concerns

Access and public rights of way	15
Promotion, awareness, education and interpretation	14
Recreation sites and country parks	12

Social policies

Minority and disadvantaged groups	5
Public transport policies	4

Other activities and land areas

Noisy and intrusive sports	6
Water recreation	5
Cycling	4
Accommodation for long-distance walks	3
Horseriding	2
Urban fringe	2

Management and implementation

Co-operation, development of countryside forums	4
Preparation of countryside recreation strategies	3
Countryside management and ranger services	3
Local/community involvement (especially in PROW work)	2
Releasing recreational potential of land	2

In enumerating these priorities, both countryside strategies and countryside recreation strategies had been successful in focusing on non-land-use issues that fell beyond the jurisdiction of the structure plan. This was particularly the case in relation to education, promotion and interpretation as well as social issues, and those concerned with management and implementation.

7.6.3 The potential of informal strategic planning

There would appear to be two principal advantages in the development of informal planning strategies for countryside recreation in England and Wales since 1988. The first of these is that they allow a fuller consideration of non-land-use policies for countryside recreation that fall beyond the remit of statutory planning. A brief review of their content indicates that most strategies have been successful in achieving this. Importantly, the underlying ethos of these informal strategies is much less restrictive than that in structure plans, with an emphasis on positive management in provision, rather than restraint.

Their success in this respect may legitimate their existence as informal plans. Although the 1991 Planning and Compensation Act considers all informal plans as an unsatisfactory basis upon which to make development decisions, strategies for recreation encompass, by and large, non-development issues and to a large degree distance themselves from matters of development control. The 1991 Act passes no comment about the legitimacy of informal plans in this context.

Second, they do appear to exhibit success in collaborative plan making, between a wide variety of interested parties, at a number of stages in the planning process. Sutcliffe's (1992) study indicates that this is one of the principal benefits of strategies as perceived by authorities themselves, alongside the ability to undertake longer term planning for countryside recreation, the opportunity to target resources effectively and the enhanced opportunity for grant-aid provision. In addition, simply doing the exercise itself assists in achieving co-operation.

But a number of problems in relation to strategies of both types endure. The first of these is the confusion in advice on strategy formulation offered by government agencies. Views on their form and purpose vary widely both in terms of the local-authority level at which they should be generated, and what they should contain. Guidance on their scope and content is lacking. The production of countryside recreation strategies appears to have been more coherent and consistent than countryside strategies in terms of both form and purpose, because of the availability of a more singular policy statement from the Countryside Commission. General countryside strategies appear to be less-well directed and more variable, driven more by uncertainties in the statutory planning system than by any clear guidance offered.

While the relationship to structure plans appears to be compatible in the case of most strategies, there is some doubt, in the content of strategies, as to whether they are really strategic planning documents at all in many cases or, rather, area-based management plans. As informal plans, too, they are always likely to be a residual attractor of resources, relative to authorities' statutory responsibilities towards structure plans.

Countryside recreation strategies in particular have been seen as necessary by the Countryside Commission as more systematic vehicles for the distribution of grant aid. Whatever the motivations for producing these strategies have generally been on the part of local authorities, the Commission has championed them principally because grant-aid allocations on the basis of statutory structure and local plans have been less than successful. This has been due, in part at least, to the residual priority and the land-use focus of countryside recreation policies in statutory plans (Countryside Commission, 1990c).

This means that countryside recreation strategies, at least, are grant-aid driven, with advice from Commission regional offices, at one extreme, summing to little more than 'no strategy, no grant' (Sutcliffe, 1992). Grant-led planning runs a grave danger of being sub-optimal relative to other considerations such as people's needs and aspirations, and local circumstances. Only in the case of the Gwent strategy has an authority been prepared to offer a critique of some of the Commission's requirements, and even here the tone is somewhat apologetic, possibly for fear of prejudicing grant allocations.

Such an approach to plan-making must also present problems for the Commission itself in two main respects. First, if a strategy is produced in exact conformity to Commission requirements, the grounds for refusing grant aid are severely weakened. Is the production of a strategy, of itself, sufficient to justify grant allocations? This could provide difficulties in allocation mechanisms if central government apportionment to the Commission is itself curtailed, with the danger of an accusation of false promises.

Second, since the geographical distribution of strategies is patchy and by no means universal, the Commission faces the dilemma as to whether grants are given only to authorities producing strategies, despite the possible obvious worth of initiatives in other areas. Is the non-production of a strategy, of itself, sufficient to refuse grant allocations? There is a danger here that grant aid is based on procedures rather than intended outcomes.

7.7 COUNTRYSIDE RECREATION AND STRATEGIC PLANNING

The story of strategic planning for countryside recreation, then, is one of a statutory process, through structure plans, which is based on presumptions about behaviour. These have been used principally to assert a growth in participation, which has been shown in Chapter 4 not to be the case, which in turn has led to, or even legitimated, a dominant presence of restrictive policies, supporting proposition 4 of this book (p. xiii). The ineffectual nature of government advice for land-use planning has done little to alter this ethos.

The importance of a fuller understanding of behaviour is not to provide social or 'people' policies within structure plans, but land-use policies that provide people with what they want. This has by and large not occurred, because of earlier fears of a recreation explosion and more recent preoccupations with environmentalism.

Rather than basing policies on an understanding of people's demands and preferences, structure plan policies have been driven by minimizing resource costs, minimizing environmental impacts, making use of underutilized land and planning standards, all of which have reinforced restrictive structure plan policies and have made helping people to enjoy themselves a low priority.

The statutory planning system also has a number of inherent limitations in the formulation of recreation policies. It is restricted to land-use considerations, when many of the issues of importance to countryside recreation do not constitute 'development' in the statutory sense. Many recreation issues also involve the management of people which are, strictly, beyond the remit of development plans. Furthermore, many countryside recreation issues are of the 'smaller scale', which are not easily dealt with in strategic planning.

Because of this last point in particular, history has repeated itself. The 1968 Countryside Act failed to anticipate the recreation issues of the 1970s and 1980s and as a result, countryside recreation management was spawned as an informal mechanism to fill the statutory void. From the late 1980s statutory strategic planning has been found wanting and the use of subject and action area local plans for recreation has been terminated. In this respect, Glyptis (1991) has been able to conclude that statutory planning has tended to adjust to, rather than anticipate, recreation demands. As a result more positive informal countryside strategies have taken over.

Thus again it would appear that statutory mechanisms have failed to anticipate recreation issues, and attempts at their resolution have been left to informal mechanisms. Such mechanisms, however, remain largely unregulated, under resourced and subject to the vagaries of individual enthusiasms. They remain a residual priority relative to statutory responsibilities and run the risk of being largely grant-aid driven. This appears a rather fragile basis for the cutting edge of recreation planning and there would seem a *prima facie* case for placing these current informal mechanisms on a firmer statutory footing.

The Countryside Commission has been instrumental in instigating both of these phases of informal planning. It was the Commission that instigated countryside management through a series of experiments, and it was the Commission too, according to Coalter (1985) that by the beginning of the 1980s had abandoned its interest in statutory planning. By the mid 1980s it had been a prime mover in proposing, even coercing through grant-aid stipulations, the development of countryside recreation strategies.

Underlying all of these developments in land-use planning has been a preoccupation with the damage that increased participation would cause to the countryside and the environmental or conservation imperative that must take precedence over such activities. The extent to which these have been legitimate concerns for the recreation planner provide the focus for the following chapter.

8

Recreation and the environment

In exploring the relationship between recreation and the environment more fully, this chapter develops two themes. First, it considers this relationship in public policy by assessing the relative importance accorded to recreation compared to conservation and other environmental factors in policy and legislation. Second, it investigates this relationship 'on the ground' by evaluating evidence in relation to the environmental impacts of recreation – the damage that it does to the countryside. It is upon the presumption of this environmental damage that the ethos of statutory land-use planning for countryside recreation has been largely based.

8.1 RECREATION AND CONSERVATION PRIORITIES IN PUBLIC POLICY

8.1.1 Amenity and scientific conservation

The history of policy and legislation for the countryside shows that recreation and conservation invariably have been considered in tandem. This is possibly because, as has been noted in the preface, the conservation of landscapes and ecosystems to a large degree constitutes the supply side of the rural leisure equation. It is concerned with those things that people wish to consume as part of the leisure experience.

But within this general area of policy, just as recreation and access have been clearly distinguished in policy formulation, amenity conservation and scientific conservation have also been disaggregated in the development of policies and the provision of statutes. By the 1930s, for example, pressures for the protection of the countryside had devolved into two distinct schools. Although they were never to be totally discrete, amenity bodies such as the National Trust and the (then) Councils for the Preservation of Rural England and Wales were championing aesthetic and ethical conservation values. The British Correlating Committee, in contrast, which had been set up in 1924 to represent a range of scientific groups, was extolling the scientific and ecological conservation cause (Woods, 1984).

In preparation for the 1949 Act, too, Hobhouse, in addition to his national parks and footpaths committees, set up a further committee to distinguish amenity from scientific conservation. He took the amenity brief himself, twinning it with recreation, and set up a separate 'nature conservation' committee, chaired by Sir Julian Huxley. Even through the passage of the Bill, nature conservation provisions were passed by both Houses of Parliament with relatively little discussion – few felt competent to dispute their scientific basis. The provisions proposed no threat to local authorities and were to cost little. It was felt that if scientists needed small corners of the countryside to get on with their research, so be it. Amenity conservation measures, on the other hand, were hotly debated. Everyone felt that they had something to say about the aesthetic worth of the countryside.

Provisions for the two types of conservation were clearly distinct as a result of the 1949 Act. National parks and Areas of Outstanding Natural Beauty were to serve the amenity interest, together with then little-used provisions to negotiate management agreements for landscape purposes, and were seen to be inextricably linked with access and public enjoyment. National Nature Reserves (NNRs) and Sites of Special Scientific Interest (SSSIs) were provisions for scientific conservation and were to be largely exclusionary. Local nature reserves, which were to be designated by local authorities, were the one scientific designation that was generally to tolerate access.

Even through the institutional framework, with the National Parks Commission (later the Countryside Commission) taking the amenity conservation role, and the Nature Conservancy (later the Nature Conservancy Council and more recently, English Nature) that of scientific conservation, the two types of conservation were clearly distinguished. By the 1968 Act the newly formed Countryside Commission was to have responsibility for the enhancement of natural beauty and amenity, but scientific conservation responsibilities were more ubiquitous – every minister, government department and public body was to have regard to the desirability of conserving fauna and flora.

The 1973 Nature Conservancy Council Act contained only scientific conservation provisions, much to do with organizational matters as a result of a split between research and advisory functions. The 1981 Wildlife and Countryside Act (and its amendments in 1985), however, represented a significant development in amenity conservation ends by introducing new-style management agreements with which to negotiate, in the last resort compulsorily, landscape changes. The renotification of SSSIs provided a discrete scientific conservation component to the Act as did a wide range of new species protection measures. The 1986 Agriculture Act extended the responsibility for amenity conservation to all government ministers.

Amenity and scientific conservation, then, as well as recreation and access, have been distinct in their legislative, policy and institutional evolution. This disaggregation has often caused ineffectiveness, animosity and the compromising of one set of objectives relative to another. In particular, it provided the opportunity for both recreation and access objectives to be residualized and conservation ones to be accorded a clear priority.

8.1.2 Residualizing the recreation and access imperative

This priority for conservation objectives began with amenity conservation being the main preoccupation in the passage of the 1949 Act. This was because, although it was agreed that controlling development would be the principal means through which amenity landscapes would be sustained in national parks and AONBs, there was much dispute about who should be vested with these development control powers – should they be nationally or locally based? Such a dispute, which has never been satisfactorily resolved, has ensured that, certainly for these two designations, amenity conservation objectives always have been at the forefront of rural leisure imperatives and subject to close scrutiny. At the same time, as has been noted in Chapter 1, the landowning interest in Parliament ensured that recreation, and particularly access provisions, were eroded.

By the 1960s, the fears of a recreation explosion allowed the elevation of conservation objectives during the passage of the 1968 Countryside Act through Parliament. Although the Bill was 'first and foremost about opportunities for the enjoyment of the countryside' (Department of the Environment, 1967), a number of conservation considerations were inserted during the Committee stage of the Bill. Principal among these was the extension of the powers of the new Countryside Commission to cover 'the enhancement of natural beauty and amenity' (Department of the Environment, 1967). As was noted in Chapter 1, the Bill itself contained only recreation and access functions for the Commission. Further amendments were proposed during the Committee stage of the Bill that were clearly attempting to adjust the relative priorities of recreation and conservation. A number of these simply attempted to reverse the order of the wording to place conservation in front of recreation when the two were considered together (Curry, 1986a).

In the early 1970s, the failure of the development control system to stem landscape deterioration adequately, brought about particularly by agriculture and forestry intensification, led to the prioritization of amenity conservation becoming more formalized. The National Park Policies Review Committee (Sandford, 1974), in reviewing the policies of national parks, proposed that where the two were in unavoidable conflict, conservation should take priority over recreation. This was reaffirmed by the Countryside Review Committee (1977) three years later which saw recreation as a 'threat' to the conserved landscape that should be 'controlled' by careful management. Conservation was seen as an objective of policy, and recreation as a land-use problem.

Into the 1980s, the continuous drafting and redrafting of the 1981 Wildlife and Countryside Act (Cloke and Park, 1985) ensured a preoccupation with amenity conservation in the debate over management agreements, and simultaneously this priority was being given formal sanction in the Countryside Commission's prospectus (Countryside Commission, 1982a) on accession to grant in aid status under the same Act:

> proportionately rather more of our resources will go into conservation [although] recreation and access will continue to receive a substantial part of our funds (p. 2).

In scientific conservation terms, 231 National Nature Reserves had been designated by 1988 and it is anticipated that there will be in excess of 6000 SSSIs when redesignation under the 1981 Wildlife and Countryside Act is complete. These were to be largely exclusionary under the 1949 Act. Of local nature reserves which were to tolerate access, only 154 have been designated to 1988 (Blunden and Curry, 1990). These designations have been far in excess of designations for country parks and picnic sites of which there are currently just over 200 of each.

During the 1980s the recreation priority was further residualized through the development of confrontation politics in the conservation sphere. This was intelligently orchestrated by articulate conservation pressure groups such as the Council for the Protection of Rural England and Friends of the Earth. The threat of a vanishing countryside engendered the support of the public. With the exception of the Ramblers' Association and the Open Spaces Society, recreation interest groups have been much more disposed to negotiating their individual interests, often with landowners directly, as has been considered in Chapter 4, and frequent disputes and territorial claims between these interest groups have served to weaken their collective cause. There has been no consolidated effort to raise the profile of recreation and access either in terms of public interest or on to the political agenda, to match that of conservation.

By the 1990s, conservation had become a more entrenched policy priority relative to recreation, due in large part to the environmental

White Paper, *This Common Inheritance* (Department of the Environment, 1990b). The principles of this Paper made conservation an entirely pervasive feature of all development plans. PPG 12 (Department of the Environment, 1992c), for example, stipulates that all development plans are to include policies in respect of the conservation of the natural beauty of the land, but, as has been noted in Chapter 6, the roles of countryside recreation and access were to command a much narrower focus.

For national parks, heritage coasts and Areas of Outstanding Natural Beauty, PPG 17 (Department of the Environment, 1991a) stipulates that recreation must always be of second-order importance to conservation objectives. This sentiment is echoed in Countryside Commission (1987b, 1987c) policy statements. Specifically for national parks, the National Parks Review Panel (Edwards, 1991) explicitly proposed the reformulation of national park purposes to give even more weight to conservation and to reduce the relative importance of 'public enjoyment' objectives. Conservation objectives were explicitly to embrace scientific as well as amenity conservation and recreation objectives were to be much more closely tied to the special qualities of parks. Sandford's (1974) priorities – where the two are in conflict conservation must have a clear priority over recreation – were reaffirmed. The report thus called conservation the 'first' purpose of national parks, and recreation the 'second'.

The principal proposals for recreation in the report focused on getting it out of the parks altogether, promoting it in areas surrounding parks, community forests and other areas, and generally 'taking the park to nearby towns and conurbations'. There is little change here in seeing recreation as a land-use problem and seeking to 'control' it in some way – in this case by shifting the burden to other areas. This was despite the fact that there was widespread agreement in the evidence received by the panel that national parks were appropriate for a wide range of active pursuits compatible with the environment.

The AONB policy review of the early 1990s (Smart and Anderson, 1990) also sustains the amenity conservation priority over recreation and access, in accordance with their statutory terms of reference. Perhaps predictably, it suggests that recreation 'pressure' (it is still largely seen as a problem) is most appropriately 'dealt with' through better education and interpretation.

8.2 RECREATION AND CONSERVATION PRIORITIES IN LAND-USE PLANNING AND MANAGEMENT

This priority of amenity and scientific conservation over recreation and access is also evident outside national policy. Even prior to the 1990 White Paper, structure plans placed considerable emphasis on both amenity and scientific conservation, relative to the generally restrictive policies for recreation considered in Chapter 7. For amenity conservation, Penning-Rowsell (1983) identifies 12 different policy instruments relating to amenity objectives across 44 different structure plans. These range from extending protected area status such as Green Belts and Areas of Great Landscape Value to the development of informal management schemes. For scientific conservation, Bain, Dodd and Pritchard (1990) consider a range of different types of structure plan policies relating to its positive development.

By the 1990s, environmental considerations were being used to qualify most recreation policies in structure plans and indeed had a role to play in all policy formulation in plans. This was found to be much more pervasive in the 1992 survey of structure plans, than in the 1985 survey, considered in detail in Chapter 7. A number of plans considered that the environment should take precedence over recreation ubiquitously, as in Berkshire (1991, p. 2):

> All provision is subject to the need to ensure that environmental interests are not damaged by recreational provision or activity.

A similar emphasis has been found in local subject plans. They have been concerned with conservation issues to a much greater extent than those of recreation (Curry, 1985a). Indeed guidance on the production of local plans (Ministry of Housing and Local Government, 1970a) sees the securing of conservation as one of their principal objectives, but where recreation is mentioned, the purpose of local plans is to 'channel and control' the demands of nearby towns. A number of local subject plans have been produced, mainly by county councils, in the late 1970s and 1980s, for the open countryside. A survey by McNab (1985) to the mid 1980s, shows the clear conservation orientation of these plans.

The most common type of rural subject plan, in fact, relates to the control of minerals development. Outside this, however, a majority of plans is concerned with the implementation of positive conservation policies. These frequently relate to Green Belts, but can range from 'Wildlife and Habitats' (for example, Barrow-in-Furness Borough Council, 1980) through 'Special Landscape Areas' (Clwyd County Council, 1979) to a wide range of conservation policies for a whole county (Cornwall County Council, 1983).

Within these conservation orientated plans, recreation is often mentioned, but invariably in the context of restriction and control, Cornwall, for example, develops the notion of 'tourism restraint areas', where recreation and tourism will not be encouraged so as not to further degrade the landscape. Within these subject plans, only a minority relate to recreation directly, and here again plans with a dominance of control policies (for example, Humberside's (1980) 'Coastal Caravans

Plan') are more common than plans mainly concerned with positive promotional policies for recreation (for example Suffolk's (1979) 'Gipping Valley Countryside and Recreation Plan').

Further, in all national parks during the 1980s, expenditure on conservation has exceeded that of recreation. For the financial year 1990/91 expenditure in all parks on conservation and planning to ensure the amenity interest approached 40%. The figure for recreation was just over 20% (Council for the Protection of Rural England, 1990; Countryside Commission, 1990b). In policy terms, where there is a straight choice between the two, the latter invariably prevails. In the North York Moors National Park (1984), quoted in Patmore (1987, p. 100), for example,

> it has never been part of the national park philosophy to match, automatically, recreational demands but rather temper these demands to the ability of the landscape to absorb them.

8.2.1 Recreation management and conservation values

In management terms too, there are understandably clear conservation priorities for AONBs and SSSIs and both national and local nature reserves but recreation objectives at designated recreation sites do not command such obvious recreation priorities. As Brotherton (1975) points out, the 1968 Countryside Act does equate designations such as country parks with protected area status, and site management plans, where they have been produced, do have specific conservation objectives. In national policy (Countryside Commission, 1974a), management for sites such as these is encouraged to have specific regard to conservation objectives, and even may determine whether a park should be broadly conservation or recreation orientated.

Management plans for such sites reflect this encouragement. The bulk of the management plan for Crickley Hill Country Park, for example (Curry, 1983), is concerned with conservation measures for specific areas and habitats within the park. There are even proposals for restrictions on public access where the habitat is considered particularly sensitive. In one possibly extreme case, a country park management plan gives clear priority to conservation objectives above those of recreation. The following from the Frencham Country Park Signpost 2000 report by Hambledon District Council (1973) is quoted in Slee (1982a):

> The first priority must be to retain the existing landscape topography and vegetation in its existing form and subsequent uses must be subordinated to this ideal.

This imbalance in recreation and conservation objectives for recreation and conservation sites might, in part at least, be attributed to a dominance of a conservation philosophy in the training of countryside managers (Slee, 1982b).

8.2.2 The legitimacy of recreation and conservation priorities

When land-use planning and individual site management are considered in tandem in national policy, both amenity and scientific conservation have been accorded a clear priority over recreation and access considerations, confirming the fifth proposition of this book. This can be seen historically to have been driven by factors that have suppressed the recreation imperative – landowning interests in Parliament and fears of a recreation explosion – as well as those that have stimulated conservation priorities, such as the environmental White Paper 'This Common Inheritance' (Department of the Environment, 1990b).

This priority, however, is to a degree questionable. First, although the importance of the conservation imperative in absolute terms is not in doubt, its principal justification lies in countering the ravages of agricultural and forestry intensification and other developments in the countryside, rather than recreation. Second, since both amenity and scientific conservation can be considered, in part at least, to represent the supply side of the recreation equation, there seems little logic in investing in conservation measures while at the same time suppressing the opportunity to consume or experience them. Even in 1942, Professor Dennison, in his minority report to the Scott Committee (Scott, 1942), could see little logic in conserving landscapes and ecosystems, unless they were to be available for the population at large, as the quote from his report in Chapter 1 clearly indicates. Third, suppressing the recreation interest for conservation ends, particularly evident in more recent structure plans, is predicated on the notion that recreation offers a real threat to the conserved countryside (Curry, 1986b). It is the legitimacy of this supposition that forms the focus for the remainder of this chapter.

8.3 RECREATION DAMAGE TO THE COUNTRYSIDE: RESEARCH EVIDENCE

Throughout this book, government and other public-sector sources have been cited as being preoccupied with a concern that a continuing growth in recreation participation would cause increasing environmental damage to the countryside. At least two factors serve to undermine this preoccupation. First, from evidence of the **public's** attitude to recreation, discussed in Chapter 4, the public does not share the concern of the policy-maker that recreation is a threat to amenity, certainly relative to development and agriculture. Second, it has been shown in the same chapter that recreation participation has not grown during the 1980s, and has in fact declined slightly.

8.3.1 The nature of research into recreation damage

The nature of these recreation participation patterns has influenced studies of environmental impact. When recreation was growing, during the 1970s, impact studies tended to focus initially on visual and aesthetic intrusion. Later (Shoard, 1978), they turned to the impacts on wildlife and ecology, focusing on vegetation and more specifically the impact of trampling, but also the impact on fauna, particularly birds. Earlier research was also concerned with the consideration and definition of 'carrying capacity', often attempting to derive unique formulae for the relationship between participation levels and damage minimization.

Glyptis (1991) defines four types of carrying capacity. **Physical capacity** relates to when a site is literally full, and although it is useful for things such as the design of car parks, of itself it says little about recreational impact. **Economic carrying capacity** can either define a level of visitor use beyond which economic damage is inflicted on associated land uses, or a minimum level below which a facility is not viable. **Perceptual or social carrying capacity** relates to people's perceptions of other users and the extent to which this affects their enjoyment. To a large degree this is self-regulating since when people's enjoyment is sufficiently impaired they will cease to remain at the site, thus reducing numbers.

It was **ecological carrying capacity**, however, that formed the principal preoccupation of researchers attempting to investigate recreation damage. It rested on the notion of attempting to define a maximum level of recreational use that could be sustained without unacceptable or irreversible damage to the site. But as Glyptis notes, the definition of 'unacceptable' was an entirely subjective concept and the notion of irreversible decline was difficult to establish until it had already taken place.

Goldsmith (1983) considered this preoccupation with ecological carrying capacity unproductive. He found many studies of different habitats and activities to be superficial and often even anecdotal. They were largely preoccupied with the analysis of problems and invariably fell short of offering any resolution to recreation and environmental conflicts. By 1987 (Goldsmith, 1987) he was able to generalize on studies of recreation damage, suggesting that because they were concerned with particular 'crisis' sites, they contributed nothing to an understanding of how widespread the recreation damage problem was.

By the mid-1980s it began to be recognized that recreation growth as a whole had abated. Such growth as there was, was in active sports and studies of environmental impact responded to this. They moved away from general studies of congestion and trampling towards the more specific effects of particular sports. Despite this, the overall level of active sports participation has been small, accounting for only about 5% of all countryside recreation trips in 1990 (Countryside Commission, 1991a), and so the spatial extent of their impact must be considered limited. In addition, Sidaway (1988) notes that most of these studies actually set out to demonstrate damage, and have been biased as a result, often again only reporting on very local situations.

8.3.2 The impact of trampling on vegetation

Early work on trampling, for example, Speight (1973) and Liddle (1975), which attempted to derive generalized models of ecological carrying capacity, has now generally fallen out of favour in recognition of the inherent variability not only of soils and vegetation in different places, but also aspect, slope, climate and frequency of use. Perhaps the most vulnerable areas in terms of recreation are the uplands. Not only do they have more fragile ecosystems and rare flora with low regenerative cycles (Edwards, Piggott and Cope, 1989), but they also constitute much of the access land in England and Wales under the 1949 National Parks and Access to the Countryside Act. They also, of course, provide the locations for nearly all of the national parks.

Path erosion in upland areas, although very localized, can be severe on popular routes, particularly under wet conditions. In the Three Peaks area in the Yorkshire Dales National Park, the 20 km path network has a mean trampled width of 11.4 m and, in places, bare widths of up to 2.7 m (Bayfield and McGowan, 1986). It has been estimated too, that almost £7 million may be needed to restore the worst sections of the Pennine Way, 20% of which is badly eroded, as well as a possible £250 000 in annual maintenance (Edwards, 1991).

In certain upland areas, too, particularly in Scotland, skiing has had a noticeable environmental impact. Wood (1987) has identified detrimental impacts that include peat compaction, the deposition of eroded material on slopes, slow regeneration of flora and the compaction of vegetation by maintenance vehicles. Selman (1992), too, has considered the damaging impacts of construction vehicles, and hydrological changes to individual sites through, for example, the construction of car parks.

But for the uplands as a whole, Selman (1992, p. 112) cautions against any broad generalizations:

given the diversity and fragility of the natural environment, and the linked roles of abrasion and erosion, it follows that footpath formation is highly variable and unpredictable except within very broad limits.

The National Parks Review Panel (Edwards, 1991), too, considered that very few paths in national parks were so heavily used as to require intensive management. It considered path erosion problems to be minor relative to changing agricultural practices, particularly increased grazing pressure. Patmore (1987) also attributed upland erosion problems not just to recreation activity, but also to diminishing resources available for management. In general terms for the uplands, Sidaway (1990b) was able to conclude that although path erosion was locally severe, 'recreation was not a threat to ecological resources'.

Where informal recreation takes place in lowland grasslands, the effects are usually less dramatic than in upland areas. They tend to be more localized in the vicinity of entry points, paths, and viewpoints, unless recreational use is particularly heavy (Green, 1985). Moreover, Harrison (1981) points to the good rates of natural recovery which have been found to be possible, given sufficient time, in semi-natural grassland and heathland plots, subject to recreation pressure, in southern England.

Wright (1989) considered the recreational impact on different vegetation types, and found that acidic grassland was lower in tolerance and had a longer recovery time than calcareous grassland, but that the slopes in the latter case could increase susceptibility to recreational impact. It is commonly the case, however, that problems in lowland areas may be exacerbated by non-recreational factors, such as a loss of habitats through agricultural intensification, and a lack of legitimate provision for some sports, which has displaced them into undesignated and ecologically more damaging sites (Sidaway, 1990a).

The ecological effects of trampling on soils and vegetation, if not their extent, are well documented. These include soil compaction, the bruising of vegetation, reductions in species diversity and the creation of bare ground leading to soil erosion (Selman, 1992). Bayfield and Aitken (1992) have defined a sequence of effects caused by increased recreational use, which moves from decreased vegetation height and slight soil compaction, through declining species diversity, severe soil compaction and structural damage, to surface erosion and exposure of the subsoil. Despite this sequence of degradation in principle, there still appears to be little evidence relating to how commonly it occurs in practice.

Because of this, Wright (1989) calls for more research on the extent rather than the type of damage caused by trampling, since assertions by Shoard (1978) claim that it is much less widespread than might be expected. She suggests that, despite the resultant changes to local ecosystems when more trample-resistant species take over, and the damage to areas such as Box Hill and Kynance Cove, where even resistant forms of vegetation cannot survive, leading to exposure of bare ground:

> very little countryside is actually trampled away (p. 93).

8.3.3 The impact of recreation on birds

For land areas, the recreational impacts on birds again lie chiefly in the uplands. The Countryside Commission (1991b) considers that intense moorland use can deter some more sensitive birds from nesting, and that their breeding success can, on occasion, be affected. It can be problematic, too, if a rare bird becomes a visitor attraction in its own right. Edwards (1991) also concludes that some sensitive species such as the golden plover and merlin are deterred from visiting areas in national parks used most intensely for recreation, but that others, such as the red grouse, are less disturbed by visitors straying from paths. He accedes, however, that more research is required in this area.

Sidaway (1988), in evaluating access impacts in Sites of Special Scientific Interest within the Peak District National Park, found that surveys had suggested a decline in some bird species. Although he accepted that recreation could affect breeding successes where the bird population was low, he concluded that recreation has not been proved to be a major cause in the decline in bird numbers, suggesting that:

> the evidence to date linking recreational access to declines in bird populations is somewhat circumstantial (p. 20).

The greatest impacts on birds in general, however, are at inland and enclosed water areas. This impact has grown during the 1980s with the extension of water recreation into the more sensitive parts of the year for bird species. Concern has particularly focused on the possible effects on overwintering and moulting birds (Goldsmith, 1987). Research such as that by Tuite (1983), Tanner (1979), and Owen (1987) suggests, however, that although there may be temporary and local disturbance of wildfowl, at the national level there is little effect on numbers.

Owen (1987) carried out a winter inventory of 1455 enclosed inland waters in England and Wales between 1979 and 1982, and a detailed study of Llangorse and Talybont Lakes in Wales. She found that intense and uncontrolled recreation had serious effects on wildfowl numbers – at Llangorse fewer birds were able to use it as a wintering area, the arrival of species in autumn was delayed, and bird numbers were depressed when recreation activity was particularly intense. In addition there was evidence of birds having to move zones on the lake because of recreation.

Water recreation was therefore seen to have both spatial and temporal effects at the local level. However, nationally she found that wildfowl numbers were actually increasing, because of an increase in the number of habitats (gravel pits and reservoirs etc.), warmer winters, and the success of zoning measures on some of the larger waters, to separate wildfowl and recreationists. Although Owen's research is rare in that it endeavours to take a national as well as local perspective into account, she nevertheless still concludes, in common with many other researchers, that:

> insufficient is still known about the exact relationship between wildlife and recreation (Owen, 1987, p. 95).

Other research focuses more on the local level – the impact on particular species at certain sites of particular activities. Green (1985) cites some unpublished research which attributes the loss of breeding populations of greyleg geese at several lakes to the fact that 5% don't return to the nest once flushed. Batten (1987) also comments on the surprisingly serious effect of sailing on populations of teal and widgeon which virtually abandoned Brent reservoir when the sailing season was extended into the winter. Although perceived as peaceful activities, sailing and windsurfing were also the most commonly mentioned causes of conflict on water in Goldsmith's (1987) survey. Earlier research by Tanner (1973) also commented on the effects of sailing, concluding that regular, even low-key activity, is probably more of a disturbance than occasional but intense recreation. However, Tanner also stated that wildfowl were probably fairly tolerant of bankside activity, as long as they had the exclusive use of the water itself.

Reviewing research in Holland, Peltzer (1989) found some strong indications of the negative effects of recreational densities on breeding birds. Again, windsurfing was found to have an effect on waterbirds, in terms of numbers and distribution of birds, even when overall numbers of boards were low. However, one survey of rare bird species tended to suggest that vegetation structure had more effect on breeding birds than recreation, and again in his conclusions, the common theme across much impact research emerges:

> some doubts about the influence of recreation are certainly justified (Peltzer, 1989, p. 148).

Moreover, not only is the evidence concerning the extent of short-term disturbance to birds by water recreation (as for land-based recreation) inconclusive, but there is also the problem of ascertaining whether this disturbance itself is actually crucial in the long term. As Watmough (1983, p. 3), quoted in Glyptis (1991) says:

It is a truism that birds will fly away when disturbed; for the successful management of enclosed waters it is necessary to know if this matters to the birds.

8.3.4 Recreational impacts on coasts and inland waterways

Research into recreational impacts on coasts reflects the same uncertainties and contradictions that are evident for trampling and birds. In terms both of erosion and bird populations, most problems appear to be on 'soft' coastlines of sands and mudflats, which provide vital overwintering grounds for large populations of migratory waders. In winter, the disturbance affecting these migratory birds overwintering in England stems from wildfowlers, and also baitdiggers who deny birds access to vital low-tide feeding grounds (Green, 1985). The extension of boating activities into the winter months is a cause for increasing concern, although boating activities at high tide are probably not such a problem as the birds are roosting on higher ground (Tanner, 1973).

Summer, informal and water recreation can disturb beach breeding birds, and sailing and motor boating have the effect of opening up to access from the sea beaches inaccessible from land. The (then) Nature Conservancy Council (1984) review of declining bird species since 1950 found that only one could be attributed to recreation. This was the little tern, which had been adversely affected through a decrease in the number of undisturbed shingle beach nesting habitats, caused by the penetration by water recreationalists of previously remote locations. Green (1985, p. 187) also remarks that:

> it is generally considered that the decline of the little tern in Europe is correlated with the disturbance of its once inaccessible breeding beaches.

Sidaway (1988) concludes that the situation on estuaries is probably more critical than that concerned with inland waters, and that the effect on breeding birds (which have traditionally been left undisturbed throughout the winter) may be crucial. However, he also believes that the effects of coastal recreation on cliff nesting seabirds are, as with birds on inland waters, local and temporary (Sidaway, 1990b).

Concern for dune systems, which are unstable and vulnerable to human disturbance, has also resulted in a substantial amount of research. Selman (1992) cites figures from a study in Anglesey which found that the passage of 200 cars in summer resulted in a reduction in dune height of over 50%. However, once again studies on dune systems have largely been local, discrete surveys, which has led Selman (1992, p. 102) to conclude that:

although much effort has gone into describing and quantifying the recreational impact on dunes . . . it is still difficult to generalise from the highly empirical individual studies.

In an early review of inland waterways, Tanner (1973) stated that although research was limited, the effects of recreation were fairly limited, apart from pollution, and that the main conflicts were more likely to develop on enclosed inland waters. Since then conflicts on certain celebrated inland waters and waterways have become well known, especially in relation to the Norfolk Broads. Pollution there led to chronic eutrophication which resulted in widespread wildlife loss (Green, 1985), but, as with many early celebrated cases, this has now been brought under control. Moreover, Wright (1989) cautions that the problems on the Broads were found to be caused by many other factors, as well as recreation, and that boating impacts are just one part in an interrelating system of causes and effects.

The restoration of the Basingstoke Canal seems to have become something of a *cause célèbre* in the literature, in terms of the unresolved conflicts and claims of both recreationalists and conservationists. It is, however, a unique case (Sidaway, 1988). High traffic densities of propeller-driven boats contribute to a loss both in the amount of aquatic vegetation and in the number of species, but at low levels of traffic, species diversity may actually be increased because keeping the water open prevents the encroachment of invasive minimal species (Sidaway, 1988).

8.3.5 Other recreational impacts

Sidaway (1988) and Broadhurst (1987) both look specifically at the effects of orienteering on woodlands and forests, and conclude that it is an activity which has been misrepresented in terms of impact on the environment. As Sidaway (p. i) states, criticisms have been based on a:

false perception of large numbers of runners trampling round a defined route.

Instead, both authors emphasize that because runners are actually well dispersed throughout the woods the impact on vegetation is minimal, and is acceptable even at sensitive sites. Broadhurst reviews Swedish literature and concludes that again minimal impact is implied, except possibly on the breeding of some bird species. Although the precise impact on ground nesting birds and mammals has still to be assessed, orienteering is found to be a highly organized sport, and one in which the organizers pay considerable attention to conservation interests. As a result there is little evidence of direct conflict.

Sidaway (1988) finds that caving has had a considerable effect on the environment of the caves (graffiti, damage to geological formations etc.) but that increasing measures have been taken to restrict this. He also examines climbing, and concludes that it affects the location of bird nesting rather than their total numbers. Moreover, climbing is cited as an example of particularly good practice by the governing body (the British Mountaineering Council), in incorporating conservation aims in their policies, imposing effective voluntary restrictions, and communicating with conservation interests.

For motorsports, Edwards (1991) found that in the evidence received by the National Parks Review Panel on recreation, the greatest problem was considered to lie in:

> those sports, particularly, but not exclusively, the motorised sports, that are environmentally intrusive – noisy, ugly, and damaging to wildlife and vegetation (p. 35).

Goldsmith's (1987) survey of recreational conflicts in National Nature Reserves and Sites of Special Scientific Interest also found that the land-based recreational activity most commonly mentioned as causing conflict was motorbike scrambling. Elson, Buller and Stanley (1986) consider a wide range of issues connected with provision for motorsports, among which they surmise that the most significant effects of motorsports **may** be the destruction of flora, the inhibition of the regeneration of vegetation, disturbance to wildlife, the compaction and destruction of topsoil, and the erosion and rutting of surfaces which lead to the channelling of surface run off and the widening and deepening of tracks. Motorsports have greater impact than recreation on foot or by horse, because of the speeds involved, and the intensity of use in some places. However, Elson, Buller and Stanley also point out that the main sites used for organized motorsports are well suited to recovery from the activity – such as the well drained, gently sloping grazing land of southern England.

In all of this evidence, it is important to make the distinction between sport and informal recreation. Sidaway (1988) concentrates in his report on the former, a less well researched area. He considers the effects of sport to be 'more specific and more acute than those of informal recreation, which are more widespread and perhaps less contentious'. Indeed, he believes that informal recreation causes fewer problems than some of the literature suggests. He also warns against the local impact of some organized sports becoming a *cause célèbre*, giving a misleading impression of widespread conflict.

The Sports Council (1992), in contrast, considers that more of the problems in the countryside come from the casual recreationist, than from active sport, mainly because casual recreation still accounts for by far the greater proportion of countryside activity:

Many of the problems in the countryside stem not from the relatively small number of countryside activity participants, but rather from casual car-borne visitors or spectators (Sports Council, 1992, p. 13).

8.4 THE PLANNING AND POLICY CONSEQUENCES OF RECREATIONAL IMPACT

Overall, then, empirical evidence concerning the damage that recreation does to the countryside is, at best, inconclusive. Studies have tended to focus on individual sites rather than overall impacts and even in these they are commonly cautious or even doubtful about the lasting damage that recreation imposes. Much more concern appears to focus on the impacts of water recreation than land-based activities.

8.4.1 Erroneous inferences from research

Unfortunately, the lack of research pointing to any systematic evidence of the extent of recreational impacts has led planners and managers to err on the side of caution (Edington and Edington, 1986). As the Sports Council (1992, p. 13) notes:

A lack of objective data and/or misleading interpretation of data on the real impacts of countryside activities has led to a sometimes inappropriate, over-restrictive approach towards the use of a resource by an activity.

Moreover, as Sidaway and O'Connor (1978) maintain, in the absence of good research, recreation pressure has often been inferred directly from recreation growth, a point echoed by Glyptis (1991, p. 137):

The effects of recreation on flora, fauna and landscape more readily engender emotion and assumption than hard evidence. All too often, the mere existence of recreational activity or the fact of temporary disturbance are taken to infer inevitable adverse impact.

Even where damage from recreation has been demonstrated, its consequences are often hard to articulate. As Goldsmith (1987) has noted, it is very difficult to tell whether such damage really matters in the long term. Sidaway (1988) accuses some conservationists of assuming that damage is necessarily important, to allow them to articulate a 'scenario of failure' and magnify the consequences of recreation. He maintains that showing that damage does occur is not sufficiently persuasive to show that it is of any real consequence.

Madgwick (1988, p. 3), too, herself a nature reserve manager, also states, in an article about open access policies for nature reserves:

on the whole, naturalists appear to have an exaggerated fear of damage caused by visitors. Often the destruction of peace and solitude is their prime objection, rather than the damage to wildlife itself.

8.4.2 Recreation damage in the wider environmental context

From the research evidence cited above, distinction can be made, of importance to public policy, between short-term recreation disturbance, on a wide scale, and more localized longer-term recreation damage. The Sports Council (1992) maintains that this distinction is of crucial importance since very few authors indeed suggest that recreation has widespread long-term effects on whole ecosystems and wildlife populations. Most research evidence suggests that recreation damage is confined, both temporally and spatially.

Edwards (1991), for national parks, notes the spatial patchiness of park use, suggesting that even at times of greatest recreation pressure, large areas of parks remain relatively empty of visitors. The growth in active pursuits in parks has created an increased perception of visitor pressure, but even here, most activity is considerably contained. Even for nature reserves, Madgwick (1988) maintains that widespread impacts are not important, since even though the intense public use of a site will eventually have some noticeable effect on habitat, the resulting adjustment to species is often insignificant.

In respect of widespread impacts, too, Sidaway (1988, p. iii) was able to state:

> Overviews of ecosystems or species groupings have concluded that recreational damage and disturbance are relatively insignificant to the survival of the species, when compared to the major environmental threats of pollution or loss of habitat.

This raises the importance of placing recreation damage in the wider environmental context of the countryside, and here, there is a consensus among many (Shoard, 1978; Harrison, 1983; Countryside Commission, 1991b; Edwards, 1991) that recreation damage is almost insignificant compared with the impacts of intensifying agriculture and forestry – overgrazing, land improvement, the use of herbicides and pesticides, industrial buildings and so on. Not only are these visually intrusive and ecologically damaging, particularly in more sensitive upland areas, but they are also pervasive. This gives them a much greater significance altogether than incidences of recreation damage that are invariably confined to localized areas.

8.4.3 Policies of restraint versus policies of good management

Whatever the uncertainties concerning recreation damage to the countryside, the consensus of its localized nature severely calls into question the blanket restraint policies of structure plans and particularly, the recreation and conservation priority in public policy. There is an increasing groundswell of opinion that suggests that policies of restraint and residualization are, in fact, less appropriate than developing effective systems of management where recreation, in a limited number of crisis areas, can be seen to have significant environmental consequences.

Several authors stress the importance of good management, and the contribution that this can make to minimizing conflicts, especially when combined with adequate (but not necessarily excessive) finances, and some form of monitoring. As early as 1972, when the perceived threat of recreation was at its greatest, the report presented before the Stockholm Conference (Department of the Environment, 1972) concluded that most of the problems caused by recreation could be solved by mutual understanding and imaginative management.

Shoard (1978) also attributes much to management, in that where effective it can allow a large numbers of visits without major damage. As she puts it:

> millions of people visit Kew Gardens each year without reducing it to dust (p. 64).

Similarly, Green (1985) maintains that with suitable management in most cases the planned use of an area for informal recreation would be perfectly compatible with the maintenance of ecological value. The Countryside Commission (1991a) reach similar conclusions. They maintain that in most cases sound visitor management and investment in suitable surfaces can ensure that people's use of a site, and their movement within it, can take place on a sustainable basis.

Goldsmith (1987), too, in his study of conflicts at National Nature Reserves and Sites of Special Scientific Interest maintained that with appropriate research, sympathetic management and modest investment, particularly in staff time, most recreation and nature conservation conflicts could be solved. He felt that the overall level of damage to sites designated primarily for nature conservation was not too serious anyway. He quotes from an internal report by the (then) Nature Conservancy Council, which stated that:

> It was not recreation that was affecting the scientific interest of the reserve but rather the lack of good habitat management.

Goldsmith also found from the survey that the investment needed was actually very little in proportion to the numbers of people using the sites. He cites (as do other authors) the example of the New Forest

where good management controlled the burgeoning recreational pressures of the late 1960s. The Three Peaks moorland footpath management
exercise is also quoted as an example of a positive approach to conflict
(Bayfield, 1987), and in terms of water recreation, Rutland Water is often
cited (for example Sidaway, 1988) as being the best example of a site
where both recreation and conservation interests were planned from the
start, and where zoning has meant that both are catered for.

The need to plan creatively from the start of a project is emphasized
by Sidaway (1988, p. iv):

> conflicts between recreation and conservation can almost in-
> variably be solved if we concentrate on a creative approach, geared
> to enhancing both the recreation and conservation values of our
> environment.

In the same study Sidaway also stresses the need for a more strategic
approach, particularly in the case of activities such as motorsports,
water recreation and upland access, and for management to be integrated with research. Actually providing in a positive way for certain
sports and activities can itself help reduce the environmental damage
which is otherwise done when they are carried out in an uncontrolled or
illegal way, especially for example for motorsports and off-road cycling
(Sidaway, 1990a; Department of the Environment, 1991a).

Sidaway (1990a) suggests that these conflicts can be reduced if management is based around five key principles. These are multiple-use and
creative conservation (i.e. few areas devoted solely to recreation or
conservation), clearly stated aims for both recreation and conservation,
consultation with all groups, impact assessment prior to any development, and monitoring and review.

8.4.4 The environmental benefits of recreation

Indeed, a number of authors, in assessing the impact of recreation, have
stressed that this impact can be beneficial, both economically and environmentally. The Sports Council (1992, p. 2) notes that countryside sport
and recreation bring direct and indirect benefits:

> which far outweigh the occasional problems which arise.

Involvement in countryside activities, too, fosters in many people an
understanding of the natural environment, and a commitment to nature
conservation. Green (1985) suggests that even ecologically not all the
effects of recreation are adverse. Beneficial effects include moderate
trampling which can help maintain some ecosystems. Work in the Scilly
Isles for example (Goldsmith, Munton and Warren, 1978) has shown
that trampling prevents the invasion of bracken over grassland.

Recreation can also enable money to be made available to protect eco-systems that might otherwise disappear, such as in the case of the restoration of the Basingstoke Canal which has itself led to wildlife flourishing again. Action and pressure by recreation groups can also benefit the environment – for example Sidaway (1988) comments of the influence of anglers in ensuring (albeit from self-interest) cleaner rivers. The creation of new golf courses also presents a real opportunity, through the reclamation of land previously of little wildlife interest; the wildlife potential of roughs on golf-courses is being increasingly realized (Schofield, 1987).

Thus the evidence that is available about recreation damage to the countryside suggests that it is not as pervasive as policy-makers might assume. Where particular crisis areas are evident, these are most likely to be successfully resolved through good management rather than re-strictive policies. Indeed a number of authors have articulated the fact that recreation activity can bring positive benefits to the conservation interest. All of this brings the historical residualization of recreation and access relative to amenity and support conservation in public policy, the fifth proposition of this book (p. xi), into question. In the context of both amenity and scientific conservation there is a case for both recreation and access, in both policy and management terms, to be accorded a higher priority.

9

Current issues for policy formulation

9.1 POLICY PROPOSITIONS

This book has explored five principal propositions relating to the formulation of recreation and access policies, principally in Britain:

1. that the fragmented nature of the organizational structure for countryside recreation has inhibited the development and implementation of comprehensive policies and plans;
2. that the provision of countryside recreation, access facilities and opportunities has exhibited a confusion between the responsibilities and functions of the public sector and those of the market place and has been piecemeal and unco-ordinated as a result;
3. that policies and plans have not paid full regard to the social composition of recreation participation and have not fully taken into account people's preferences for recreation and access in the countryside;
4. that policy has generally been preoccupied with fears of a recreation explosion and the rights of the landowner, rather than the development of recreation opportunities and has been unduly restrictive as a result;
5. that policies for recreation and access have had an unduly low priority in pressures for change in the countryside, particularly in relation to those in the conservation interest.

This final chapter examines the consequences of these propositions for public policy, and makes suggestions for the reformulation of policy if their impacts are to be ameliorated.

9.2 FRAGMENTED ORGANIZATIONAL STRUCTURES

The first proposition of this book suggests that the fragmented nature of the organizational structure for countryside recreation has inhibited the development and implementation of comprehensive policies and plans. Chapter 2 has highlighted the fact that this structure is complex at the level of ministries, government agencies and even within local authorities. There is clearly scope for reappraising the responsibility for countryside recreation at all three of these levels.

Although a new 'Ministry for Leisure' proposed in the Labour Party Manifesto in 1987 seems an unrealistic proposition, a clearer demarcation in the portfolios of the ministries of Education, Environment, Employment, Agriculture, Heritage and Trade and Industry in respect of rural leisure is important. Since the majority of rural leisure activities as was noted in Chapter 3 depend in some way on the citizens' rights of access over (usually) private land, it would seem appropriate that recreation responsibilities should centre on the Department of the Environment (and the Welsh Office) to sit alongside its other land-use control functions, principally in relation to the town and country planning system. Giving a more singular responsibility to one ministry in this way is itself likely to facilitate an increasing importance for countryside recreation and access on the political agenda.

The disparate responsibilities for recreation and access among government agencies is central to its residualization in policy terms. In this respect, consideration could be given to the creation of a singular 'Countryside Recreation Commission'. This is a less naive proposition than the notion of a Ministry for Leisure, since organizational structures among agencies with part responsibilities for rural leisure are currently in a particular state of flux. In Wales and Scotland, the functions of the two Countryside Commissions have been merged with those of the (then) Nature Conservancy Council. The future of the English Countryside Commission must now be open to particular speculation and the possibility of a Countryside Recreation Commission, separated from an English Nature that adopts the existing Commission's amenity conservation portfolio, becomes a real possibility. The proposed reorganization of the Sports Council, too, in 1993, whilst it is on hold, provides a good opportunity for portfolio reassessment.

The role of the Countryside Commission and the National Parks Commission before it have remained substantially altered since 1949 (despite revisions to its geographical areas of jurisdiction in 1968 and its change in status to a 'public service' in 1981) and its dual responsibilities for amenity conservation and recreation and access have become increasingly less easy to reconcile over time. By the 1990s, achieving a realistic balance between these two responsibilities has become almost impossible as ubiquitous governmental imperatives in the conservation sphere have successively residualized the recreation role.

Despite this, the Countryside Commission remains the only body at a national level with a comprehensive and holistic recreation and access portfolio. This contrasts with its role as a conservation agency increasingly competing with both English Nature and the Ministry of Agriculture in the wake of the 1986 Agriculture Act. Only with its realignment as a Countryside Recreation Commission will it be able to develop recreation priorities unfettered by externally imposed conservation obligations.

Such a Countryside Recreation Commission could adequately represent the recreation interest throughout the continuing reformulation of the Common Agricultural Policy, to ensure that recreational land use did not again become a residual function of changing agricultural practice. Such a Commission could play a less ambiguous lobbying role to put countryside recreation further up the political agenda (in this respect, acting more like a pressure group) and improve the allocation of public monies to recreation and access, particularly at a time of significant reallocations of public funds in rural areas as a result of agricultural restructuring. For a Commission of this nature, the choice of commissioners would be critical, particularly in respect of their collective attitudes to public access rights over private land.

Farm-based recreation is likely to provide an important part of future provision, and such a Commission could seek a central role within the agricultural sector. Consideration could be given to the introduction of county farm recreation advisors along the lines of the Farming and Wildlife Advisory Group officers – their conservation counterpart. A new Commission would not only be able to adopt a more constructive position with private landowners, but also with more commercial concerns, voluntary organizations and other public agencies. In this respect, the Commission could clarify and seek to influence the roles of the Forestry Commission, the Sports Council, the National Rivers Authority and others in rationalizing responsibilities and provision.

Local authorities, too, could be given more exacting guidance from a singular Countryside Recreation Commission. The uneasy relationship between their 'recreation' functions in county planning departments and 'access' functions in highways departments could be more readily integrated and prioritized to reflect the importance of rural leisure to the public at large, focusing more clearly, in management terms at least, on access and rights of the citizen. In this respect, jurisdiction over access should probably fall to planning departments, in order that conflicts over rights of way can be more effectively dealt with. The responsibilities of rights of way officers in such departments should be clarified.

This would perhaps facilitate a clearer recreation role for footpaths, and would allow, for example, the publication of footpath leaflets which would in themselves allow some form of control over use. Such leaflets could be devised with a clear understanding of a recreation system within one locality.

A Countryside Recreation Commission could also do much to ameliorate the problems associated with the plethora of government advice for recreation land-use planning evaluated in Chapter 6. If singular responsibility for the production of advice was given to one such body, even if eventually transmitted through the Department of Environment and the Welsh Office, current contradictions in the collective nature of such advice could be substantially reduced. It could be made temporally more consistent and unified, and clearer advice could be given in its adoption overcoming many of the problems that currently exist. Such a Commission could produce notes for guidance on the recreation components of structure, local and informal plans along the lines of those notes produced in the 1970s by the Countryside Commission for national park and country park plans. In particular, a Countryside Recreation Commission would allow the faltering Regional Councils for Sport and Recreation and their ineffectual regional sport and recreation strategies to be abandoned.

9.3 PUBLIC VS PRIVATE PROVISION

The second proposition of this book suggests that the provision of countryside recreation and access facilities and opportunities has exhibited a confusion between the responsibilities and functions of the public sector and those of the market place and has been fragmented and unco-ordinated as a result. In Chapter 3, it was noted that public provision can be justified on at least four grounds. The first two of these relate to the citizen's rights of access: that customary opportunities are not eroded and that *de facto* rights are upheld. The second two relate more specifically to recreation facilities: it is hard in practice to exclude people from certain facilities because they don't have defined access points and provision is often undertaken for social purposes.

The first two of these reasons certainly legitimate the public provision of access opportunities, but the second two are less persuasive. Access to a large number of facilities can be controlled, and, as has been noted in Chapter 5, the provision of social policies for countryside recreation has been seen to be less than effective in practice. In clarifying the role of state provision for countryside recreation and access, there appears to be some legitimacy in considering separately the provision of access opportunities on the one hand and individual facilities on the other. In fact, there are a number of characteristics of facility provision that suggest to a large degree that they might more rationally be considered as market commodities.

9.3.1 Facilities as market commodities: principles

The first of these characteristics is that the social structure of recreation participation suggests that it is market demands, rather than any expressions of social need, that provide the principal triggers to all types of recreation participation. Second, because tastes or preferences are often stronger influences over participation than prices, charging prices could move the social structure of participation towards the less affluent. This is because, as has been noted in Chapter 5, free 'solitude' activities tend to be consumed more than proportionately by the more affluent than 'events' such as village fêtes, agricultural shows and exhibitions, which are usually charged for and attract a wider social spectrum of the population. Thus, charging market prices, particularly as a result of changing the product towards more 'activity'-orientated pursuits, could make countryside recreation participation more egalitarian.

Related to this, a third characteristic of facility provision is that free access to individual local-authority-owned sites, required under Section 43 of the 1968 Countryside Act, is socially regressive because a greater proportion of the more affluent visit such countryside recreation sites than the less affluent. Free access thus benefits those who need it least, and charging market prices to individual facilities is more likely to accord to notions of social justice. Certainly, charging market prices does not change the pattern of consumption towards the more affluent. The importance of tastes and preferences, as well as transport costs, as triggers to participation may render the free access criterion unimportant as well as inappropriate. In any event, the 'free access' criterion may be more apparent than real since many local-authority facilities, while allowing free access for entry to the site, charge, quite legitimately, for car parking.

Fourth, free access to some publicly owned facilities appears inappropriate, when there is a tradition of charging for access to other publicly owned sites, such as ancient monuments in the charge of the Heritage Ministry, and to sites owned by the voluntary sector, such as those of the National Trust.

A final characteristic of facility provision that suggests their consideration as market commodities is that at the margin, the properties of facilities provided by the public sector, particularly where this is manifest in an intensity of facilities, many of which are sub-contracted to private operators anyway, are indistinguishable from private facilities.

How many countryside recreation participants really distinguish between the recreation experience offered by an intensively managed country park and, say, a privately owned butterfly park?

9.3.2 Facilities as market commodities: practice

In addition to these characteristics that suggest the consideration of recreation facilities as market commodities, their provision, particularly by the public sector, has perceptibly moved towards market principles during the 1980s and into the 1990s. As well as the underlying ethos of a government generally committed to market principles, the policies of various government agencies, and indeed many local authorities, have begun to mimic the market more closely.

As Harrison (1991) notes, the Countryside Commission's (1987b, 1987c) 'Enjoying the Countryside' initiative provided a clear indication of a government agency moving towards a market orientation in facility provision. By 1992 (Countryside Commission, 1992a) its further commitment to identifying market needs and market potential for countryside recreation, through market research, reinforces this ethos. Notions of improving customer care and improving the quality of the welcome for visitors are again derived from the principles of the market place.

These policies, therefore, are beginning to accede to a recognition of the market characteristics of countryside recreation facilities outlined above. In practice, the consideration of market attributes, particularly in relation to pricing, can have a number of advantages, even when used by the public sector. Bovaird, Tricker and Stoakes (1982) have suggested that there are three distinct advantages to charging at recreation sites. First and most obviously, revenues can be generated for the further development of the facility.

In addition, however, charging can be used to regulate or manipulate the number of people visiting a site, perhaps to protect the site from over-use, or to even out the spread of visitors during the day, week or season through differential pricing. A closer study of pricing by the same authors (Bovaird, Tricker and Stoakes, 1984) revealed that for (then) Department of the Environment ancient monuments and National Trust properties, increases in prices of around 10% in real terms caused a reduction in participation of between 5% and 8% at higher-priced sites, and smaller reductions in participation at lower-priced sites. Price sensitivity was thus sufficient to be able to control visitors, while often being sufficiently inelastic to increase overall revenues even with increases in prices. At peak periods, price increases would have to be quite considerable if significant numbers of visitors were to be deterred.

A third advantage of charging at publicly owned sites is that it allows the collection of information on levels of use, and to a degree people's preferences, so that planning and management can become more customer-orientated. In addition to these three advantages, the notion of creating a market image can also be considered a benefit of pricing. As has already been noted, many people have a different perception of a visit to a facility that has a positive price, than if it is 'free'. Prices can thus help to identify facilities as 'market' as opposed to 'non-market' ones (Curry, 1991b).

Flexibility can be deployed in the means by which charging takes place. As well as paying admission charges at the gate, peak-period pricing, car-park charging and donations boxes have been commonly deployed by local authorities. Memberships, licences and permits have been less commonly employed, because they are more difficult to police.

Certainly, there are management costs associated with charging. There are often significant costs associated with the start-up of such schemes, and running costs may be high because, apart from paying attendants, for car parks at least, they may be subject to some form of positive rating when charging takes place, which they otherwise would not be. In addition, revenues may reduce the priority for grant-aid allocations and they commonly accrue to the local authority rather than the individual site and may not be returned to the facility for further developments. Revenue targets are also commonly based on the previous year's performance and good summers may cause unrealistic targets for subsequent years.

For individual sites, charging may be inappropriate for frequent users, it may dissuade voluntary effort and may have a negative impact on adjacent sites which are free. Charging for car parking may also cause traffic management problems associated with people trying to park at the perimeter of the paying area. All of these problems, however, do not negate the principle of treating facilities as market commodities. This notion of pricing deserves consideration at a national level and should itself, perhaps, provide an element of national policy for market-based recreation facilities.

9.3.3 Policy proposals for facilities

For facilities, then, there is evidence to suggest that a more market orientated approach to their provision might be an appropriate means of overcoming the confusion which surrounds the way in which they are currently provided. This raises difficult issues as to whether they should be provided by the public or private sectors, but it seems likely that both historical patterns of ownership, and jurisdiction and pressures for local authorities to develop an enterprise culture, will leave the responsibility for many facilities in public hands. Despite this, there is scope for public policies for facility provision that ease the operation of the market, rather than necessarily create direct intervention. Some limited grant-aid or preferential loan finance to the private sector, the former of which has been available for capital projects in country parks and picnic sites since the 1968 Countryside Act, might be extended to other types of facility in this respect, provisions for which have been available since the 1974 Local Government Act, but which have rarely been taken up.

In addition to policies of market easement, public policies that reconsider public facilities along market lines appear to be appropriate, if somewhat curious. Certainly such policies would not impair the 'social' motive for intervention since the evidence suggests that this is, at best, ineffectual. Market-orientated policies might even be more egalitarian, particularly if they are designed to provide facilities that the public actually wants, rather than those that the policy-maker feels that they ought to have. In terms of the motive for state intervention based on non-excludability, this will always remain for certain facilities, where access realistically cannot be policed.

An increasing market orientation of such facilities in public policy, whether they be publicly or privately provided, also brings benefits to the rural economy, which themselves can have positive social impacts, this time for the rural population. Certainly compared to the agriculture and forestry sectors which are, at the margins, uneconomic and the water sector monopolistic (Curry *et al.*, 1986), rural leisure provides a relatively attractive proposition for rural areas as a free market enterprise. It offers the opportunity for economic activities in rural areas without continuing subsidization. All components of the rural leisure sector certainly are more labour-intensive than the resource sectors and thus provide greater employment opportunities per pound of expenditure. The Countryside Commission (1992a), in recognition of this, proposes the development of new opportunities to attract and retain visitor spending within rural communities which should be developed in ways that include the promotion of rural skills and products.

In 1992, an estimated £13 000 million was spent on leisure-day visits from home between April and September inclusive. Spending took place on 7 out of 10 visits and on average £14 per visit was spent specifically on visits to the countryside (Walker, 1993). In addition to day visits, despite declining visitor nights in the countryside during the late 1980s, tourism facilities also offer an obvious market potential, particularly in relation to farm diversification. Some 10% of all farms in Britain had some form of tourism enterprise in 1985, and this figure undoubtedly has increased into the 1990s. Some 5 million people camp in caravans or tents during any one year and net income from these is around £25 per annum per pitch (Carruthers, 1986). The English Tourist Board provides up to 25% grant aid for fixed capital associated with the setting up of such sites. For farmhouse tourism, current returns on capital in the free market are low (Crocker, 1986), but developments in the marketing of farmhouse tourism elsewhere in Europe, for example, the growth of gites in France, provide models of a more structured approach to the supply of more market-orientated recreation opportunities in Britain.

Market provision for sports in the countryside also offers economic potential. To the extent that they are organized they can be charged for easily and the growth in new types of sports (for example, hang gliding, windsurfing and motor sports) during the 1980s offers new areas of exploitation as long as traditional access rights are not compromised. For traditional sports, Cobham Resource Consultants (1983) estimated total expenditure on them in Britain in 1982 to be in excess of £950 million.

For countryside recreation facilities, non-excludability remains a problem in exploiting market potential, but where this prevails, since such facilities provide an essential infrastructure for the tourism sector, their maintenance and development could be sustained through some form of tourism tax, a notion endorsed by the Countryside Commission (1992a). Where excludability can be achieved, woodlands, water areas, war games and pick your own (Carruthers, 1986) are considered to offer most market potential.

Again in this respect, the challenge for public policy in maximizing the market potential of recreation facilities, whether publicly or privately provided, lies in giving the public what they actually want. In this respect, there is scope for a Countryside Recreation Commission to provide business advice to rural entrepreneurs about people's preferences, market potentials and operational strategies. Indeed, the Countryside Commission (1992a) is committed to continuing market research, to identify people's needs more closely, and to make this information more readily available, through publications, seminars and training events.

In terms of both national and strategic level land-use policies, facilities should be treated as any other market commodity. Such policies should be **promotional** rather than simply facilitating, something that is reflected in recent policies of both the Sports Council (1992) and the Countryside Commission (1992a). The control of the development of these 'market' facilities in the public interest should be through strong policies in Planning Policy Guidance notes and development plans and through development control mechanisms to ensure, through sympathetic design, siting and layout, that they are sensitive to their countryside surroundings. They should not, however, overestimate recreation damage to the countryside and should be aware of the fact that there is a natural limit to the demand for recreation facilities anyway.

9.3.4 Public provision: responding to citizens' rights

There is thus a case to be made for the 'privatization' of specific recreation facilities whether publicly or privately provided: they exhibit many of the features of market commodities anyway and form only a minority interest on the part of countryside recreationists in general (Harrison, 1991), accounting for around 25% of all countryside recreation trips (Countryside Commission, 1992a). Developing policies towards access to the countryside, particularly in respect of public rights of way, however, is a very different matter.

Despite the fact that many organized sporting groups in particular are keen to consider access as a market commodity as a means of enhancing their access opportunities (Centre for Leisure Research, 1986), such access represents a basic citizen's right, through custom, legislation and negotiation. Since national participation surveys suggest that the exercising of these citizens rights is a much more frequent preoccupation among participants than visiting facilities, it is in this area that the most significant policy implications arise. This is important since, historically, there has been a policy preoccupation with sites and facilities in recreation terms, rather than the rights of citizenship, undoubtedly due to the relative ease with which such site-based policies can be implemented on land in public control. There is a need for a reappraisal of the balance of policy effort towards these rights.

Despite access being the right of all citizens, the exercising of these rights is still exploited more by the more affluent, as has been noted in Chapter 4. This would suggest, perhaps, that unlike policies for facilities, access policies, at least those promulgated by the public sector, should not focus on promotion, but rather **facilitation.**

9.3.5 Policy proposals for access

Policies for defending the rights of the citizen for access can be considered in two broad strands: national and strategic policies, and policies for the management of access opportunities. The former should ensure the rights of access through a number of mechanisms.

First, there is a need for a better understanding of public access rights, particularly legislation, on the part of the public at large. The limited impact of the Access Charter (Countryside Commission, 1985a) suggests that this understanding might most usefully be promoted at the level of the county council as part of an orchestrated policy for public rights of way. Such a policy might embrace the 'packaging' of rights of way in the manner considered in Chapter 3, to sit alongside policies for the completion and review of the definitive map, and rights of way maintenance. The Countryside Commission (1992a) is committed to developing this better understanding through more integrated information services that are both practical and accessible and are produced at a local level.

It is important too, that such information is available not only in the countryside. Even in 1975, Law (1975) suggested that such information was likely to be more effective if located in areas where the population live. She suggested that a countryside information centre should be located in Hyde Park, to maximize the dissemination of such information to the London population. In view of the inherent limitations of site-based information and interpretation facilities considered in Chapter 2, this more general approach to information dissemination needs to be further developed. Again, the Countryside Commission's (1992a) commitment to environmental education in schools in relation to the countryside, to embrace such things as map reading, is likely to enhance the understanding of access rights in the population as a whole.

Second, more extensive use of existing powers for exercising access rights should be encouraged. The ability of local authorities to secure access for public enjoyment by either agreement, order or acquisition has been available for open country since 1949. Historically, it has not been used to any great extent, particularly in lowland Britain. These are almost forgotten powers every bit as potent and long-standing as management agreements for conservation measures which have been so much in the public eye, which have stimulated Acts of Parliament (1981 Wildlife and Countryside Act) and which have been significant mechanisms in securing both landscape and nature conservation ends. The opportunity to use management agreements under the 1981 Act for recreation purposes has also not been widely exploited and represents a further opportunity for securing access rights, particularly since such agreements can relate to any type of land, and not just open country.

It would seem appropriate to review the effectiveness of all of these types of agreement with a view to developing ways in which the responsibility for such arrangements could be given to the occupier. This would be of particular interest in remoter upland areas of marginal agricultural significance since any shifts in agricultural policy away from food production in these areas is likely to be towards the roles of positive management for recreation and rural custodianship (Melchett, 1985). The potential for embracing such agreements within Ministry of Agriculture grant aid should be given consideration. The possibility of developing access systems involving more than one landowner, and co-existing with more than one land use, should be explored. Funding for such agreements may be more appropriately subsumed under agricultural improvement schemes managed jointly by the Agricultural Development Advisory Service, and local authorities, but must be for positive management and not compensation for doing nothing. The voluntary sector may have a legitimate role to play in aspects of this management.

At the national level, too, the Countryside Commission's powers to buy land, at least for experimental purposes including recreation, under the 1968 Countryside Act have never been exercised, and this represents a further opportunity for securing access. It would certainly be cheaper than negotiating agreements or making orders, as English Nature have found in respect of nature conservation. In addition, further consideration should be given to the designation of more recreation footpaths, particularly Regional Routes and National Trails. Currently, for example, the Countryside Commission is considering National Trail status for the Cotswold Way and Hadrians Wall.

In extending the use of all of these existing powers, however, care must be taken to ensure that the creation of new *de jure* access rights by these means does not simply lead to a loss of existing *de facto* rights. In this respect, once *de jure* rights have been placed on a clearer footing, there is a need for local authorities to recognize more overtly, and take responsibility for, *de facto* access. This might embrace the development of some form of register of *de facto* access in parallel with the definitive map, and a more comprehensive management service for such areas. Currently, *de facto* access exists within a policy vacuum.

Third, there is scope for legislative reform in the whole area of rights of way, access to open country and common land. It is perhaps unrealistic to suggest that any new legislation could radically alter the rights of public access over private land in terms of severely diminishing landowners rights, in the manner that Shoard (1987) and others have proposed. There is certainly, however, a need for legislation simply to clarify access rights over common land along the lines of the recommendations of the Common Land Forum (Countryside Commission, 1986), and to consolidate various provisions relating to public rights of way. At the margins, perhaps, some changes could be made, for example, to the definition of open country, to allow access agreements to be negotiated more widely. This definition could be extended to include parkland (Shoard, 1978), but particular potential lies in defining the new National Forest, community forests and woodland areas more generally as open country, to allow their recreation potential to be more fully exploited.

Recent proposals from the Ramblers' Association (1993) do suggest new legislation specifically for access to open country. Claiming a consensus of views for their proposals from the Country Landowners Association, the National Farmers' Union, English Nature and others, stemming from the deliberations of the Common Land Forum, they are seeking to alter the law on trespass. The proposed legislation would reverse the presumption of trespass unless permission had been gained from the landowner. Instead, it calls for a freedom to roam in open country, where trespass, within that freedom, is much more closely defined and in the main restricted to damage and wilful interference. This is coupled, in the proposals, with a series of 'sweeteners' relating to the suspension of access for periods of game shooting and lambing and for the protection of various habitats and wildlife.

Other proposals include a more comprehensive provision of wardens as facilitators, compensations for economic loss, and payments to upland farmers in their role as environmental custodians. Although these trespass proposals do appear to diminish landowners rights, and they are still at variance with County Landowners' Association (1992) views on access to open country, the sweeteners offered may just be sufficient, at a time of severe economic crisis in upland agriculture, to make such legislative proposals a realistic proposition. Certainly they would be significant since they would achieve a freedom to roam in open country that has been a frustrated cause in Parliament ever since James Bryce's Access to Mountains (Scotland) Bill of 1884.

Management policies should also concentrate on ensuring access rights, through keeping paths open and through the completion of the definitive map. In view of the principal problems in both of these areas, it seems that a priority for management should be the allocation of additional resources, to allow these functions to be executed more effectively, a notion that is central to the most recent policy statement of the Country Landowners' Association (1992). In fact, spending on public rights of way nationally doubled in cash terms (a 50% increase in real terms) between 1987 and 1991 (Countryside Commission, 1993).

It might even be in this respect that more explicit account should be taken of the potential of landowners as land managers for public rights of way and their maintenance. Grant aid could be extended within agricultural improvement schemes for this purpose, to allow farmers a more explicit and directly paid for custodianship role in relation to access at a time of declining agricultural incomes. Local authorities may contract private landowners in this respect through Environmental Land Management Services (ELMS) agreements, and these should be extended. Liaison over such management could take place through monitoring groups such as the Countryside Recreation and Access Groups proposed by the Country Landowners Association (1992).

In 1992 the government has responded to management requirements for public rights of way by allocating an additional £0.9 million to the Countryside Commission's budget for allocation under the Parish Paths Partnership. This is designed to stimulate local improvement schemes through voluntary parish council effort and the activities of other local interest groups, specifically for public rights of way. It is designed to relieve local highways authorities of an element of this responsibility to allow them to concentrate on legal disputes and the completion of the definitive map (Department of the Environment, 1992g).

The extent to which this is legitimate hinges on whether the use of such paths is essentially by the local population. The use of public rights of way by non-locals, since countryside recreation is essentially a migratory activity, may sap the enthusiasm for locally based maintenance. The notion of villages and parishes providing better information services about local countryside access opportunities (Countryside Commission, 1992a) may also meet with limited success if its principal effect is simply to encourage use by non-locals.

Above all, there is scope to place countryside management, particularly in relation to access, on a firmer statutory footing. It is management that lies at the cutting edge of provision and yet, as has been noted in Chapter 2, countryside management has grown, despite rather than because of, legislative provisions. It has been dependent on the skills of individual project officers, voluntary effort, experimental schemes and fragile resources. And where it has been planned it has been through informal mechanisms such as countryside strategies, rather than statutory plans.

Individual initiatives like the Parish Paths Partnership can only perpetuate this fragility. Clearer and longer-term resources and administrative structures need to be set into a statutory management framework, placing the responsibilities and benefits of provision for access more clearly on the public authority on the one hand and the landowner on the other.

This co-ordinated management action could be greatly facilitated by a reconsideration of government employment schemes to allow the reintroduction of programmes along the lines of the Community Programme and Employment Action that would allow permanent employment and income-generating work forces, much needed in rural areas, to contribute to the management of access. Only with the amelioration of the ambiguities and responsibilities for the management of access though such statutory mechanisms will the enduring conflicts between the landowner and those citizens seeking access be reduced.

9.3.6 Access rights and the market place

At the margins between market-based facilities and citizens rights lies the area of paying market prices for access opportunities. Where these opportunities have not existed historically, either in *de jure* or *de facto* terms, this may be legitimate. Indeed, the introduction of Access Agreements under the 1949 National Parks and Access to the Countryside Act establishes this as a precedent. Farm diversification will bring increasing pressures or opportunities for this means of securing access as the growth in the use of bridleway tolls, considered in Chapter 3, illustrates. In these developments it is important that appropriate regulation is enforced, for which provision is made in the negotiation of access agreements, to ensure that *de jure* and *de facto* rights are not impaired.

It is where access provision lies on the cusp between the market and citizens rights, however, that the greatest difficulties in policy development lie. On the one hand, rights of access give the landowner legal responsibilities without a guarantee of income to fulfil those responsibilities. On the other hand, access agreements for open country and payment for the maintenance of access rights over a five-year agreed management plan under the Countryside Stewardship Scheme, ELMs and so on, encourage farmers faced with declining incomes to consider access rights as market commodities.

Certainly under these changing circumstances a closer investigation is required, over the longer term, into rights, externalities, public goods and the cost of sound management. Here too, closer liaison is required between the various agencies, the Ministry of Agriculture, local authorities and so on, that are responsible for the promulgation of individual initiatives.

9.4 THE SOCIAL COMPOSITION OF PARTICIPATION AND PEOPLE'S PREFERENCES

The third proposition of this book suggests that policies and plans have not paid full regard to the social composition of recreation participation and have not fully taken into account people's preferences for recreation and access in the countryside. It has been suggested in the previous section that the social structure of participation, skewed as it is towards the more affluent members of society, is a key feature in the reassessment of recreation facilities as market commodities, as a component of public policy.

The nature of people's preferences, however, also has consequences for public policy in the social sphere. It has been noted in Chapter 5 that a number of attempts at promulgating social policies have been less than successful because there is a strong element of preference in people's propensity not to participate in countryside recreation, particularly among lower social groups. This has led certain social policies actually to be regressive as the more affluent take advantage of them more than the less affluent. Despite these instances does the development of social policies for countryside recreation nevertheless have a role? In answering this question, three generic types of social policy can be considered.

9.4.1 Demand management policies

The core of the development of social policies for rural leisure, as they have been manifest, lies in the fact that they are policies that are inherently restricted to influencing the type and extent of recreation supply, when inhibitions to participation arise as a result of a lack of access to characteristics that influence demand. It might be argued from this that it is demand management policies, rather than supply-based policies, that are likely to be most effective in manipulating the social structure of participation.

Unfortunately, it is unlikely to be the case that demand management policies can have an effective role in countryside recreation since the factors that influence the demand for it are much too broad and fundamental to come under the influence of recreation policy *per se*. It is difficult to envisage recreation policies which, in themselves, will significantly alleviate the time constraints of upper social groups and the material constraints (such as income and car ownership levels) of lower social groups.

These constraints are more likely to be changed by broader social policies and the nature of economic growth. A number of authors have therefore argued, (Roberts, 1979) that it is the improvement of more general social conditions that will allow people to make their own choices over leisure, that is more likely to solve the problem of need. Young and Willmot (1973, p. 127) to consider that:

> Without more equality in general . . . more and more kinds of leisure will be shut off from the poor and carless, young and, even more, old.

The Countryside Review Committee (1977, p. 16) also maintains that countryside recreation should be a more general part of government social policy, rather than specifically focused on individual recreation initiatives:

> This surely is an important social objective, particularly in relation to the underprivileged, for the contribution, physical, mental and emotional, which countryside recreation can make to the quality of urban life as a whole is self-evident.

Certainly in the leisure context, it has been policies of this wider social nature, such as the universal holidays with pay development in the earlier part of this century, that have had the greatest impact on people's ability to participate in rural leisure opportunities. The fact that participation in countryside recreation does not feature strongly as an objective of social policy generally may derive from an understanding that an interest in it is not universal. It is more likely, however, that countryside recreation is simply not important enough either to people or, perhaps, policy-makers, relative to other deprivations, such as housing and employment, to merit a specific priority in general social policy.

9.4.2 Supply-led policies: stimulating preferences

The potential of demand management policies for countryside recreation, then, is likely to fall beyond the remit of the recreation policy-maker. But while supply-led policies are a more feasible option for recreation provision, their effect is likely to be more limited in terms of influencing the social structure of participation. Do supply-led policies nevertheless have a role as social policies?

A first consideration for supply-led policies might be to further stimulate people's preferences for the countryside. Since preference is less among lower social groups, certainly for more passive types of recreation, then a stimulation of preference could provide a more than proportionate increase in participation among lower social groups. It does seem inherently, however, that policies designed to encourage people to do things in which they show little interest have little application. Certainly, without the consideration of people's preference, there is always the danger of basing social policy on the 'middle-class-professional' values approach to policy formulation which is based on presumptions about people's behaviour, rather than observation.

Accommodating preferences, on the face of it, seems to be the thinking behind the Countryside Commission's 'Operation Gateway' project (Ashcroft, 1986) which aims to 'widen people's horizons so that the countryside becomes more naturally used by people from all walks of life'. Certainly, such a policy may engender the interest of 'disadvantaged' groups, but it does appear to be at variance with the government statements, noted in Chapter 3, that all maintain that public policies for recreation should be developed in line with people's 'wishes', 'interests' and 'choices', rather than be developed to change any of these parameters of preference.

It might perhaps be more appropriate if preferences are to be the concern of supply-led policies, and the encouragement of less advantaged social groups is considered important, that policies are developed that cater for facilities in which these social groups are most interested – zoos, safari parks, theme parks, and so on. The Operation Gateway project tries to overturn this notion (Ashcroft, 1986, p. 6):

> Some disadvantaged people's traditional enjoyment comes from a high intensity of experience, with lots of things to do, entertainment and excitement. A challenge . . . is whether the slower pace but rich contents of the countryside can be interesting and enjoyable.

Harrison (1991, p. 130) also notes in respect of Operation Gateway, an element of coercion in trying to make the project successful:

> although cheap transport might prove one constraint on partici-
> pation, other community services would need to be employed as
> well if recreation trips were to become enjoyable experiences for
> people who had no tradition of countryside visiting.

Despite this public effort and expenditure, Harrison (1991, p. 132) concludes by noting how enduring people's preferences not to partici-pate in countryside recreation had been in Operation Gateway:

> When a trip was arranged on public transport . . . for a group who
> had already enjoyed a coach excursion to the countryside, only
> fifteen of an anticipated party of seventy arrived at the bus station.
> Even when the bus was diverted to people's homes, the organisers
> were unable to encourage people to join them.

The danger in developing supply-based policies to alter people's leisure preferences, then, lies in misplaced philanthropy. Those types of provi-sion that exploit the leisure preferences of lower social groups, for example more commercial activities, perhaps ironically are traditionally not within the jurisdiction of the public sector. When a group under the Operation Gateway project undertook to organize its own recreation trip, it went to the Blackpool Illuminations! (Harrison, 1991). In this respect, the Countryside Commission's (1992a) changing emphasis towards identifying people's preferences more closely, and then provid-ing for them along market lines, is likely to be more successful than social policies based on coercion.

9.4.3 Supply-led policies: overcoming constraints

A second consideration for supply-led policies might be to focus on reducing the constraints on participation experienced by various social groups. This notion of targeting is put forward by the Centre for Leisure Research (1986):

> Non-participants could more appropriately be the targets of any
> public policy which seeks to promote participation. Mobility is a
> particular policy area here, particularly for the elderly and the
> disabled.

But the examples of recreation transport policies, policies for location and policies for free access considered in Chapter 5 have shown that such policies are simply too blunt a set of instruments for differentiating either between constraints and interests or between one social group and another.

Indeed the House of Lords Select Committee on Sport and Leisure (1973, p. 12) questions the need to differentiate between social groups in leisure provision:

> leisure activities should be available to all, whether they can afford to pay for them or not and whether their neighbourhood is rich or poor.

But the naivity of this blanket approach is captured well by Ravenscroft (1991) who notes that even in the context of the 'Sport for All' policies of the Sports Council, inequalities in the structure of sports participation have persisted. He suggests that such social policies, aimed at reducing constraints on participation, have principally allowed those who would have been active in any event, to participate more and at a considerably lower cost than they might have been otherwise prepared to pay. He cites Gratton and Taylor (1985, pp. 215–16) in this respect:

> Even if we regard recreation as a 'need', it is naive to expect that . . . offering recreation services at subsidised prices is an ideal way to cater for that need. The inefficient way to spend public money is to subsidise every consumer, since some consumers will consume above the desired minimum without subsidy. It is not only inefficient but also inequitable when the main beneficiaries of the subsidies are the better off.

It is this problem, too, that has exercised the concern of government agencies on both sides of the Atlantic where both the Department of the Environment's (1975b) *Recreation and Deprivation in Inner-Urban Areas* and the US Department of the Interior's (1978) *National Urban Recreation Study* felt that public policy in recreation provision may well be inadvertently concentrating on the needs of the better off, and neglecting those of poorer sections of society.

Despite these compelling problems, the Countryside Commission's (1987b) *Policies for Enjoying the Countryside*, contains a number of social policies, under the guise of 'Policies for People', which were updated in 1992 (Countryside Commission, 1992a). In terms of improving people's awareness, proposals included 'marketing' recreation at the places people live and work, including in newspapers and on the local radio. Since, however, from the 1984 National Survey of Countryside Recreation the vast majority of people are informed of recreation opportunities either through word of mouth or familiarity, and the media (radio, TV and newspapers) appear to have no direct impact at all, this proposal is likely to have little direct effect.

Policies for promoting an understanding among the public are also likely to be of limited value where they simply enhance the interpretation facilities at individual sites, as has already been noted in Chapter 2. Of more value, perhaps, is the notion of enhancing environmental education in schools within the national curriculum, considered in the previous section, since this policy is generally more one of demand management, influencing the attributes of the population at large.

Ultimately, it may be that countryside recreation policy overall has a limited role to play as a 'social' policy influencing people's behaviour patterns. It could perhaps be more constructive to accept that these patterns are more likely to be influenced by exogenous social policies and that the real role of recreation policy lies in the development of land-use and land-management systems to cater for a predetermined profile of participation.

9.5 RESTRICTIVE POLICIES

The fourth proposition of this book suggests that policies for country-side recreation, particularly in land-use terms, have generally been preoccupied with fears of a recreation explosion and the rights of the landowner rather than the development of recreation opportunities, and have been unduly restrictive as a result. This proposition has been justified throughout the book in historical terms, but particular focus has been given to the nature of land-use planning process in Chapters 6 and 7. The facts that recreation participation has declined during the 1980s, and that recreation damage to the countryside is largely unproven, do suggest that a policy agenda for the 1990s might be more progressive than has historically been the case, particularly for strategic land-use plans.

Rather than basing structure plan policies on presumptions about recreation behaviour, these should now be disposed to providing people more directly with what they want. Policies for recreation facilities, particularly if considered in their market context as proposed in the previous section, should be more clearly **promotional**. This is not to suggest that they should compromise environmental objectives but should, rather, be clearly concerned to identify the most appropriate areas within counties where market goods for rural leisure purposes can most appropriately be developed. The renewed strength of structure plans provided by the 1990 Town and Country Planning Act and the 1991 Planning and Compensation Act allows this promotion to take place with appropriate environmental safeguards. Policies for the access rights of the citizen should be more clearly based upon facilitation rather than promotion, since such opportunities cater for a more affluent sector of the population and promotional policies of direct state intervention, therefore, constantly run the risk of being socially regressive. The notion of facilitation does not deny inherent access rights and at the same time allows public authorities to fulfil their statutory obligations.

As with countryside management, the more progressive and promotional countryside strategies and countryside recreation strategies should be given statutory recognition. This would serve not only to place strategies that are at the cutting edge of recreation and access implementation and management on a firmer footing, but would also allow non-land-use policies to be given some formal legal status. This is important, since the development of informal strategies has shown that many of the central issues for strategic recreation planning, considered in Chapter 7, fall outside of the land-use planning framework and are therefore not susceptible for inclusion in statutory structure plans.

To a degree, some of these principles are finding their way into policy reappraisals for the 1990s, heralding a shift, in some quarters at least, from policies of restriction and control to policies of encouragement and sound management. The Central Council for Physical Recreation (1991), for example, calls for the Countryside Commission, the Countryside Council for Wales, and English Nature to initiate further research into possible conflicts in the countryside between recreation and conservation. Any real problems thrown up by such research should be overcome by management plans and management agreements which accommodate all interests.

The Department of the Environment (1992d) takes a clear promotional stance in respect of multiple recreation uses of the countryside, as long as there is no harm to the countryside itself. English Nature (1992), in collaboration with the Countryside Commission, is also seeking to create wider opportunities for quiet enjoyment as long as it is coupled with suitable management to minimize impacts. The Sports Council (1992), too, in producing for the first time a nationally orchestrated policy for the countryside, believes that throughout most of the countryside there is scope to increase the number of people taking part, without leading to conflict with other countryside uses. In pursuit of this, it promotes a policy of 'sustainable promotion', which is defined as:

> the encouragement of people to take part in countryside activities while having regard to the long term need to maintain the natural resources. The long term conservation of the finite 'natural' resources of the countryside is essential for the long term continuation and development of countryside activities (p. 9)

Thus, active sport and recreation in the countryside are to be positively promoted in ways which allow increases in participation to be sustainable with respect to natural resources. For the very small number of critical areas where recreation has been shown to be clearly damaging, the Sports Council calls for 'alternative sites' to be made available so that recreation opportunities as a whole are not diminished. For other areas, land-use designations should be encouraged that signal clearly, recreation as a priority land use.

By 1992 the Countryside Commission (1991b, 1992a) had come round to supporting the lead taken by the Sports Council and some sports governing bodies in promoting recreation, but with appropriate environmental safeguards. Specifically the Commission commits itself, as part of its policy, to agree with the Sports Council a code of practice for sport and the conservation of the countryside, to carry out with others further research into the relationship between sport, recreation and conservation, and to carry out an environmental assessment of its own recreation policies to ensure compatibility with the sustainable use of natural resources. In all of this it urges that the reflations between sport and recreation 'be assessed realistically and not defensively'.

The Commission also proposes to revise its previous objective in relation to enjoying the countryside (Countryside Commission, 1991b, p. 11) to reflect the need for sustainable promotion:

> to improve and extend opportunities for the public to enjoy the countryside in ways that help to sustain both its environmental quality and the social and economic well-being of rural communities (p. 11).

The challenge for the 1990s is to ensure that this shifting policy stance finds its way into implementable strategic policies at the local-authority level.

9.6 RECREATION AS A RESIDUAL INTEREST

The final proposition of this book suggests that policies for recreation and access have sustained a residual priority in pressures for change in the countryside, particularly in relation to those of the conservation interest. The policy proposals contained in this chapter will undoubtedly go some way towards ameliorating this imbalance. Clearer ministerial responsibilities, a singular Countryside Recreation Commission and the rationalization of countryside recreation and access responsibilities in local authority departments will do much to reduce the confusion over agency roles and will allow a clearer identification of a small number of agencies and departments less ambiguously disposed towards championing the recreation and access cause.

Second, a clearer recognition of the potential of recreation facilities as market commodities will reduce uncertainties in their provision. It will allow those currently in the control of the state sector to be operated more clearly along market lines rather than being fettered by the often conflicting objectives of attempting to cater for market demands and social needs simultaneously. Simply put, it will allow policy-makers to provide people with what they want, measured through the market, rather than any philanthropic notions of what they ought to have. The market orientation of facilities will also provide a clearer focus for strategic planning, where facilities can be treated as any other market commodity and in this respect they can be positively promoted within the context of the environmental safeguards of strong development plans.

Third, this 'privatization' of facilities will allow the public sector to focus its responsibilities of provision on the access rights of the citizen. In facilitating these rights, improving public understanding, making more extensive use of existing powers and new legislation relating to rights of way and common land will all assist in clarifying the legitimacy of where the public may, and may not exploit access opportunities more fully as a right. Placing management for access on a firmer statutory footing and making it less reliant on voluntary effort and individual personalities will further serve to clarify, and reduce the ambiguity of, such access rights.

Fourth, a recognition of the inherent limitations of supply-based recreation and access policies in manipulating the social structure of participation will reduce the possibility of the development of public policies that constantly run the risk of being socially regressive. Because such policies are not a sufficiently important part of national social policy priorities they do not offer the potential for demand management and as such, except in exceptional and selective circumstances, they should cease to be pursued.

Fifth, in the light of declining overall levels of participation during the 1980s, policies at both the national level and in strategic planning should become less restrictive. Chapter 8 has shown that basing restrictive policies on presumptions about the damage that recreation might cause to the countryside generally is largely unfounded, and that, rather, sound management principles, based upon notions of sustainability, might more appropriately form a component part of progressive policies. Placing such management principles on a firmer statutory footing and more formally involving the landowner in their execution will make a valuable contribution to the development of recreation and access opportunities more closely aligned to amenity and scientific conservation interests.

A further challenge relates to a political realignment , particularly in the shire counties, that no longer serves to suppress recreation interests in the way that it has done historically. As Harrison (1991, p. 14) notes:

> in practice, a powerful alliance between landed interests, environmentalists and rural local authorities gained ground throughout the 20th century and together they were often aligned against recreationists.

Overcoming this alliance certainly will be difficult. As has been considered in Chapters 1 and 2, it has been one of the principal causes, historically, of the suppression of recreation and access opportunities. Public policy will need to stress the minimal damage of recreation, particularly relative to agriculture and forestry practices, and even some of the environmental benefits that can accrue, particularly in the context of sustainable management. If such notions might go some way towards convincing the environmentalist, appeasing landed interests and local authorities might focus on the market potential of recreation facilities and the fact that an active interest in countryside recreation is probably witnessing a structural decline anyway. The elevation of the importance of management, particularly for access opportunities, to a legitimate and paid-for function of the farmer and landowner, as custodians, and therefore a central part of their work, may do much to ameliorate the historical antipathy towards access on their part, where it has invariably been seen as an intrusion into their legitimate economic activity.

In this respect, if a lesson is to be learned from history it is that policy should no longer attempt to resolve just the recreation and access issues of the past, so that it is more or less out of date as soon as it is formulated. It should, instead, be anticipatory.

In anticipating the late 1990s, it is probably a fundamental reformulation of the Common Agricultural Policy that provides the biggest challenge for recreation and access policy-makers. Agricultural (and indeed forestry) land can no longer be considered sacrosanct for recreation and access, as national policies and the policies of structure plans in the 1970s and 1980s considered it. There is in the 1990s, by dint of European policy, an agricultural land surplus. This provides a whole new canvas upon which to develop market policies for countryside recreation and public policies for the citizens rights of access, central to the economic activities of the farmer and landowner, that has never been available before.

References

Aldridge, D. (1975) Principles of countryside interpretation and interpretive planning, Part I of *A Guide to Countryside Interpretation*, Countryside Commissions for England and Wales and Scotland, HMSO, London.

Applied Leisure Marketing (1985) *Culture, Nature or White Knuckle? A Research Survey of Visitors to Commercial Leisure Attractions*, ALM, London.

Ashcroft, P. (1986) Gateway to the countryside. *Countryside Commission News*, **20**, March/April.

Ashley, P.P. (1978) Barbed wire entanglement. *Guardian*, 14 October, p. 13.

Association of Metropolitan Authorities (1986) *Leisure Policy Now*, AMA, London, March.

Atkins, R. (1991) *Review of Sport and Active Recreation*, Department of Education and Science, London.

Avon County Council (1982) *Avon County Structure Plan*, explanatory memorandum, County Planning Dept, Bristol.

Avon County Council (1991) *Structure Plan, Third Alteration*, draft on deposit, County Planning Dept, Bristol.

Bain, C., Dodd, A. and Pritchard, D. (1990) *RSPB Planscan: a Study of Development Plans in England and Wales*, Conservation Topic Paper No. 28, October, Royal Society for the Protection of Birds, London.

Baker, E. (1924) *The Forbidden Land: A Plea for Access to Mountains, Moors and Other Wastelands in Great Britain*, Witherby, London.

Barrow-in-Furness Borough Council (1980) *Barrow-in-Furness Wildlife and Habitats (Subjects Plan)*, Borough Planning Dept, Barrow-in-Furness.

Batten, L.A. (1987) Sailing on reservoirs and its effects on water birds, *Biological Conservation*, **11**.

Bayfield, N.G. (1987) Positive approaches to management of the uplands, in *Recreation and Wildlife: Working in Partnership*, Countryside Recreation Research Advisory Group Conference, 25–7 September, York University.

Bayfield, N.G. and Aitken, R. (1992) *Managing the Impacts of Recreation on Vegetation and Soils: a Review of Techniques*, Report to the Countryside Commission, Countryside Commission for Scotland, Countryside Council for Wales and English Nature, Institute of Terrestrial Ecology.

Bayfield, N.G. and McGowan, G.M. (1986) *Footpath Survey, 1986. The Three Peaks Project*, Institute of Terrestial Ecology Report No. 1 to the Yorkshire Dales National Park, YDNP, Grassington.

Bedfordshire County Council (1980) *The Structure Plan for Bedfordshire*, County Planning Department, Bedford.

Bedfordshire County Council (1990) *Bedfordshire's Countryside: A Strategy for Action*, County Planning Dept, May, Bedford.

Benson, J.F. (1986) Integrating conservation and recreation priorities in the rural landscape, *Landscape Issues*, **3**(1), April.

Benson, J.F. and Willis, K.G. (1990) *The Aggregate Value of the Non-Priced Recreation Benefits of the Forestry Commission Estate*, A Report to the Forestry Commission, Environmental Research Consultants, University of Newcastle upon Tyne, January.

Berkshire County Council (1991) *Berkshire Structure Plan, 1990–2006* submission document, Royal County of Berkshire, Dept of Highways and Planning, Reading, November.

Big Farm Weekly (1990) ELMS takes route in Devon, 15 February.

Blunden, J. and Curry, N. R. (eds) (1985) *The Changing Countryside*, The Open University/Countryside Commission, Croom Helm, Birkhamstead.

Blunden, J. and Curry, N. R. (eds) (1988) *A Future for Our Countryside*, Basil Blackwell, Oxford.

Blunden, J. and Curry, N. R.(eds) (1990) *A People's Charter? 40 Years of the 1949 National Parks and Access to the Countryside Act*, HMSO, London.

Bonyhady, T. (1987) *The Law of the Countryside: The Rights of the Public*, Professional Books, Abingdon.

Bovaird, A. G., Tricker, M. T. and Stoakes, R. (1982) *The Role of Charging Policies in Countryside Recreation Management Facilities*, Paper to the Management and Compulsion in the Countryside Symposium, Institute of British Geographers, University of Southampton, January.

Bovaird, A. G., Tricker, M. T. and Stoakes, R. (1984) *Recreation Management and Pricing*, Aldershot, Gower Publishing.

Bracken, I. (1980) *A Policy Analytic Framework for Structure Plans*, Department of Town Planning, University of Wales Institute of Science and Technology, Cardiff, June.

Bracken, I. (1982) Towards an analytical framework for land use planning, *Urban Studies*, **19**.

Bradshaw, A.D. (1979) Derelict land: is the tidying up going too far?, *The Planner*, **65**.

British Tourist Authority (1990) *Digest of Tourist Statistics*, No. 14, BTA, London.

Broadhurst, R. (1987) Forest recreation: orienteering in woodlands and forests, in *Recreation and Wildlife: Working in Partnership*, Countryside Recreation Research Advisory Group Conference, 25–7 September, York University.

Bromley, P. (1990) *Countryside Management*, E & F N Spon, London.

Broom, G. (1991) Pricing the countryside: the context, Countryside Recreation Research Advisory Group. *Our Priceless Countryside, Should It Be Priced?*, Annual Conference Report, Manchester, University of Manchester Institute of Science and Technology, 25–7 September.

Brotherton, I. (1975) The development and management of country parks in England and Wales. *Journal of Biological Conservation*, **7**.

Bruton, M. and Nicholson, D. (1987) *Local Planning in Practice*, The Built Environment Series, Hutchinson, London.

Buckinghamshire County Council (1989) *Buckinghamshire Countryside Strategy, Countryside Recreation*, County Planning Dept, Aylesbury.

Bureau of Outdoor Recreation (1967) *Outdoor Recreation Trends*, BOR, Washington.

Burton, T. L. and Wibberley, G. P. (1965) *Outdoor Recreation in the British Countryside*, Research Report, Wye College, University of London.

Cabinet Office (1985) *Pleasure, Leisure and Jobs: The Business of Tourism*, Enterprise Unit, HMSO, London.

Cambridgeshire County Council (1980) *The Structure Plan for Cambridgeshire*, approved plan, County Planning Dept, Cambridge.

Carruthers, S. P. (ed.) (1986) *Land-use Alternatives for U.K. Agriculture*, Centre for Agricultural Strategy, University of Reading, CAS Report No. 12, April.

Central Council for Physical Recreation (1960) *Sport and the Community*, The Report of the Wolfenden Committee on Sport, CCPR, London.

Central Council for Physical Recreation (1991) *Sport and Recreation in the Countryside* (May), CCPR, London.

Central Statistical Office (1985) *Social Trends No. 15*, HMSO, London.

Centre for Leisure Research (1986) *Access to the Countryside for Recreation and Sport*, CCP 217, Countryside Commission, Cheltenham; Sports Council, London.

Chairman's Policy Group (1983) *Leisure Policy for the Future*, discussion paper.

Cherry, G. (1975) *Environmental Planning 1939–1969, Volume II: National Parks and Recreation in the Countryside*, Peacetime History of Environmental Planning, HMSO, London.

Cherry, G. (1985) Scenic heritage and national park lobbies and legislation in England and Wales. *Leisure Studies*, **4**.

Cheshire County Council (1979) *The Structure Plan for Cheshire*, approved plan, County Planning Dept, Chester.

Cheshire County Council (1991) *A Rural Strategy for Cheshire*, County Planning Dept and others, January, Chester.

Clark, G. (1992) Rural tourism in Britain in the 1990s, in Bowler, I., Bryant C. and Nellis D., *Contemporary Rural Systems in Transition*, **2**, CAB International, Oxford.

Clayden, P. (1992) *Our Common Land, the Law and History of Commons and Village Greens*, Open Spaces Society, Henley, Oxfordshire.

Cleveland County Council (1977a) *The Structure Plan for Teeside*, approved plan, County Planning Dept, Middlesbrough.

Cleveland County Council (1977b) *The East and West Cleveland Structure Plans*, approved plans, County Planning Dept, Middlesbrough.

Cleveland County Council (1978) *River Tees Plan for Access and Recreation*, local subject plan, County Planning Dept, Middlesbrough.

Cleveland County Council (1990) *Approved Replacement Structure Plan*, County Planning Dept, Middlesbrough.

Cloke, P. J. (1983) *An Introduction to Rural Settlement Planning*, London, Methuen.

Cloke, P. J. and Park, C. C. (1985) *Rural Resource Management*, Croom Helm, Birkhamstead.

Clwyd County Council (1979) *Clwyd Special Landscape Area Subject Plan*, County Planning Dept, Mold.

Clwyd County Council (1990) *Recreation in the Countryside: a Strategy for Clwyd*, County Planning Dept, Mold.

Clwyd County Council (1991) *Approved Structure Plan Alteration Number One*, County Planning Dept, Mold.

Coalter, F. (1985) The defence of public leisure services: professional rationality or political struggle? *Leisure Management*, **5**(5).

Coalter, F., Long, J. A. and Duffield, B. S. (1986) *The Rationale for Public Sector Investment in Leisure*, report prepared for the Sports Council and the Social Science Research Council Joint Panel on Recreation and Leisure.

Cobham Resource Consultants (1983) *Countryside Sports: their Economic*

Significance, The Standing Conference of Country Sports, the College of Estate Management, Reading.

Cobham Resource Consultants (1988) *A Holiday Village in the Cotswold Water Park: Environmental Statement,* CRS, Abingdon, Oxfordshire.

Coopers Lybrand Associates (1979) *Rufford Country Park Marketing Study,* CCP129, Countryside Commission, Cheltenham.

Cornwall County Council (1983) *Cornwall Countryside Local Plan,* written statement, April, County Planning Dept.

Cotswold Water Park Joint Advisory Committee (1983) *Cotswold Water Park Review,* CWPJAC, Cirencester.

Council for National Parks (1990) *A Vision for National Parks,* evidence to the National Park Review Panel, CNP, London.

Council for Nature (1965) *Outdoor Recreation, Active and Passive,* Countryside in 1970 Conference, Report of Study Group 6, Royal Society of Arts, London.

Council for Nature (1966) *The Countryside in 1970: Proceedings of the First Conference,* Second Report, Royal Society of Arts, London.

Council for the Protection of Rural England (1990) *Our Finest Landscapes*: CPRE Submission to the National Parks Review Panel, CPRE, London.

Country Landowners' Association (1984) *Agreeing on Access,* CLA, London.

Country Landowners' Association (1992) *Recreation and Access in the Countryside: A Better Way Forward,* CLA, London.

Countryside Commission (1970) *Planning for Informal Recreation on the Sub-regional Scale: the Sherwood Forest Study,* CCP 69, CC, London.

Countryside Commission (1972) *Policy on Country Parks and Picnic Sites,* CC, February, London.

Countryside Commission (1974a) *Advisory Notes on Country Park Plans,* CCP 80, CC, Cheltenham.

Countryside Commission (1974b) *Advisory Notes on National Park Plans,* CCP 81, CC, Cheltenham.

Countryside Commission (1976a) *The Lake District Upland Management Experiment,* CCP 93, CC, Cheltenham.

Countryside Commission (1976b) *The Bollin Valley: A Study of Land Management in the Urban Fringe,* CCP 97, CC, Cheltenham.

Countryside Commission (1977) *Grants to Local Authorities and Other Public Bodies for Conservation and Recreation in the Countryside,* CCP 78, January, CC, Cheltenham (reprinted from May 1974).

Countryside Commission (1979a) *Digest of Countryside Recreation Statistics,* CCP 86, CC, Cheltenham (reprinted from 1975).

Countryside Commission (1979b) *The Snowdonia Upland Managment Experiment,* CCP 122, CC, Cheltenham.

Countryside Commission (1979c) *Leisure and the Countryside,* CCP 124, CC, Cheltenham.

Countryside Commission (1981) *Recreational Public Transport,* AS 5, CC, Cheltenham.

Countryside Commission (1982a) *Countryside Issues and Actions: Prospectus for the Countryside Commission,* CCP 151, CC, Cheltenham.

Countryside Commission (1982b) *Participation in Informal Countryside Recreation,* CCP 152, CC, Cheltenham

Countryside Commission (1983) *A Management Plan for the Green Belt Area in Barnet and South Hertfordshire, 1982–1987,* CCP 147, CC, Cheltenham.

Countryside Commission (1985a) The Access Charter, *Countryside Commission News,* January.

Countryside Commission (1985b) *National Survey of Countryside Recreation 1984*, CP 201, CC, Cheltenham.

Countryside Commission (1986) *Report of the Common Land Forum*, CC, Cheltenham.

Countryside Commission (1987a) *New Opportunities for the Countryside: Countryside Policy Review Panel*, CCP 224, CC, Cheltenham.

Countryside Commission (1987b) *Policies for Enjoying the Countryside*, CCP 234, CC, Cheltenham.

Countryside Commission (1987c) *Enjoying the Countryside: Priorities for Action*, CCP 235, CC, Cheltenham.

Countryside Commission (1987d) *A Compendium of Recreation Statistics 1984–6*, CC, Cheltenham.

Countryside Commission (1989a) *Recreational Cycling in the Countryside*, CCP 259, CC, Cheltenham.

Countryside Commission (1989b) *Planning for a Greener Countryside*, CCP 264, CC, Cheltenham.

Countryside Commission (1989c) *Paths Routes and Trails: Policies and Priorities*, CCP 266, CC, Cheltenham.

Countryside Commission (1989d) *Managing Rights of Way, an Agenda for Action*, CCP 273, CC, Cheltenham.

Countryside Commission (1989e) *Common Knowledge?*, CCP 281, CC, Cheltenham.

Countryside Commission (1990a) *Annual Report 1989–1990*, CC, Cheltenham.

Countryside Commission (1990b) *National Park Supplementary Grant in England for 1991/92*, CC, Cheltenham.

Countryside Commission (1990c) *Ten Critical Years: an Agenda for the 1990s*, CC, Cheltenham.

Countryside Commission (1990d) *Capital Tax Relief for Outstanding Scenic Land*, CCP 204, CC, Cheltenham.

Countryside Commission (1990e) *National Rights of Way Condition Survey 1988* CCP 284, CC, Cheltenham.

Countryside Commission (1991a) *Caring for the Countryside: A Policy Agenda for England in the 1990s*, CC, Cheltenham.

Countryside Commission (1991b) *Visitors to the Countryside: a Consultation Paper*, CCP 341, CC, Cheltenham.

Countryside Comission (1992a) *Enjoying the Countryside: Policies for People*, CCP 371, CC, Cheltenham.

Countryside Commission (1992b) *Rights of Way: and Action Guide*, CCP 375, CC, Cheltenham.

Countryside Commission (1993) *1990/91 Survey of Local Authority Public Expenditure on Public Rights of Way*, CC, Cheltenham.

Countryside Commission News (1989) *Commons Assurance*, Issue No. 37, May/June, CC, Cheltenham.

Countryside Commission for Scotland (1974) *A Parks System for Scotland*, CC, Perth.

Countryside Commission for Scotland (1982) *Promoting Lochore Meadows Country Park*, CC, Perth.

Countryside Review Committee (1977) *Leisure in the Countryside*, London, HMSO.

Crocker, S. (1986) Diversification: pitfalls or profits? *The Royal Agricultural College Journal*, **14**.

Cross, D. T. and Bristow, M. R. (eds) (1983) *English Structure Planning, A Commentary on Procedure and Practice in the 1970s*, Pion, London.

Cumbria County Council (1983) *The Cumbria and Lake District Joint Structure Plan*, approved plan, County Planning Dept, Carlisle.

Curry, N. R. (1980) A review of cost-benefit techniques in rural recreation planning. *Gloucestershire Papers in Local and Rural Planning*, Issue No. 7, April.

Curry, N. R. (1983) Crickley Hill Country Park 1982, A Visitor Survey and Review of Management Implications. *GlosCAT Working Paper No. 4*, Gloucester.

Curry, N. R. (1985a) Countryside recreation priorities in the rural landscape. *Landscape Issues*, **1**(1), January.

Curry, N. R. (1985b) Countryside recreation sites policy, in Rural Symposium. *Journal of Agricultural Economics*, **36**(1), January.

Curry, N. R. (1985c) Countryside recreation sites policy, a review. *Town Planning Review*, **56**(1), January.

Curry, N. R. (1986a) Recreation Policy and Legislation, unpublished Report to the Countryside Commission, August.

Curry, N. R. (1986b) New country code: don't touch? *Town and Country Planning*, February.

Curry, N. R. (1988) Recreation and tourism, in Gilg, A. (ed.), *International Yearbook of Rural Planning*, Elsever Applied Science, London.

Curry, N. R. (1991a) Visitors to the Countryside: the Analysis of Responses, unpublished report to the Countryside Commission, Cheltenham, September.

Curry, N. R. (1991b) *Charging the Customer to Raise Funds*, workshop to the Countryside and Recreation Research Advisory Group annual conference, Our Priceless Countryside, Should it be Priced?, University of Manchester Institute of Science and Technology, 25–7 September, Manchester.

Curry, N. R. (1992a) Nature conservation, countryside strategies and strategic planning, *Journal of Environmental Planning and Management*, **35**(1).

Curry, N. R. (1992b) Recreation, access, amenity and conservation in the United Kingdom: the failure of integration, in Bowler I., Bryant C. and Nellis D., *Contemporary Rural Systems in Transition*, Vol. 2, CAB International, Oxford.

Curry, N. R. and Comley, A. (1985) Countryside Recreation Policies in Structure Plans, unpublished report to the Countryside Commission, the Commission, Cheltenham.

Curry, N. R. and Comley, A. (1986) Who enjoys the countryside? *Strathclyde Papers in Planning*, Department of Urban and Regional Planning, University of Strathclyde.

Curry, N. R., Edwards, D., Gratton, C., Ravenscroft, N., Roberts, K. and Taylor, P. (1986) Recreation 2000: Perspectives on the Future Recreation Policies of the Countryside Commission, unpublished report to the Countryside Commission, Cheltenham.

Curry, N. R. and Edwards, D. (1991) *Development Control in National Parks*, Royal Agricultural College, Centre for Rural Studies, Occasional Paper No. 16, Cirencester.

Curry, N. R. and Gaskell, P. T. G. (1989) *The Transition from the Community Programme to the Employment Training Programme: A Survey of its Impact on Environmental Work in the Countryside*, Working Paper CCD 37, Countryside Commission, Cheltenham.

Curry, N. R., Gaskell, P. T. G. and Turner, K. (1992) *Towards an Environmental Policy for the Hereford and Worcester Training and Enterprise Council*, report to HAWTEC, May, Worcester.

Curry, N. R. and Pack, C. M. (1992) Government advice for rural leisure planning, *Landscape Issues*, **9**(1 and 2).

Curry, N. R. and Pack, C. M. (1993) Planning on presumption: the case of strategic planning for countryside recreation in England and Wales. *Land Use Policy*, **10**(2), April.

Daily Telegraph (1990) Charge of the landowning brigade, 14 June.

Daily Telegraph (1992) Under wraps: your right to roam, 1 August.

Dartington Amenity Research Trust (1978) *Interpretation at Visitor Centres*, Countryside Commission, CCP 115, Cheltenham.

Department of Employment (1991) *Tourism and the Environment: Maintaining the Balance*, report of the Countryside Working Group, May.

Department of the Environment (1967) *Parliamentary Notes on Clauses to the 1967 Countryside Bill*, Department of the Environment Parliamentary Library, London.

Department of the Environment (1971) *Town and Country Planning Act, 1968*, Part I: Town and Country Planning (Structure and Local Plans) Regulations 1971 and Memorandum, Circular 44/71, HMSO, London.

Department of the Environment (1972) *Sinews for Survival: A Report on the Management of Natural Resources*, HMSO, London.

Department of the Environment (1974) *Structure Plans*, Circular 98/74, HMSO, London.

Department of the Environment (1975a) *Sport and Recreation*, White Paper, Cmd 6200, HMSO, London.

Department of the Environment (1975b) *Recreation and Deprivation in Inner Urban Areas*, HMSO, London.

Department of the Environment (1976a) *Report: National Parks Review Committee*, Circular 4/76, HMSO, London.

Department of the Environment (1976b) *Regional Councils for Sport and Recreation*, Circular 47/76, HMSO, London.

Department of the Environment (1977) *Regional Recreation Strategies*, Circular 73/77, HMSO, London.

Department of the Environment (1979) *Local Government and Tourism*, Circular 13/79, HMSO, London.

Department of the Environment (1980) *Development Control, Policy and Practice*, Circular 22/80, HMSO, London.

Department of the Environment (1981) *Local Government Planning and Land Act, 1980: Town and Country Planning: Development Plans*, Circular 23/81, HMSO, London.

Department of the Environment (1983a) *Public Rights of Way*, Circular 1/83, HMSO, London.

Department of the Environment (1983b) *Caravan Sites and Control of Development Act 1960*, Circular 23/83, HMSO, London.

Department of the Environment (1984) *Green Belts*, Circular 14/84, HMSO, London.

Department of the Environment (1988a) *Unitary Development Plans and the Town and Country Planning (Unitary Development Plans) Regulations 1988*, Circular 3/88, HMSO, London.

Department of the Environment (1988b) *Green Belts*, Planning Policy Guidance Note PPG 2, HMSO, London.

Department of the Environment (1988c) *Strategic Planning for the West Midlands*, Planning Policy Guidance Note PPG 10, HMSO, London.

Department of the Environment (1988d) *Strategic Guidance for Merseyside*, Planning Policy Guidance Note PPG 11, HMSO, London.

Department of the Environment (1989) *The Future of Development Plans*, Cm 569, HMSO, London.

Department of the Environment (1990a) *Regional Policy Guidance, Structure Plans and the Content of Development Plans*, Planning Policy Guidance Note PPG 15, HMSO, London.

Department of the Environment (1990b) *This Common Inheritance*, White Paper, Cm 1200, HMSO, London.

Department of the Environment (1991a) *Sport and Recreation*, Planning Policy Guidance Note PPG 17, HMSO, London.

Department of the Environment (1991b) *Regional Guidance for East Anglia*, Regional Planning Guidance Note RPG 6, HMSO, London.

Department of the Environment (1992a) *General Policy and Principles*, Planning Policy Guidance Note PPG 1, HMSO, London.

Department of the Environment (1992b) *The Countryside and the Rural Economy*, Planning Policy Guidance Note PPG 7, HMSO, London.

Department of the Environment (1992c) *Development Plans and Regional Guidance*, Planning Policy Guidance Note PPG 12, HMSO, London.

Department of the Environment (1992d) *Sport and Recreation*, Planning Policy Guidance Note 17, HMSO, London.

Department of the Environment (1992e) *Nature Conservation*, draft PPG, the Department, London.

Department of the Environment (1992f) *Tourism*, Planning Policy Guidance Note 21, HMSO, London.

Department of the Environment (1992g) *Action for the Countryside*, HMSO, London.

Derbyshire County Council (1991) *Countryside Strategy*, DCC, Derby.

Devon County Council (1981) *The Devon County Structure Plan*, approved plan, County Planning Dept, Exeter.

Devon County Council (1989) *Approved Structure Plan Alterations Numbers 1 and 2*, County Planning Dept, Exeter.

Donelley, P. (1986) The paradox of parks: politics of recreational land use before and after the mass trespass. *Leisure Studies*, 5(2).

Dower, J. (chairman) (1945) *National Parks in England and Wales*, Cmd 6628, HMSO, London.

Dower, M. (1965) The fourth wave: the challenge of leisure, A Civic Trust Survey. *Architect's Journal*.

Dower, M. (1978) *For Whom Have We Aimed to Provide, and How Is It to Be Achieved?*, Countryside Recreation Research Advisory Group, 1978 Conference, Countryside for All? A Review of the Use People Make of the Countryside for Recreation, Countryside Commission, CCP 117, CC, Cheltenham.

Duffield, B. (1982) A review of mobility and countryside recreation, in *Countryside Recreation in the 1980s, Current Research and Future Challenges?*, Countryside Recreation Research Advisory Group Conference, University of Bath, September.

Durham County Council (1981) *The Durham (with Darlington) Structure Plan*, approved plan, County Planning Dept, Durham.

Durham County Council (1989) *Countryside Recreation Strategy, 1989–1993*, County Planning Dept, Durham.

Dyfed County Council (1989) *Countryside Recreation and Access Strategy*, County Planning Dept, December, Carmarthen.

Edington, J. M., and Edington, M. A. (1986) *Ecology, Recreation and Tourism*, Cambridge University Press.

Edwards, R., Piggott, C. and Cope, R. (1989) An appraisal of the ecological effects of gill scrambling in the English Lake District, in Brown, B. (ed.),

Leisure and the Environment, Proceedings of the Leisure Studies Association Annual Conference, 1987, Bournemouth, LSA, Eastbourne.

Edwards, R. (Chairman) (1991) *Fit for the Future*, report of the National Parks Review Panel, Countryside Commission, CCP 334, CC, Cheltenham.

Elson, M. J. (1977) *A Review and Evaluation of Countryside Recreation Site Surveys*, Working Papers, Cheltenham, Countryside Commission.

Elson, M. J. (1986) *Green Belts: Conflict and Mediation in the Urban Fringe*, Heinemann, London.

Elson, M. J., Buller, H. and Stanley, P. (1986) *Providing for Motorsports: from Image to Reality*, Research Study 28, Sports Council, London.

English Nature (1991) Rural Strategies, internal memorandum, January.

English Nature (1992) *Enjoying Our Natural Heritage*, English Nature with the Countryside Commission, Peterborough.

English Tourist Board (1988) *Visitors to the Countryside*, ETB, London.

English Tourist Board and the Countryside Commission (1989) *Principles of Tourism in the Countryside*, ETB, London.

English Tourist Board and the Trades Union Congress (1976) *Holidays: the Social Need*, ETB, London.

Enjoying the Countryside Newsletter (1990) Ignore access at your peril, no 2, Winter.

Essex County Council (1982) *The Essex Structure Plan*, County Hall, Colchester.

Exmoor National Park (1981) *Visitor Survey Analysis 1980*, Park Authority, May.

Farming News (1990a) *Paying for Footpaths*, 26 January.

Farming News (1990b) *Footpath Signs May Have to Come Down*, 25 February.

Ferguson, M. J. (1979) A strategic choice approach to recreation site resource allocation. *Town Planning Review*, **50**(3), July.

Fitton, M. (1976) The urban fringe and the less privileged. *Countryside Recreation Review*, **1**, Countryside Commission, Cheltenham.

Fitton, M. (1978) The reality: for whom are we actually providing? *Countryside for All? A Review of the Use People Make of the Countryside for Recreation*, Countryside Recreation Research Advisory Group Conference, CCP 117, Countryside Commission, Cheltenham.

Fitton, M. (1979) Countryside recreation: the problems of opportunity. *Local Government Studies*, July/August.

Forestry Commission (1983) *Forestry Commission Census of Woodlands and Trees, 1979–1982*, FC, Edinburgh.

Gibbs, R. S. and Whitby, M. C. (1975) *Local Authority Expenditure on Access Land*, Research Monograph No. 6, Agricultural Adjustment Unit, University of Newcastle upon Tyne.

Gloucestershire County Council (1979) *The Structure Plan for Gloucestershire*, approved plan, County Planning Dept, December, Gloucester.

Glyptis, S. (1991) *Countryside Recreation*, Longman/Institute of Leisure and Amenity Management Series, London.

Glyptis, S. (1992) *Rural Recreation*, in Bowler I., Bryant C. and Nellis D., *Contemporary Rural Systems in Transition*, **2**, CAB International, Oxford.

Godwin, F. (1990) *Our Forbidden Land*, Jonathan Cape, London.

Goldsmith, F. B. (1983) The ecological effects of visitors and the restoration of damaged areas, in Warren, A. and Goldsmith, F. B. (eds), *Conservation in Practice*, John Wiley & Sons, Chichester.

Goldsmith, F. B. (1987) The wildlife perspective. *Recreation and Wildlife, Working in Partnership*, Countryside Recreation Research Advisory Group, annual conference report, 25–7 September, University of York.

Goldsmith, F B., Munton, R. J. C. and Warren, A. (1978) The impact of recreation on the ecology and amenity of semi-natural areas; methods of investigation used on the Isles of Scilly. *Biological Journal of the Linnean Society*, **2**.

Gosling (Chairman) (1967) *Report of the Footpaths Committee*, Ministry of Housing and Local Government, London, HMSO.

Gratton, C. and Taylor, P. (1985) *Sport and Recreation: An Economic Analysis*, E & F N Spon, London.

Grayson, A. J., Sidaway, R. M. and Thompson, F. P. (1973) *Some Aspects of Recreation Planning in the Forestry Commission*, Forestry Commission Research and Development Paper No. 95, FC, Edinburgh.

Greater London County Council (1976) *The Greater London Development Plan*, approved plan, County Planning and Transportation Dept, London.

Greater Manchester County Council (1981) *The Greater Manchester Structure Plan* approved plan, County Planning Dept, Manchester.

Green, B. H. (1985) *Countryside Conservation*, E & F N Spon, London.

Groome, D. (1991) Recreational traffic in the countryside. *Planning Transatlantic, Global Change and Local Problems*, Association of Collegiate Schools of Planning and the Association of European Schools of Planning Joint International Congress, July, Oxford.

Groome, D. and Tarrant, C. (1985) Countryside recreation: achieving access for all? *Countryside Planning Yearbook 1985*, Geo Publications, Norwich.

Gwent County Council (1981) *The Gwent Structure Plan*, written statement of policies and proposals, County Planning Dept, Cwmbran.

Gwent County Council (1989) *Enjoying the Gwent Countryside: 1990–1994*, a joint countryside recreation strategy, County Planning Dept, Cwmbran.

Hambledon District Council (1973) *Frensham Country Park: Signpost 2000*, HDC, Surrey.

Hampshire County Council (1983) *The Structure Plan for South West Hampshire*, approved plan, County Planning Dept, Winchester.

Hantrias, L. (1984) Social inequalities in leisure and French government policy. *Leisure Politics and Planning*, Leisure Studies Association International Conference.

Harrison, C. M. (1981) Recovery of lowland grassland and heathland in southern England from disturbance by seasonal trampling. *Biological Conservation*, **19**.

Harrison, C. M. (1983) Lowland heathland: the case for amenity land management, in Warren, A. and Goldsmith, F. B. (eds), *Conservation in Practice*, John Wiley & Sons, Chichester.

Harrison, C. (1991) *Countryside Recreation in a Changing Society*, TMS Partnership Ltd, London.

Harrison, C., Burgess, J., and Lumb, M. (1986) Popular Values for the Countryside, unpublished report to the Countryside Commission, CC, Cheltenham.

Healey, P. (1983) *Local Plans in British Land Use Planning*, Urban and Regional Planning Series, Vol. 31, Pergamon Press, Oxford.

Heart of England Tourist Board (1976) *Tourism in Rural Areas*, HETB, June, Worcester.

Heart of England Tourist Board (1989) *Quality First: A Tourism Strategy for the Heart of England into the 1990s*, HETB, Worcester.

Hereford and Worcester County Council (1991a) *Hereford and Worcester County Structure Plan*, Second Alterations to the Written Statement and Explanatory Memorandum, County Planning Dept, September, Worcester.

Hereford and Worcester County Council (1991b) *Countryside Recreation Strategy 1991–2001*, County Planning Dept, Worcester.

Hill, H. (1980) *Freedom to Roam: the Struggle for Access to Britain's Moors and Mountains*, Moorland Publishing, Ashbourne.

Hillman, M. and Whalley, A. (1978) *Fair Play for All*, Political and Economic Planning, Broadsheet No. 571, PEP, London.

HMSO (1944) *The Control of Land Use*, White Paper, Cmd 6537, HMSO, London.

HMSO (1972) *Forest Policy*, White Paper, June, HMSO, London.

Hobhouse, Sir Arthur (Chairman) (1947a) *Report of the National Park Committee (England and Wales)*, Cmd 7121, HMSO, London.

Hobhouse, Sir Arthur (Chairman) (1947b) *Report of the Special Committee on Footpaths and Access to the Countryside*, Cmd 7207, HMSO, London.

House of Lords (1973) *Second Report of the Select Committee on Sport and Leisure* (the Cobham Report), HL, 193, I–III, HMSO, London.

Humberside County Council (1980) *Coastal Caravans Plan*, Technical Services Department, Hull.

Humberside County Council (1988) *Humberside Structure Plan*, explanatory memorandum, Technical Services Department, March, Hull.

Illbury, B. W. (1989) Farm-based recreation: a possible sollution to falling farm incomes? *Journal of the Royal Agricultural Society of England*, **150**.

Kelly, J. R. (1978) Family leisure in three communities. *Journal of Leisure Research*, **10**(1).

Kent County Council (1990a) *Kent Countryside Strategy*, County Planning Dept, May, Maidstone.

Kent County Council (1990b) *A Planning Strategy for Kent*, Approved Kent Structure Plan and Explanatory Memorandum, County Planning Dept, Maidstone.

Kerry-Smith, V. (1976) Re-examining an old problem: the identification of demand curves in outdoor recreation. *Journal of Leisure Research*, **9**(4).

Lancashire County Council (1983) *Central and North Lancashire Structure Plan*, approved plan, County Planning Dept, Preston.

Lancashire County Council (1988) *A Countryside Recreation Strategy for Lancashire*, County Planning Dept, October, Preston.

Law, S. (1975) Leisure and recreation: problems and prospects. *Planning Outlook Special Issue, Planning for Recreation*, Summer.

Leicestershire County Council (1989) *Countryside 2000: Planning for Change in the Leicestershire Countryside: Action Strategy*, County Planning Dept, Leicester.

Liddle, M. J. (1975) A selective review of the ecological effects of human trampling on natural ecosystems, *Biological Conservation*, **7**.

Lincolnshire County Council (1979) *The Structure Plan for Lincolnshire*, Lincoln.

Lowe, P. (1983) A question of bias: appointments to rural planning agencies. *Town and Country Planning*, **52**.

Lowe, P., Clark, J. and Cox, G. (1991) *Reasonable Creatures: Rights and Rationalities in Valuing the Countryside*, paper to the Rural Economy and Society Study Group annual conference, University of York, 16–18 December.

Lowe, P. and Goyder, J. (1983) *Environmental Groups in Politics*, Allen & Unwin, Resource Management Series No. 6, London.

Lowerson, J. (1980) Battles for the countryside, in Gloversmith, F. (ed.) *Class, Culture and Social Change: New Views of the 1930s*, Harvester Press.

MacEwen, M. and MacEwen, A. (1982) *National Parks: Conservation or Cosmetics?* The Resource Management Series No. 5, George Allen & Unwin, London.

MacEwen, M. and MacEwen, A. (1987) *Greenprints for the Countryside? The Story of Britain's National Parks*, George Allen & Unwin, London.

McConaghy, R., Ogle, S. and Stott, A. (1992) *Northern Ireland Leisure Day Trips Survey, 1990–1991*, Northern Ireland Sports Council, Northern Ireland Tourist

Board and the Department of the Environment, Northern Ireland, HMSO, Belfast.

McIntosh, P. and Charlton, V. (1985) *The Impact of Sport for All Policy, 1966–1984, and a Way Forward*, Sports Council, London.

McLaughlin, B. P. and Singleton, D. (1979) Recreational use of a nature reserve: a case study in north Norfolk. *Journal of Environmental Management*, **9**.

McNab, A. (1985) Subject plans for the open countryside: a national survey, GlosCAT Working Paper, July, unpublished.

Madgwick, J. (1988) Nature reserved for whom? *Countryside Commission News*, **30**, Jan/Feb.

May, G. H. and Green, D. H. (1980) *Technology, Change and Planning: Content Analysis of Structure Plans with Reference to Employment*, Leeds Polytechnic, Planning Research Unit, Summer.

Melchett, P. (1985) Conservation gets a platform, *Farming News*, 22 November.

Ministry of Housing and Local Government (1970a) *Development Plans: a Manual of Form and Content*, HMSO, London.

Ministry of Housing and Local Government (1970b) *Sports Facilities and Planning Acts*, Circular 59/70, HMSO, London.

Ministry of Land and Natural Resources (1966) *Leisure in the Countryside of England and Wales*, Cmd 2928, HMSO, London.

Morrisey, J. (1986) Tourism and the public sector, *The Planner*, June.

National Farmers' Union (1990) *Land Use Policy Review*, NFU, London.

National Rivers Authority (1991) *Corporate Plan 1991/1992*, NRA, London.

National Trust for Places of Historic and Scientific Interest (1965) *Annual Report 1964–1965*, NTPHSI, London.

Nature Conservancy Council (1984) *Nature Conservation in Britain*, NCC, Peterborough.

Northamptonshire County Council (1985) *The Northamptonshire Structure Plan*, 1st Alteration, County Planning Dept, Northampton.

Northamptonshire County Council (1990) *A Rural Strategy for Northamptonshire*, County Planning Dept, Northampton.

Northumberland County Council (1980) *The Structure Plan for Northumberland*, approved plan, County Planning Dept, Morpeth.

North West Regional Council for Sport and Recreation (1989) *Progress Through Partnership: A Strategy for the Development of Sport and Recreation in the North West, 1990–1993*, NWRCSR, Manchester.

North York Moors National Park Committee (1984) *North York Moors National Park Plan*, First Review, Helmsley.

North Yorkshire County Council (1981) *North Yorkshire County Structure Plan*, approved plan, County Planning Dept, March, Northallerton.

Office of Population Censuses and Surveys (1976) *The General Household Survey 1973*, Social Survey Division, OPCS, HMSO, London.

Office of Population Censuses and Surveys (1979) *The General Household Survey 1977*, Social Survey Division, OPCS, HMSO, London.

Office of Population Censuses and Surveys (1982) *The General Household Survey 1980*, Social Survey Division, OPCS, HMSO, London.

Office of Population Censuses and Surveys (1985) *The General Household Survey 1983*, Series GHS 13, Social Survey Division, OPCS, HMSO, London.

Office of Population Censuses and Surveys (1988) *General Household Survey 1986*, Social Survey Division, HMSO, London.

Office of Population Censuses and Surveys (1991) *General Household Survey 1987*, Supplement B, HMSO, London.

Office of Population Censuses and Surveys (1992) *General Household Survey 1990,* Social Survey Division, HMSO, London.

Open Spaces Society (1988a) *Open Space,* Journal of the OSS, **23**(1), Spring

Open Spaces Society (1988b) *Open Space,* Journal of the OSS, **23**(2), Summer.

Open Spaces Society (1988c) *Our Common Right: the Story of Common Land,* OSS, Henley, Oxfordshire.

Open Spaces Society (1988d) *Annual Secretary's Report,* July, OSS, Henley, Oxford.

Outdoor Recreation Resources Review Commission (1962) *Outdoor Recreation for America,* Washington.

Owen, M. (1987) The impact on waterbirds of recreation on lowland wetlands. *Recreation and Wildlife, Working in Partnership,* Countryside Recreation Research Advisory Group annual conference report, 25–7 September, University of York.

Palmer, J. (1975) Recreation structure planning, *Planning for Recreation,* Planning Outlook Special Issue, Summer.

Patmore, A. (1983) *Recreation and Resources,* Blackwell, Oxford.

Patmore, A. (1987) A case study in national park planning, in Cloke, P. (ed.), *Rural Planning, Policy into Action?,* Harper & Row, London.

Patmore, A. (1989) Land and leisure: a contemporary perspective, in Patmore, A. (ed.), *Recreation and Conservation: Themes in Applied Geography,* University of Hull.

Patmore, A. and Rogers, H. B. (1973) *Leisure in the North West,* North West Sports Council, Stockport.

Pearson, L. F. (1977) Leisure facilities: use and under-use, *Town and Country Planning,* **45**(1).

Peltzer, R. H. M. (1989) The impact of recreation on nature in the Netherlands, in Brown, B. (ed.), *Leisure and the Environment,* proceedings of the Leisure Studies Association Annual Conference, 1987, Bournemouth, LSA, Eastbourne.

Penning-Rowsell, E. (1983) County landscape conservation policies in England and Wales. *Journal of Environmental Management,* **16**.

Prince, D. R. (1980) Countryside interpretation in the North York Moors National Park: a socio-psychological study. Unpublished Ph.D thesis, University of Hull.

Qualitative Consultancy (1986) Qualitative research to explore motivations behind visiting the countryside. Report to the Countryside Commission, unpublished.

Ragheb, M. O. and Beard, J. G. (1982) Measuring leisure attitude. *Journal of Leisure Research,* 2nd quarter.

Ramblers' Association (1982) *A Policy for Footpaths,* briefing note for the Countryside, No. 8, RA, London,

Ramblers' Association (1985) *Rights of Way Legislation, 1st Monitoring Report,* CCP 202, Countryside Commission, Cheltenham.

Ramblers' Association (1987) *Rights of Way Legislation, 2nd Monitoring Report,* CCP 242, Countryside Commission, Cheltenham.

Ramblers' Association (1993) *Harmony in the Hills,* RA, London.

Rapoport, R. and Rapoport, R. N. (1975) *Leisure and the Family Life Cycle,* Routledge & Kegan Paul, London.

Ravenscroft (1991) The place of leisure facilities in the provision of public leisure services. *Journal of Property Research,* **8**.

Redburn, M. W. (1985) Water authorities and leisure provision in England and Wales. *Reading Geographical Papers* No. 88, The University of Reading.

Redcliffe-Maud, Lord, (Chairman) (1969) *Report of the Royal Commission on Local Government*, Cmnd 4040, HMSO, London.

Redmond, M. (1991) Freedom of access to forests. *Landscape Design*, November.

Reid, I. (1977) *Social Class Differences in Britain, a Source Book*, Open Books, London.

Riddell, J. and Trevelyan, J. (1992) *Rights of Way: a Guide to Law and Practice*, Charlesworth, London.

Roberts, K. (1979) Countryside recreation and social class. Unpublished report to the Countryside Commission, Cheltenham.

Rogers, H. B. (1968) *Pilot National Recreation Survey*, Report No. 1, British Travel Association/University of Keele, July.

Roome, N. J. (1983) The use of national nature reserves by access permit holders. *Journal of Environmental Management*, **14**.

Rosmah, G. H. and Girling, S. (1976) The identification of outdoor recreation market segments on the basis of frequency of participation. *Journal of Leisure Research*, **8**(4).

Rothman, B. (1982) *The 1932 Kinder Trespass*, Willow Publishing, Altrincham, Cheshire.

Royal and Ancient Golf Club of St Andrews (1987) *The Demand for Golf*, Development Panel, Royal and Ancient, St Andrews, Scotland.

Royal Commission on Common Land (1958) *Common Land*, Cmd 462, HMSO, London.

Rubenstein, D. and Speakman, C. (1969) *Leisure Transport and the Countryside*, Fabian Research Series, 277, Fabian Society, London.

Rural Development Commission (1991a) *Tourism in the Countryside: A Strategy for Rural England*, RDC, December, London.

Rural Development Commission (1991b) *Meeting the Challenge of Agricultural Adjustment, A New Rural Development Commission Initiative*, RDC, June, London.

Rural Development Commission (1991c) *Rural Development Strategies*, internal memorandum, RDC, London.

Rural Voice (1991) *Rural/Countryside Strategies*, Internal Memorandum, November.

Ryan, J. (1978) *The Scope for Private Investment for Countryside Recreation*, in *Economic Aspects of Countryside Recreation Management*, Countryside Recreation Research Advisory Group Annual Conference 1976, CCP 101, Countryside Commission, Cheltenham.

Sandford, Lord, (Chairman) (1974) *Report of the National Park Policies Review Committee*, Department of the Environment, HMSO, London.

Schofield, M. (1987) Golf courses: maximising ecological interest, in *Recreation and Wildlife: Working in Partnership*, CRAAG Conference, 25–27 September, York University.

Scott, Mr Justice, (Chairman) (1942) *Report of the Committee on Land Utilisation in Rural Areas*, Cmd 6378, HMSO, London.

Scott Planning Services (1990) A review of countryside recreation strategies in Wales. Unpublished report to the Countryside Commission Committee for Wales.

Scott Planning Services (1991) *Local Authorities' Involvement with Rights of Way in England and Wales*, CCD 43, Countryside Commission, Cheltenham.

Seckler, D. W. (1966) On the uses and abuses of economic science in evaluating public outdoor recreation. *Land Economics*, **43**(4), November.

Selman, P. H. (1982) The use of ecological evaluations by local planning authorities. *Journal of Environmental Management*, **15**.

Selman, P. H. (1992) *Environmental Planning: The Conservation and Development of Biophysical Resources*, Paul Chapman, London.

Shoard, M. (1978) Access: can present opportunities be widened? *Countryside for All?: A Review of the Use People Make of the Countryside for Recreation*, Countryside Recreation Research Advisory Group annual conference, CCP 117, Countryside Commission, Cheltenham.

Shoard, M. (1987) *This Land is Our Land*, Paladin Books, London.

Shoard, M. (1989) Turnstiles on the trail. *The Times*, 4 February.

Shropshire County Council (1987) *Approved Structure Plan Alteration No. 1*, SCC, Telford.

Shropshire County Council (1991) *A Countryside Strategy for Shropshire*, consultation draft, County Planning Dept, Telford.

Shucksmith, D. M. (1979a) The demand for angling at the Derwent Reservoir, 1970–1976. *Journal of Agricultural Economics*, **30**(1).

Shucksmith, D. M. (1979b) Petrol prices and rural recreation in the 1980s. *National Westminster Bank Quarterly Review*, February.

Sidaway, R. (1982) Trends and issues in countryside recreation in the 1970s and 1980s: analysis and interpretation of recent large-scale surveys, in *Countryside Recreation in the 1980s*, Countryside Recreation Research Advisory Group Conference Report, Sports Council, London.

Sidaway, R. (1988) *Sport, Recreation and Nature Conservation*, Study Number 32, Sports Council, London.

Sidaway, R. (1990a) *Good Conservation Practice in Sport and Recreation*, Sports Council, Countryside Commission, Nature Conservancy Council and Worldwide Fund for Nature.

Sidaway, R. (1990b) The birds are more adaptable than the birdwatchers, in Tomlinson, A. (ed.), *Leisure, Labour and Lifestyles: International Comparisons*, Vol. 7, Parks and Outdoor Recreation: Themes and Issues, LSA Conference Paper No. 38, LSA, Eastbourne.

Sidaway, R. and O'Connor, F. B. (1978) Recreation pressures in the countryside. *Countryside for All? A Review of the Use People Make of the Countryside for Recreation*, Countryside Recreation Research Advisory Group 1978 Conference, Countryside Commission, CCP 117, Cheltenham.

Sillitoe, K. K. (1969) *Planning for Leisure*, HMSO, London.

Slee, R. W. (1982a) Country parks: a review of management and policy issues. *Gloucestershire Papers in Local and Rural Planning*, No. 17, October.

Slee, R. W. (1982b) New approaches to countryside management. *Parks and Recreation*, April.

Slee, R. W. (1985) Stover Country Park Visitor Survey 1984, Seale-Hayne College, unpublished.

Slee, R. W. (1989) *Alternative Farm Enterprises*, 2nd edn, Farming Press, Ipswich.

Smart, G. and Anderson, M. (1990) *Planning and Management in Areas of Outstanding Natural Beauty*, Countryside Commission, CCP 295, Cheltenham.

Social and Community Planning Research (1986) *British Social Attitudes, the 1986 Report*, Gower Publishing, Aldershot.

Social and Community Planning Research (1987) *British Social Attitudes, the 1987 Report*, Gower Publishing, Aldershot.

Social and Community Planning Research (1988) *British Social Attitudes, the 5th Report*, Gower Publishing, Aldershot.

Social and Community Planning Research (1992) *British Social Attitudes, Cumulative Sourcebook, the First Six Years*, Gower Publishing, Aldershot.

Somerset County Council (1986) *Somerset Structure Plan*, written statement incorporating alteration No. 1, County Planning Dept, Taunton.

South Glamorgan County Council (1990) *Countryside Recreation Strategy*, County Planning Dept, Swansea.

Southern Regional Council for Sport and Recreation (1990) *Strategy for Sport, 1990–1993*, SRCSR, Reading.

Speight, M. C. D. (1973) Outdoor recreation and its ecological effects. Discussion *paper in Conservation No. 4*, University of London.

Sports Council (1982) *Sport in the Comunity: the Next Ten Years*, SC, London.

Sports Council (1987) *Which Way Forward?*, SC, London.

Sports Council (1988) *Sport in the Community: into the 1990s*, SC, London.

Sports Council (1991a) *Sport and Recreation Content of Unitary Development Plans (U.D.Ps) in London*, SC, London.

Sports Council (1991b) *District Sport and Recreation Strategies: A Guide*, SC, London.

Sports Council (1992) *A Countryside for Sport: A Policy for Sport and Recreation*, SC, London.

Spray, M. (1984) Keeping some of it a bit rough, *Town and Country Planning*, **53**(1).

Staffordshire County Council (1984) *The Structure Plan for Staffordshire*, replacement plan, County Planning Dept, Stafford.

Stansfield, K. (1990) Going for green. *Public Service and Local Government*, **20**(3).

Stephens, T. (1978) The development and role of interpretation in upland Britain, in Tranter, R. (ed.), *The Future of Upland Britain*, Centre for Agricultural Strategy, University of Reading, paper No. 2, November.

Stephenson, T. (1989) *Forbidden Land: the Struggle for Access to Mountain and Moorland*, Holt, A. (ed.), Manchester University Press and Ramblers' Association, Manchester.

Sterelitz, Z. (1978) The city dweller and the countryside. *Countryside Recreation for All? A Review of the Use People Make of the Countryside for Recreation*, Countryside Recreation Research Advisory Group Conference 1978, CCP 117, Countryside Commission, Cheltenham.

Stoakes, R. (1979) *Oil Prices and Recreation Travel*, WP 20, Countryside Commission, Cheltenham.

Stoakes, R. and Champion, D. (1982) *Participation in Informal Countryside Recreation*, Countryside Commission, Cheltenham.

Struthers, W. A. K. and Brundell, M. J. (1983) The West Midlands: from reconstruction to regeneration, in Cross, D. T. and Bristow, M. R. (eds), *English Structure Planning, a Commentary on Procedure and Practice in the 1970s*, Pion, London.

Suffolk County Council (1979) *Gipping Valley Countryside and Recreation Plan*, County Planning Dept, Ipswich.

Suffolk County Council (1992) *Suffolk Countryside Strategy:* Issues Discussion Paper, County Planning Dept, Ipswich.

Surrey County Council (1980) *The Structure Plan for Surrey*, County Planning Dept, Kingston upon Thames.

Surrey County Council (1990) *Surrey Countryside Strategy: Key Issues and Proposals*, consultation draft, County Planning Dept, November, Kingston upon Thames.

Sutcliffe, T. H. (1992) An assessment of countryside recreation strategies in England. Unpublished MA (Landscape Management) dissertation, Department of Planning and Landscape, University of Manchester, April.

Tanner, M. F. (1973) *Water Resources and Recreation*, Sports Council, London.

Tanner, M. F. (1979) *Wildfowl, Reservoirs and Recreation*, Research Report 5, Water Space Amenity Commission.

Telling, A. and Smith, R. (1985) *The Public Right of Navigation*, a Report to the Sports Council and the Water Space Amenity Commission.

Thomas, K. (1983) *Man and the Natural World: Changing Attitudes in England, 1500–1800*, Allen Lane, London.

Torkildsen, G. (1986) *Leisure and Recreation Management*, 2nd edn, E & F N Spon, London.

Tourism and Recreation Research Unit (1980) *A Study of Four Parks in and Around Glasgow*, Research Report No. 44, University of Edinburgh.

Town and Country Planning Association (1979) The greening of politics, *Town and Country Planning*, **42**(2).

Treasury, HM (1972) *Forestry in Great Britain: An Interdepartmental Cost Benefit Study*, HMSO, London.

Tuite, C. H. (1983) *The Impact of Water-based Recreation on the Waterfowl of Enclosed Inland Waters in Britain*, Wildfowl Trust, Nature Conservancy Council and the Sports Council.

US Department of the Interior (1978) *National Urban Recreation Study*, Executive Report, Washington DC, US Government Printing Office.

University of Reading (1985) *Ploughing Footpaths and Bridleways*, Joint Centre for Land Development Studies, a Report to the Countryside Commission, CCP 190, Cheltenham.

Veal, A. J. (1979) *Sport and Recreation in England and Wales, an Analysis of Participation Patterns in 1977*, Centre for Urban and Regional Studies, University of Birmingham, Research Memorandum No. 74, July.

Veal, A. J. (1980) The future of leisure, *Tourism Management*, **1**(1), March.

Veal, A. J. and Travis, A. S. (1979) *Local Authority Leisure Services, the State of Play*, University of Birmingham, Centre for Urban and Regional Studies, July/August.

Walker, S. (1993) The 1992 UK Day Visits Survey (UKDVS). *Countryside Recreation Network News*, No. 2, June.

Watmough, B. (1983) *The Effects of Wildfowl on Recreation at Reservoirs in the Mid-Trent Valley*, Severn Trent Water Authority.

Welsh Water (1991) *Conservation, Recreation and Access, an Overview 1989–1991*, Welsh Water, Brecon, Powys.

White, J. (1981) *A Review of Tourism in Structure Plans in England*, Occasional Paper, University of Birmingham, Centre for Urban and Regional Studies.

William, Ellis C. (1928) *England and the Octopus*, Bles, London.

Wiltshire County Council (1983) *The Structure Plan for South Wiltshire*, approved plan, County Planning Dept, Trowbridge.

Wood, T. F. (1987) Methods of assessing relative risk of damage to soils and vegetation arising from winter sports development in the Scottish Highlands. *Journal of Environmental Management*, **25**(3), October.

Woods, A. (1984) Countryside conservation: the development of policy from 1880 to 1980, *Gloucestershire Papers in Local and Rural Planning*, Gloucestershire College of Arts and Technology, Issue No. 24.

Worth, J. (1984) What we think of the countryside. *ECOS*, **5**(1).

Wright, S. (1989) a review of the impacts of recreation on vegetation, in Brown, B. (ed.), *Leisure and the Environment*, Proceedings of the Leisure Studies Association Annual Conference, 1987, Bournemouth, LSA, Eastbourne.

Yorkshire and Humberside Regional Council for Sport and Recreation (1989) *A Sporting Chance, 1989–1993*, YHRCSR, Leeds.

Young, M. and Willmot, P. (1973) *The Symmetrical Family: A Study of Work and Leisure in the London Region*, London, Routledge & Kegan Paul.

Index

Page numbers referred to in **bold** represent figures, those in *italics* represent tables